A FAMILY WORSHIP RESOURCE:
Devotionals for parents and youth, plus stories for children.

HOWARD BEAN

Christian Light Publications, Inc.
Harrisonburg, VA 22802

FRUITFUL FAMILIES

Christian Light Publications, Inc.,
Harrisonburg, Virginia 22802
 Published 2010
Printed in the United States of America

Cover Design and Inside Art: Diane Burkholder

ISBN 978-0-87813-682-7

Cover and Interior Graphics
Vineyard: © iStockphoto.com/Benjamin Goode
Grapes: © iStockphoto.com/MvH
Family: © Diane Burkholder
Leaves: © iStockphoto.com/Lezh

13934

DEDICATION

I dedicate this book to my parents, Gordon and Lillian (Richardson) Bean, who taught me not just by word but also by example. I learned not only from listening in family worship but especially from observing their lives.

On the farm they instructed me about types of fruit, crops, weeding, and gardening. In the spiritual sense, they taught me the themes explained in this devotional book for families.

They have taught me about love and commitment in marriage, having recently celebrated seventy-one years of happy, harmonious marriage. Both of them are presently ninety-seven years of age and they continue to teach me about being "faithful unto death."

My father has demonstrated what has priority in life, what it means to stand for truth, and what is involved in submitting to God's chastening hand. My mother—a naughty, insecure orphan—yielded to Christ in her youth and has been transformed into a child of God who has demonstrated the fruit of the Spirit more than any other person I know.

Howard Bean
May, 2010

ACKNOWLEDGEMENTS

- I am thankful to the four writers of stories for this book: Juliann Ropp Good, Katrina Hoover, Janelle Erb Kuepfer, and Danette Schrock Martin. Each was a student of mine at the Christian school or the winter Bible school where I teach. I am grateful that they use their abilities in God's service.

- I am grateful to my wife Barbara for her helpful suggestions and typing skills.

- Thanks to the personnel at Christian Light Publications for their skills in editing, typesetting, and publishing.

- I am thankful to God, who blessed me with wonderful experiences in family living.

Table of Contents

Dedication *iii*
Acknowledgements *v*
How Parents Can Use This Book *xiii*

LOVE *1*

The Importance of Love *3*
Love God *5*
Love Your Neighbor *7*
Love Your Enemies *9*
Love the Stranger *11*
Love Your Spouse *13*
Love Your Children *15*
Winter Storm Love *17*

JOY *29*

Jesus and Great Joy *31*
Attempts to Find Joy *33*
Steps to Salvation's Joy *35*
The Joy of the Prodigal's Return *37*
Be of Good Cheer *39*
Joy Amidst Trials *41*

The Joy of the Lord Is Your Strength *43*
Joyful George *45*

PEACE *57*

Jesus, Prince of Peace *59*
Peace From the Prince of Peace *61*
Peace in Spite of Grief *63*
Peace at Home *65*
Restoring Peace *67*
Making Peace, Not Pieces *69*
Though Trials Should Come *71*
Zeke's Revenge *73*

LONGSUFFERING *81*

I Want It *Now* *83*
Patience of God *85*
Learn Patience from James and Job *87*
Causes of Impatience *89*
Developing Patience *91*
Sweet Fruit of Patience *93*
Patience in Daily Life *95*
Patience Is a Virtue *97*

GENTLENESS *107*

God's Kindness *109*
Kindness of Christ *111*
Kindness at Home *113*
Kindness to Siblings *115*
Kindness to the Handicapped *117*
Kindness in the Community *119*
Kindness at Church *121*
Gentleness Comes Back *123*

Goodness *135*

Barnabas: A Good Man *137*
Brave Esther *139*
Helpful Aaron *141*
Lydia: A Good Businesswoman *143*
Jethro: A Wise Advisor *145*
President of the Dorcas Society *147*
Jonathan: A True Friend *149*
Envious Ben *151*

Faith *157*

Jesus Is Faithful *159*
Faith in Abraham's Shield *161*
Holy and Wholly Committed *163*
A Dying Leader's Challenge: Be Faithful *165*
Diligent Deborah *167*
Let Your Heart Be Steadfast *169*
Faithful Unto Death *171*
A Dog's Last Name *173*

Meekness *183*

Meekness of Jesus *185*
The Need for Meekness *187*
Meekness in Relation to God *189*
The Value of Meekness *191*
Meekness Demonstrated *193*
Meekness in Action *195*
Meekness in Building Relationships *197*
Picnic Day *199*

TEMPERANCE *213*
Be Temperate *215*
Developing Self-Control *217*
How to Grow the Fruit of Temperance *219*
What Esau Saw *221*
Importance of Self-Control *223*
The Slavery of Indulgence *225*
Temperance at Home *227*
Everyone Needs Temperance *229*

GARDENING LESSONS *241*
Gardening: Past and Present *243*
Lessons From Gardening *245*
What to Plant *247*
Fruit-Bearing *249*
Parable of the Laborers *251*
Parable of Two Sons *253*
Parable of the Wicked Farm Manager *255*
The Miracle Garden *257*

WONDERS OF PLANTS *271*
The Biggest Trees *273*
The Fiercest Plants *275*
The Most Useful Plant *277*
The Largest Seed *279*
A Very Fragrant Plant *281*
The Tallest Grass *283*
The Thickest Plant *285*
The Greatest Plants *287*

WEEDS 297

Weeding Your Garden 299
Weeds Grow Fast 301
Weeds Choke 303
Identifying Weeds 305
Keep Weeding 307
Weeding Is Work 309
Weeding Is Worth It 311
The Ugly Weed 313

SOWING AND REAPING 325

The Results of Sowing 327
Getting What You Don't Want 329
The Weight of the Crop 331
Helping Yourself by Helping Others 333
Grim Education 335
Not a Defective Detective 337
Reaping a Good Crop 339
Sowing and Reaping—You Get What You Plant 341

Themes, Titles, Verses, and Readings 355

How Parents Can Use This Book

Fruitful Families is a resource for the family altar. I hope it helps to meet a need my wife and I felt when we were rearing our four children—the need for something on a child's level that would interest and instruct them.

The book consists of two parts for each day. The first part is for Mom and Dad and the older children in the family. It consists of a suggested Scripture reading, a theme verse, and a devotional meditation on the topic introduced by the Scripture reading.

The second part consists of a story for children incorporating the same weekly theme as the adult lesson. You as parents (or an older child) may read the story. Here are various possibilities about how you could use the story.

- You may read a portion of the story each day. A leaf indicates a suitable stopping place.
- You may wait to read the story portion until evening (assuming your family worship is in the morning).

- You may read several portions or the whole story on days when you have a more relaxed schedule (such as Saturday for some families).

The goal of these stories is to create interest and enthusiasm for family worship in the hearts of children while making application of Bible principles. This is hard for parents to do if the devotional thoughts are solely on an adult level.

I have provided ten questions based on each week's story that you may use if you wish. The *Questions for Review* are easier, largely factual questions that younger children may be able to answer. *Questions for Discussion* are intended for older children and provide opportunities for applying the theme to your family life.

You will notice there are thirteen themes divided into seven days each, thus encompassing ninety-one days—approximately one quarter of a year.

God bless your family worship time that you may all "grow in grace, and in the knowledge of our Lord and Saviour Jesus Christ" (2 Peter 3:18) and be "filled with the fruits of righteousness, which are by Jesus Christ" (Philippians 1:11).

— Howard Bean

LOVE

The Importance of Love

And walk in love, as Christ also hath loved us,
and hath given himself for us an offering and a sacrifice
to God for a sweetsmelling savour.
— Ephesians 5:2

READ JOHN 15:12-17

Ripley's *Believe It or Not* reports that Marcel Leclure, a painter from Paris, France, wrote a very lengthy love letter. He wrote *Je vous aime* ("I love you") 1,875,000 times (1,000 times the year 1875). He was enthralled by the sound of the words, so he dictated the letter to his scribe, who wrote it, and had his hired helper repeat the phrase each time it was written. Thus the phrase was repeated in oral and written form 5,625,000 times. The story concludes with the words, "Never was love made manifest by as great an expenditure of time and money."

But I know a greater expression of love. Calvary was a much greater demonstration of love. And Christ, in our daily reading, declares what is the greatest expression of human love (v. 13). Christ commands us to "love one another," but He also gives the example "as I have loved you" (v. 12).

The essence of Christianity can be stated in one word: love. That includes God's love to us and our response of love to Him and others. John, writing in 1 John 4:19, 21 connects the two: "We love him, because he first loved us. . . . And this commandment have we from him, That he who loveth God love his brother also."

It is not by accident that the first fruit of the Spirit that Galatians 5:22 mentions is love. In a sense, love encompasses the eight fruit that follow. Joy is love's cheerfulness; peace is love's confidence; longsuffering is love's composure; gentleness is love's consideration; goodness is love's character; faith is love's trustworthiness; meekness is love's strength; and temperance is love's discipline.

The Old Testament emphasizes love. The words of Jesus in our daily reading contain two quotations: Deuteronomy 6:5 and Leviticus 19:18. The best known verse of the New Testament (John 3:16) is about God's great love; and 1 Corinthians 13, perhaps the best known chapter in the New Testament, is about the supremacy and endurance of love. Duty makes us do things well, but love makes us do them beautifully.

We love the gifts that God gives us. Let's love the Giver. The wise lover values not so much the gift of the lover as the love of the giver.

Love God

I will love thee, O Lord, my strength.
— Psalm 18:1

READ MATTHEW 22:34-40

The young son of a Bible scholar said, "Papa, what do the words *cherubim* and *seraphim* mean?"

His dad explained that *cherubim* comes from a Hebrew word meaning "knowledge," and *seraphim* has to do with "flame." He added that it is commonly thought the cherubim are angels who excel in knowledge and the seraphim are those who excel in love.

"Then I hope," the boy said, "that when I die I will be a seraphim. I'd rather love God than know everything."

The boy's theology of the afterlife may not have been the best, but his desire to love God was excellent. As shown by the daily reading, the first and foremost command is to love God. Psalm 31:23 says, "O love the Lord, all ye his saints."

Jesus made clear that the basic way we show love to God is by obeying Him. John 14 records that Jesus explained this truth three times during His last words to the disciples on the eve of the Crucifixion. Verse 15 says, "If ye love me, keep my commandments." Verse 21 says, "He that hath my commandments, and keepeth them, he it is that loveth me: and he that loveth me shall be loved of my Father, and I will love him, and will manifest myself to him." Verse 23 says, "Jesus answered and said unto him, If a man love me, he will keep my words: and my Father will love him, and we will come unto him, and make our abode with him."

Isaac Watts said, "Love so amazing, so divine, demands my soul, my life, my all."

A. W. Tozer wrote, "Our Lord told His disciples that love and obedience were organically united. The final test of love is obedience."

John, the apostle of love, understood what Jesus meant. He wrote, "This is the love of God, that we keep his commandments: and his commandments are not grievous" (1 John 5:3).

An early church leader wrote, "How shall we become lovely? By loving Him who is ever lovely."

Love Your Neighbor

If a man say, I love God, and hateth his brother, he is a liar:
for he that loveth not his brother whom he hath seen,
how can he love God whom he hath not seen?
— 1 John 4:20

Read Luke 10:25-37

The height of our love for God will never exceed the depth of our love for our brother. Augustine said, "What does love look like? It has the hands to help others. It has the feet to hasten to the poor and needy. It has the eyes to see misery and want. It has the ears to hear the sighs and sorrows of men. That is what love looks like."

Because love to one's neighbor, as shown by the daily reading, may get inconvenient, risky, messy, costly, and time-consuming, love in practice is more difficult than thinking about it in principle. Love is appealing, but its practice is appallingly hard. Love is not just a warm fuzzy feeling; it involves action. It is essentially unselfishness.

Paganism does not value selfless love. I have read that the Inuit of Greenland had no word for love prior to the missionaries bringing the Gospel. The Japanese language had no word to express Christian love, so the translators needed to coin a word. The natives of Tasmania had no word for love either, but they had numerous words for infanticide.

Sacrificial love originates in God, for it is a fruit of the Spirit. 1 John 5:1 says, “Whosoever believeth that Jesus is the Christ is born of God: and every one that loveth him that begat loveth him also that is begotten of him.”

Christian love is like the moon—it has no light of its own. It is a reflection of the Sun of righteousness.

Love never asks, “What will I get?” but it asks, “What can I give?” It does not ask, “What must I do?” but, “What can I do?”

Let your love to others be open and obvious. As Jesus said, “By this shall all men know that ye are my disciples, if ye have love one to another” (John 13:35).

As George Herbert said, “Love and a cough cannot be hid.”

Love Your Enemies

Therefore if thine enemy hunger, feed him; if he thirst,
give him drink: for in so doing
thou shalt heap coals of fire on his head.
— *Romans 12:20*

READ MATTHEW 5:38-48

From the land in which our Lord walked comes a story of mercy and forgiveness. In 1989, Sergeant Zeev Traum was patrolling the beachfront road south of Gaza City. He and another Israeli soldier were ambushed in their Jeep by Palestinian gunmen. The forty-year-old's death brought a unique dilemma for his widow. She could simply bury her husband, or donate his heart to an ailing Palestinian. A measure of revenge could be found if she denied the request and let the man die, since a Palestinian had killed her husband. Instead she opted to forgive. She literally had a heart for her enemy. So outside the city walls where Jesus Christ died of a broken heart, 54-year-old Hanna Khader, who had waited four months for a heart, received new life from his political enemy.

Our daily reading tells us how Jesus wants His followers to love, bless, and do good to their enemies. Don't only love those that love you.

Love will be shown by one's speech. The tongue is a terrible weapon. It is quicker and more easily wielded than a sword. It is as sharp as a sword and can cause much pain. It can be deadly to reputations, friendly relationships, and peaceful living. People who would not think of using a sword may use their tongue in a way that violates nonresistance as much as some forms of military service. How sad! How inconsistent!

Do not trade insult for insult, argument for argument, barb for barb, deceit for deception, tit for tat.

A nonresistant spirit may be shown not only in big ways but also in daily life. At a men's conference, a truck driver was asked what difference becoming a Christian made in his life. He thought for a moment then said, "Well, when I find someone tailgating my truck, I no longer drive on the shoulder of the road to kick up cinders at him."

LOVE THE STRANGER

I was a stranger, and ye took me in.
— Matthew 25:35

READ EXODUS 22:21-27

A former Hindu explained to a missionary why he went to church. He said, "Years ago when I was a boy we heckled a missionary preaching in the bazaar—threw tomatoes at him. He wiped the tomato juice from his face and then after the meeting took us to the sweet shop and bought us sweets. I saw the love of Christ that day, and that's why I'm here."

Repeatedly the Old Testament teaches that consideration and love should be shown to a stranger, as in verse 21 of our daily reading. Leviticus 19:34 gave this instruction: "The stranger that dwelleth with you shall be unto you as one born among you, and thou shalt love him as thyself; for ye were strangers in the land of Egypt." If an Israelite observed someone experiencing hard times, he was commanded to help even if he was a stranger (see Leviticus 25:35.) Boaz reaped a lifetime blessing (Ruth) because he kindly let a stranger from Moab reap in his fields. Deuteronomy 27:19 says, "Cursed be he that perverteth the judgment of the stranger, fatherless, and widow."

In the New Testament, Jesus expressed His displeasure with those who failed to welcome the stranger. "I was a stranger, and ye took me not in" (Matthew 25:43). A widow worthy of church support was one who had "lodged strangers" (1 Timothy 5:10). And Hebrews 13:2 says, "Be not forgetful to entertain strangers: for thereby some have entertained angels unawares."

Today helping a stranger may involve friendliness to a visitor at church, assistance to an immigrant family, befriending a foreign student at a local university, hosting a visiting speaker at church, or welcoming a neighbor to the community.

I am impressed with an Indian in the White Pigeon, Michigan, area who showed love to newcomers. In 1830, when white settlers came to the area, some of the local Indians converted to Christianity, and one of their members became very devoted to the white people. When he learned of a plot by some hostile Indians to raid the little village and massacre the whites, he ran sixty miles to warn his Christian friends. His valor was great, but the dash was too much of a strain for his body. As he staggered into the settlement shouting a warning, he fell dead. Today there's a monument in the village to White Pigeon. The inscription says simply, "Greater love hath no man."

Love Your Spouse

That they may teach the young women to be sober,
to love their husbands,
to love their children.
— Titus 2:4

Read Ephesians 5:25-33

King Cyrus, king of Persia (Isaiah 45:1), decided to put a stop to the trouble caused by Cagular, a rebel chieftain, who kept harassing the Persian troops. Cyrus sent out his forces to capture Cagular and his family, intending to get revenge.

Cagular and his wife were brought before Cyrus in the throne room. The monarch asked, "Cagular, if I were to save your life, what would you do?"

"King, I would serve you the rest of my days," he replied.

Cyrus then said thoughtfully, "What would you do if I spared the life of your wife?"

He replied, "Your Majesty, if you spared my wife, I would die for you."

This so impressed King Cyrus that he pardoned Cagular and his wife and placed him in charge of the royal troops on the southern border of Persia.

As Cagular returned home with his family, he began to talk of the stunning wealth and splendor of Cyrus's throne room. "Did you see all the marble?" he asked his wife. "The guard's armor was made of silver. And the throne was made of shining solid gold. And did you see the magnificent ornaments?"

His wife replied, "No, I didn't see any of that."

Cagular was dumbfounded that she had not noticed the splendor and riches that were so impressive. "What did you see?" he asked in surprise.

She said, "I saw only the face of the man who said he would die for me."

Jesus died for His bride. According to our daily reading, husbands should love their wives even as Jesus loves and cares for the church, and wives should be taught to love their husbands. This means there should be mutual appreciation and respect. The love needs to be expressed in practical, daily terms.

The times when spouses are most universally appreciated seem to be before the wedding and after the funeral. Husbands and wives, let's show unselfish love day by day between those two events. The mystery of love is that the more you give, the more remains in your heart.

LOVE YOUR CHILDREN

And lo a voice from heaven, saying,
This is my beloved Son, in whom I am well pleased.
— Matthew 3:17

READ TITUS 2:1-8

Our daily reading indicates that parents should love their children. This can be expressed in a variety of ways: sympathy, forgiveness, provision of food and clothing, listening, and caring. However, one area of possible neglect is in telling our children, "I love you."

God verbalized His love to His Son. At Jesus' baptism He said, "Thou art my beloved Son; in thee I am well pleased" (Luke 3:22).

What's the application for parents?

1. Personally express your love. God spoke to Jesus, "*Thou* art." It's fine to tell other folks you love your child, but it's more important to tell the child. This may be done with your voice or your pen. I was in a home where a daughter's birthday cards were hung on a door. I noticed one from her dad, communicating his love and appreciation to her. Verbalizing your love gives a sense of *recognition* to your child.

2. Stress words like *my*. God said, "Thou art my beloved Son." This helps give a sense of *belonging* and *security*.
3. Specifically and repeatedly tell your children you love them. This meets a basic human need of *affection*. The Father called Jesus "my beloved Son." When our first child was small, my wife often placed her on her lap, saying, "I love you," and the little one happily responded, "I wuv you too."
4. Express appreciation and commendation. God said of Jesus, "in whom I am *well pleased*." Giving words of praise affirms a child's sense of *significance*.

We can take a lesson from a study of a large high school in Oklahoma. The faculty were asked to identify the ten best-adjusted students. Each of these students was asked, "How long has it been since your parents told you they loved you?"

The best-adjusted students said, "Yesterday," "This morning," or "Last evening." In fact, all ten had been verbally assured of parental love in the preceding twenty-four hours.

To the same question, the worst-adjusted students gave a much different answer. In fact, only one of the ten remembered hearing a parent ever say they loved him, and he couldn't remember when.

What would your child say? God verbalized His love to His Son and to His children (via the Bible). Go and do thou likewise.

Winter Storm Love

by Katrina Hoover

Stevie settled into his seat at school and watched as Miss Russell arranged her papers and prepared for her devotional talk. But his mind was far from school. At breakfast that morning, Mom had said that a winter storm was predicted for the next day, and Stevie already counted on having a day off from school. Oh, he liked school for the most part; but it was February, and it seemed as if school would never end.

"Can someone tell me what holiday is coming up soon?" Miss Russell asked as she began.

Someone gave the obvious answer: Valentine's Day.

"Yes," said Miss Russell. "You can't go into a store anywhere without seeing pink and red hearts and chocolates and flowers and valentines of all sorts. But I have a question: Do you think all the people who buy those things really understand the true meaning of love?"

The fifth graders grinned and squirmed just a little.

"I don't mean love like boyfriends and girlfriends," Miss Russell said. "I mean love like the Bible talks about. Did you ever think what love meant to Jesus? To Jesus, love meant a lot of hard work, not much sleep, hours in prayer, and finally pain and death." Miss Russell gave out five Bible verses for students to find and read. Each verse showed a little more about the true Bible meaning of love.

"Now," said Miss Russell, "I have a little assignment for you. Valentine's Day comes the day after tomorrow. I want all of you to see if you can show someone the Bible kind of love between now and then. On Valentine's Day, I'll ask you to report on what you did. Maybe you can offer to do something special for one of your parents or help one of your brothers or sisters. Did you ever realize that it's usually the hardest to love the people we live with all the time? It's easy to say we love people we don't see very often. But it's really hard to show true love to the people we see every day."

The rest of the day at school, Stevie and his friends talked about the hoped-for winter storm. Surely they would get the day off from school! Only a few of them remembered Miss Russell's assignment.

After school, while washing his lunchbox, Stevie thought of Miss Russell's devotions again. "Mom," he said, "you know what Miss Russell said this morning? She said it's harder for us to love people we're with all the time than people we don't see very often. I don't believe that."

"Why not?" Mom asked.

"Well, I don't have any problem loving my friends, and I'm with them all the time," Stevie said.

"So you think six hours a day in school is all the time?" Mom asked with a smile. "Miss Russell probably meant loving your brothers and sisters."

Stevie thought of fourteen-year-old Karen, two years older than himself. And of Philip, three years younger. Of six-year-old Elizabeth and "baby" sister Alexis. "Do they count?" he asked. He laughed a little. Of course he loved his brothers and sisters. But did they really matter as much as other people?

"That's just what your teacher meant," said Mom. "Since you're with them all the time, they don't seem as important as other people."

Stevie laughed again. "Well, the most important thing right now is the weather. Will we get to stay home from school or won't we?"

Before Stevie went to bed, he peered out the window at the sky. A few lazy snowflakes drifted down. Surely they would start coming faster and thicker before morning!

"I hope we get three feet of snow," Philip said as they lay in bed listening to the wind.

"We won't get *that* much," Stevie said wisely. "I just hope we get enough to cancel school."

In the night, Philip had a coughing spell that woke Stevie. Stevie turned sleepily on his pillow and looked at the clock: 4:45. Then he remembered: The snowstorm! Had it come? He sat up in bed and looked out into a white world. Wind tossed the snow in whirling patterns and threw drifts against the lawn mower shed. Sometimes an extra-strong gust made a roaring sound against the walls of the house. Stevie lay down and pulled up the covers. "They have to cancel school," he told himself.

The next thing Stevie heard was the ringing of the phone. He checked the clock again: 6:30. He heard Dad answer, but could not hear what he said. Stevie slipped out of bed and went to the top of the stairs. He held his breath until his father opened the stair door and called, "Boys, no school today!"

"Yippee!" Stevie tore back to his bedroom and turned a cartwheel. A whole day to just do stuff at home! "Wake up, Phil. No school!"

After they ate breakfast and waved Dad off to work, Philip and Stevie decided to play farm. Both of the boys had a small collection of miniature John Deere tractors they had gotten for Christmas or birthdays. Stevie had a combine and two tractors with machinery to pull behind. Philip had only one tractor and did not have as many pieces of machinery. The boys also had a huge set of Lincoln logs. Usually they began the fun by building log cabins and sheds to park their tractors in. Then they divided the carpet into plots of land for each boy to farm.

Stevie began building an elaborate log cabin with several wings. He left space for windows and doors. He chose two matching plastic roof pieces and shingled the roof with long boards.

"Stevie, you always take the best roof pieces," Philip said. "Why can't I ever have them?"

"Well, why didn't you get them if you wanted them?" Stevie asked.

"You always take them before I have a chance," Philip said. "I can never make a nice big cabin like you do."

"Too bad," said Stevie carelessly, starting a shed for his farm equipment. He did not put a roof on this one, because he wanted to reach in and drive the pieces out of the shed. He left a door opening wide enough for even his combine to go through. After he finished the shed, he tried to park his equipment inside.

"Bother," he mumbled.

"What's wrong?" Philip asked.

"I didn't make the shed big enough for all my stuff."

"I have an idea," said Philip. "Give me one of your tractors. I need another one to pull my wagon anyway."

"Oh, no. I might need it," said Stevie. "I'll just park my gravity wagon outside the shed."

"But you have a combine and two tractors!" protested Philip. "You can't use those all at once anyway!"

"Look, Philip, if you want to farm with me, then stop complaining about stuff and begging for my things," said Stevie. He ignored his brother's sad look and began marking out his cornfield on the living room carpet. Then he said, "This time I'm going to combine every inch of carpet. I never did that before." With a Lincoln log slat, he drew a field lane in the carpet. He drove his combine out of the shed and down the field lane. He began to drive up and down his cornfield.

Mom stepped into the living room, leading their little sister.

"You have some neat buildings, boys," she said. "I remember when you used to make only little square boxes for your cabins. But now, Stevie, I want you to watch Alexis while I get lunch."

"Aw, come on, Mom," Stevie complained. "Can't Karen take care of her? She'll knock our buildings over."

"Not if you watch her," said Mom. "Karen is doing laundry."

"Okay," grumbled Stevie. "But she'd better not spoil our farms." He gathered all the leftover Lincoln logs and vehicles into a pile. Then he set the toddler next to them and said, "Here, Alexis, you can play with these. But don't touch our buildings." He pointed to them and firmly said, "No."

Stevie made up his mind to finish combining his cornfield. He wanted to see how long it would take him.

Just as he emptied another load of corn into a truck, he heard a crash. He turned around; Alexis had knocked in the roof of Philip's cabin.

"Alexis!" Stevie yelled.

"Stevie, you were supposed to watch her!" Philip howled.

Alexis took one look at her two angry brothers and began to cry.

Mom appeared in the living room doorway.

"Stevie, I think it's time you take Alexis out of this room and read to her," Mom said.

"But, Mom, I haven't finished—"

"Stevie, do it now. You didn't watch her, so you must solve the problem you created for yourself," said Mom.

"Come, then." Stevie grabbed Alexis and hauled her into the toy room. She howled even louder when he plopped her on the floor and went to find a picture book to show her.

By lunch, things had calmed down. Philip had cleared away the Lincoln logs and farm equipment as Mom had told him to do. Stevie had resigned himself to amusing his little sister and had her laughing at the funny way he read the story. He patted her head, wishing he had not been so rough with her.

"Hey, look!" Stevie said, looking out the window. "The snow's about stopped. Look at how much we got! That looks like good snow for an igloo!"

It seemed strange to eat lunch at home on a weekday. Mom set a bowl of potato soup and a basket of apple muffins on the table. After prayer, Stevie split a steaming muffin with his fork, spread it with butter, and drizzled honey over it. "I like this better than eating lunch out of a lunchbox!" he said.

"Okay," said Mom after lunch, "Karen, I want you to put Elizabeth and Alexis to bed for their naps. Philip, you can lie down for a while too, or help Stevie with the dinner dishes."

"What?" said Stevie. "I'm doing the dishes?"

"That's right," said Mom.

"Oh, well, at least there aren't many," Stevie said, looking at the soup bowls and spoons with relief.

"How's your loving experiment going?" Mom asked him as she cleared the table.

"What?"

"You know, you were supposed to show the Bible kind of love and tell about it tomorrow in devotions."

"Oh, I forgot about that! You mean that's tomorrow? Well, I didn't even go to school today, so how can I show anyone love?"

"Stevie," Mom sighed. "You missed at least two chances to show love this morning already. Both of them would have made great stories to share in class."

"What do you mean?" Stevie asked.

"Well, what about sharing some of your farm machinery with Philip? That would have showed love. What about taking good care of your baby sister right away instead of waiting until she smashed your buildings and then yelling at her?"

"Oh-h-h," said Stevie. "Well, I just never really thought about showing love to *them.* They're just family."

"Just family." Mom sighed again.

"Come to think of it, Miss Russell did mention doing something for our brothers and sisters," said Stevie. "Maybe I'll have a chance to do something yet this afternoon."

After finishing the dishes, Stevie put on his boots, winter jacket, hat, and gloves. He slipped out the door.

The sun glistened on the snow so brightly that it hurt Stevie's eyes. He stood for a moment enjoying the perfection of the drifts and snow-capped shrubs. He almost hated to take a step and spoil the beauty.

Stevie took a handful of snow and formed a snowball. It was a little dry, but still good for packing. He decided to build an igloo up against the lawn mower shed. The drifts there would give him plenty of snow to work with. First he tugged open the door of the shed and found several shovels of different sizes. He used them to scoop the snow into piles and cut it into blocks.

As he worked, Stevie thought about how nice it was to work on his project without having a baby sister ruining it. That reminded him of Mom's idea that he might have a chance to show love to someone.

But I can't show love to anyone if they're inside taking naps, Stevie thought.

Just then the front door opened. Out came Philip and Elizabeth.

Good, thought Stevie, *I'll let them help me with my house even though I don't feel like it. That would be a good way to show love.*

"That's a neat igloo," said Philip when he and Elizabeth had waded through the snow to Stevie's house.

"You can help me if you want to," said Stevie.

"No, we're going to build snowmen," Philip answered. Philip and Elizabeth walked away to the middle of the yard.

Stevie felt relieved, because he knew he could do a better job on the igloo without Philip and Elizabeth. But he also felt disappointed that they had not even wanted to help him.

Stevie kept building, but he watched Philip and Elizabeth too. Philip had no trouble rolling balls and stacking them on top of each other. Elizabeth, though, struggled with her snowman's head. Whenever she tried to put it on, she knocked off its middle. Then she had to reshape the middle, put it back on the bottom, and try all over again.

"Here, Elizabeth, let me help you," Stevie called. He plunged through the snow and helped Elizabeth steady the snowman's head.

Elizabeth looked at it in delight. "Oh, thank you, Stevie," she said.

"Look at my cool snowman!" Philip yelled. His snowman had arms made of branches. The arms had little twigs at the ends that almost looked like fingers. Philip had dug through the snow to the gravel lane and collected a handful of stones to make the snowman's eyes, nose, and mouth.

Elizabeth looked sadly at her snowman. It didn't look nice anymore; it had no arms, no nose, no eyes, and no mouth.

"I'm going to find some bark to make a hat for mine!" Philip hollered.

Elizabeth looked even sadder.

"Here, Elizabeth, I'll help you fix him up," Stevie said. "Let's go look in the lawn mower shed."

They didn't find much in the shed until Stevie found his bird nest bucket from last summer.

"Look, Elizabeth. Do you want a beard on your snowman?" he asked. "You can have one of these birds' nests to make a beard."

"Oh, yes!" Elizabeth carefully picked through the bucket and found a nest that looked almost like hair.

"You put his beard on while I go and see what Mom can give us," said Stevie.

Mom found several large buttons and a handful of smaller ones. She also gave him an old scarf and hat. "I see you are showing love to your sister," she said, giving him an approving smile.

"Something smells really good," Stevie said. "What are you making, Mom?"

"It's a surprise," Mom said. "Wait and see."

Back outside, Stevie helped Elizabeth wrap the scarf around the snowman's neck and put on the hat. The big buttons made great eyes and the smaller ones they arranged in a big smile. The beard covered most of his mouth anyway.

By that time, all three children were cold and ready to go in.

"Is your igloo done?" Philip asked Stevie.

"No," Stevie said. "But that's okay; I had fun watching you guys."

"You *helped* me," said Elizabeth.

"And helping you," agreed Stevie.

The three shook off as much loose snow onto the porch as possible. Once inside, they helped each other undo their jackets, scarves, and coats.

"Hang your things in the basement to dry," Mom called.

"What smells so good?" Philip asked.

"A surprise," Stevie told him.

Mom was stirring the surprise when they finally walked into the kitchen.

"Caramel corn!" Stevie exclaimed. "We haven't had that in ages. Mom makes the best caramel corn," he added.

"It's not quite done," said Mom. "Stevie, if you'll watch Alexis for a bit, I'll wash the dishes here, and then we'll have some caramel corn all together."

"Come, Alexis," Stevie said. "I'll read you another story."

Stevie added noises and motions to the story until Alexis shrieked with delight. Before long, they all sat in the living room with bowls of caramel corn and mugs of hot chocolate.

"This is the best day ever," said Stevie.

"I liked the afternoon better than the morning," said Philip.

"Me too," said Mom.

"I guess I did too." Stevie gave Mom a sheepish smile.

The next day, Miss Russell started the devotional time with a few verses about the love of Jesus.

"Now," she said, "who can tell me something loving you did for someone else on your day off school?"

Groans and "I forgot!" came from all over the room.

"No one did anything loving for *anyone?*" Miss Russell asked.

Finally Stevie raised his hand. "Well, I sort of did," he said, "but I started the day off really badly, so I don't know if it counts."

Miss Russell laughed. "Tell us," she said.

Stevie explained how he had refused to share with Philip and how he had been rough with Alexis. Then he told how he had helped Elizabeth with her snowman and read a story to Alexis.

"Very good," said Miss Russell. "Even if you started all wrong, you definitely showed love to others yesterday. Anyone else?"

No one else could think of anything.

Miss Russell ended the devotional time with a prayer. Then she said, "Well, I brought a prize to share with everyone who did the assignment." She reached into a paper bag beside her desk and pulled out a large box of Valentine candy. "But since Stevie was the only one, I suppose he gets the whole box!"

The class oohed and aahed as Stevie walked up for the candy.

At lunchtime Stevie had started to open the box of candy when he thought of something. He put the box in his backpack.

"Did you tell any 'loving' stories at school today?" Mom asked Stevie that afternoon as he cleaned his lunchbox.

"Yes," said Stevie. "I was the only one who remembered, but I wouldn't have if you hadn't reminded me. So you should get some of the prize she gave me." Stevie got the box of candy from his backpack and set in on the table.

"Oh, Stevie, that's really a good kind of candy," said Mom. "Are you really going to share with us?"

"Yup," said Stevie. He split the plastic wrap with a knife and slipped the cardboard lid off the box. The warm, sweet smell of chocolate rose from the box before anyone touched a piece.

Philip and Elizabeth just picked any old piece and ate it right away. Mom and Karen read carefully on the box lid the description of each different shape. Alexis took the piece Stevie gave her and took tiny bites out of it, as if it were an apple. Stevie smiled as he watched her.

"Aren't you going to have a piece yourself?" Mom asked.

"Oh, yes," said Stevie. "I was watching Alexis and almost forgot to get my own."

"That's exactly what love does," said Mom. "It forgets itself." Stevie laughed and took a piece of candy.

Questions for Review

1. What assignment did Miss Russell give her class?
2. How did Stevie fail to show love to Philip?
3. How did Stevie fail to show love to Alexis?
4. In what ways did Stevie show love in the afternoon?
5. How did Stevie feel after showing love to his family?

Questions for Discussion

1. Do you agree with Miss Russell that it is usually hardest to show love to the people you live with all the time?
2. What should you do when you realize you failed to show love to someone?
3. What are some ways love was shown to you among family members in the last day or two?
4. How might you show love to your siblings in the next twenty-four hours?
5. How might you be rewarded as you show love to family members?

JOY

Jesus and Great Joy

Looking unto Jesus the author and finisher of our faith;
who for the joy that was set before him endured the cross,
despising the shame,
and is set down at the right hand of the throne of God.
— Hebrews 12:2

Read Luke 15:3-10

"The fruit of the Spirit is . . . joy" (Galatians 5:22). After His baptism in which the Holy Spirit descended in a bodily shape upon Him (Luke 3:21), "Jesus being full of the Holy Ghost returned from Jordan, and was led by the Spirit into the wilderness" (Luke 4:1). Because joy is a fruit of the Spirit, we know Jesus was a joyful person. The daily reading portrays Him seeking the lost and rejoicing when the lost is found.

Not only was He joyful, He brought joy throughout His life. At His birth, an angel brought "good tidings of *great joy.*" At His resurrection, two women who heard the angel explain that Jesus had arisen from the dead "departed quickly from the sepulcher with fear and *great joy*" (Matthew 28:8). At His ascension, Luke 24:51, 52 says, "It came to pass, while he blessed them, he was parted from them, and carried up into heaven. And they worshipped him, and returned to Jerusalem with *great joy.*"

Do you have great joy because of Christ's birth? He descended from Heaven to earth so that we can rise from earth to Heaven.

Do you have great joy because of Christ's resurrection? He descended into the earth but rose from the dead to enable us to live above sin.

Do you have great joy because of Christ's ascension? He descended to preach unto the spirits in prison (1 Peter 3:18, 19), and then "when he ascended up on high, he led captivity captive, and gave gifts unto men" (Ephesians 4:8).

A fourth time the New Testament mentions great joy relates to the conversion of the Gentiles. On the way to the Jerusalem Conference, Paul and Barnabas "passed through Phenice and Samaria, declaring the conversion of the Gentiles: and they caused *great joy* unto all the brethren" (Acts 15:3). How appropriate that great joy resulted from knowing that folks were transformed because of the birth, resurrection, and ascension of Christ!

In Samuel Shoemaker's opinion, "The surest mark of a Christian is not faith, or even love, but joy." If a dipstick could be placed into the depths of your being, what level of joy would it record?

The fruit of the Spirit is not lemons, chokecherries, or sour apples.

If your level of joy is low, why not add some meditations about the things that caused "great joy" to New Testament believers?

Attempts to Find Joy

For my people have committed two evils;
they have forsaken me the fountain of living waters,
and hewed them out cisterns, broken cisterns, that can hold no water.
—Jeremiah 2:13

Read Luke 15:11-20

Nero, emperor of Rome, who is believed to be responsible for the Apostle Paul's death, searched for joy. And he used a lot of money in his quest. He commanded that porches a mile in length be built around his palace. His crown was worth millions of dollars. His mules were shod with silver. His visitors were sprayed lightly with perfume from hidden showers installed at great expense. He refused to wear the same garment twice. Wherever he travelled, a thousand chariots accompanied him.

In his desperate search for joy, he paid huge sums of money to anyone who could think of new ways to entertain him. Instead of finding joy by committing his life to Christ, he found death by committing suicide.

The prodigal son was likewise unsuccessful in finding joy. He tried purchasing and partying. Other members of the human family resemble him in a number of ways. Like the prodigal, all we have has been provided by the Father. Like the prodigal, we have gone into a "far country"

(v. 13); "we have turned every one to his own way" (Isaiah 53:6). Like the prodigal, we have wasted the Father's gifts, living in spiritual riot and rebellion. The prodigal spent all and began to sense his desperate need. Our return to the Father, likewise, begins as we sense our need and acknowledge that we are spiritually bankrupt.

The prodigal was dead, in effect, in relation to his father who, upon his return, said, "This my son was dead, and is alive again" (v. 24). Thankfully, like the prodigal, we who have been "dead in trespasses and sins" (Ephesians 2:1), can become alive by being reconciled to the Father through Jesus. Our Father, like the prodigal's, will respect our choice to walk away from His favor and fellowship, but will also welcome us with love and rejoicing.

Augustine said, "There is a joy which is not given to the ungodly, but to those who love Thee for Thine own sake, whose joy Thou Thyself art. And this is the happy life, to rejoice in Thee, of Thee, for Thee; this is it, and there is no other."

One penitent sinner from the United States said, "There is more joy in Jesus in twenty-four hours than there is in the world in 365 days. I have tried them both."

Steps to Salvation's Joy

The Lord is not slack concerning his promise,
as some men count slackness; but is longsuffering to us-ward,
not willing that any should perish,
but that all should come to repentance.
— 2 Peter 3:9

Read Luke 15:21-32

If you were hungry, which would you choose: a plate with an engraved picture of tasty food, or a hamburger? If you were thirsty, would you like a billboard advertising a thirst-quenching drink, or a glass of water? The prodigal son made unwise choices that resulted in hunger for food and a thirst to see his father. What were the steps that led him back to his father?

1. *Be honest.* "He came to himself" (v. 17). This statement implies that he was only fooling himself before, that material things don't bring satisfaction, and that his situation was hopeless unless he returned to his father.

A sinner today must admit his need, his spiritual bankruptcy, and his hopeless condition outside of the Father's provision.

2. *Be humble.* It takes humility to say plainly, "I have sinned" (v. 21). He now had a lower opinion of himself. Previously he had said to his father, "*Give me* my inheritance." Upon returning, he said, "*Make me* a slave."

A sinner today needs to confess his sin and be ready to serve the Lord.

3. *Be resolved.* He had a determined desire and made a definite decision to seek reconciliation. Note the progression: "I will arise" (v. 18); "and he arose" (v. 20); "and came" (v. 20). He not only had a good purpose but also a good performance.

A sinner today needs to decide to come to God and then follow through with repentance and faith.

4. *Be accepting.* He received his father's welcome and embrace. He accepted the best robe—clothing given to the guest of honor. He accepted the ring—a symbol of authority. He accepted the shoes—a sign of his status as a son. (Slaves went barefoot.)

The penitent sinner today accepts the heavenly Father's pardon and is clothed richly, in spiritual terms. This brings him great joy. As Isaiah 61:10 says, "I will greatly rejoice in the Lord, my soul shall be joyful in my God; for he hath clothed me with the garments of salvation, he hath covered me with the robe of righteousness."

Jesus is the source of salvation and its attendant joy. "I am the way, the truth, and the life" (John 14:6). The prodigal (like us) was lost—Jesus is the way. The prodigal was ignorant—Jesus is the truth. The prodigal was dead—Jesus is the life.

The Joy of the Prodigal's Return

Likewise, I say unto you, there is joy in the presence of the angels of God over one sinner that repenteth.
— Luke 15:10

Read Acts 16:26-34

A Christian woman was given a Bible by John Vassar as he traveled across America on behalf of a tract society during the last half of the nineteenth century. Her husband was an atheist. When he saw the Bible in their home, he became angry. He took the Bible and his ax to the woodpile. He placed the Bible on the chopping block and hacked it in two. Then he threw half of the Bible at his wife, saying, "As you claim a part of all the property here, there is your share of this." He tossed the other half into his toolshed.

Months later on a damp winter's day, he went to the toolshed to get away from his Christian wife. Bored, he looked around and saw half of the Bible As he thumbed through it, he began to read the story of the prodigal son. He became absorbed by the story, but then discovered that the end of the story belonged in his wife's half of the book. He went into the house and furtively looked for it but couldn't find where his wife had hidden it.

Finally, he humbled himself and asked his wife for the other half. He read the story again and again and soon came to his heavenly Father, finding salvation and joy.

Joy is experienced on several levels when the prodigal comes home. First, there is joy within the prodigal's heart—sins forgiven, peace given, hope established, and reconciliation effected.

Second, there is joy on the part of the Father. In the parable, the father said to the elder son, "It was meet that we should make merry, and be glad: for this thy brother was dead, and is alive again; and was lost, and is found" (Luke 15:32).

Third, there is joy in Heaven among the angels. "There is joy in the presence of the angels of God over one sinner that repenteth" (Luke 15:10).

Fourth, there should have been rejoicing on the part of the elder brother. However, he was envious of all the attention given to his wasteful brother. Joy and jealousy do not mix. Instead, he was angry, bitter, and stubborn. Romans 12:15 tells us to "rejoice with them that do rejoice."

There is joy exquisite and everlasting in Heaven. Happily, there is joy already on earth if we are on the path to Heaven.

Be of Good Cheer

But straightway Jesus spake unto them, saying,
Be of good cheer; it is I; be not afraid.
— Matthew 14:27

Read Matthew 9:1-8

Cheerfulness is an important expression of joy. With it in your home you can have a feast, day after day, even if it is vegetable soup, grits, or leftovers on the table. Proverbs 15:15 says, "He that is of a merry heart hath a continual feast."

Smiles are a valuable aspect of cheerfulness. Only a few people (about 1,000 in the U.S.) cannot smile because of a medical condition known as Moebius syndrome. It impairs the facial muscles to the extent that the victim cannot smile. The remedy is for physicians to graft muscles and nerves from another part of the body, such as the leg, to the muscles used for chewing.

Children of God should not be affected with spiritual Moebius syndrome. Our Great Physician wants to make a graft of joy into our lives. He said, "These things have I spoken unto you, that my joy might remain in you, and that your joy might be full" (John 15:11).

Jesus gives the believer three cheers. One is in today's Scripture passage. This is the good cheer of forgiveness. Another is in the verse at the top of page 39. This is the good cheer of Christ's presence. A third is in John 16:33: "These things I have spoken unto you, that in me ye might have peace. In the world ye shall have tribulation: but be of good cheer; I have overcome the world." This is the good cheer of victory.

Besides pleasant smiles, how can a family express cheerfulness? We can have a positive outlook, anticipating God's grace. We can be thankful, remembering God's gifts and kindnesses. We can be optimistic, trusting the Lord to work things out. I don't know of any cases of eyestrain that have developed from looking on the bright side of things.

Get a grip on griping and eliminate grumbling. Speak pleasant words. Proverbs 16:24 says, "Pleasant words are as an honeycomb, sweet to the soul, and health to the bones." Have an attitude of contentment, for "godliness with contentment is great gain." The truly rich person is the one who is content with what he has.

Cheerfulness is contagious. Be a carrier in your home and beyond.

Joy Amidst Trials

My brethren, count it all joy when ye fall into divers temptations.
—James 1:2

Read Acts 16:19-25

Amy Carmichael, missionary to India, who faced numerous trials, wrote, "Joys are always on the way to us. They are always travelling to us through the darkness of the night. There is never a night when they are not coming." She had caught the thrust of today's verse.

Paul and Silas, bound in stocks in a Greek jail, knew how to experience joy in trial too. Later Paul wrote to his Philippian friends, "Rejoice in the Lord alway: and again I say, Rejoice" (Philippians 4:4). I can imagine the Philippian jailor, who found joy that night (Acts 16:34), reading Paul's command to rejoice *always* and thinking, *Ah, yes, I remember that night. I was amazed at those two fellows. They were as jubilant as a person being pardoned and released from prison. However, their backs were bleeding, because I had really laid it on. They were in the inner prison where there was no chance of escape. Their feet were in stocks.*

They were so happy singing and praying that it caught the attention of the other prisoners. And I was listening to what they were praying and praising before I fell asleep. Yes, Paul sure lived up to his admonition to rejoice always.

I'm impressed by what I read in *Martyrs Mirror* about George Wagner, an early Anabaptist of Munich, Germany, who likewise had joy in jail. He was severely tortured. The prince personally came to the prison to offer him freedom, saying that he would call George his friend for life if he renounced Christ. George's wife and child were brought to prison in an effort to make George turn from Jesus.

Martyrs Mirror says, "Having been delivered into the hands of the executioner, and led into the middle of the city, he said: 'Today I will confess my God before all the world.' He had such joy in Christ Jesus, that his face did not pale, nor his eyes show fear; but he went smilingly to the fire. And having smilingly bid farewell to a Christian, who was there, he was thrust into the fire by the executioner, and happily offered up his spirit."

The Joy of the Lord Is Your Strength

The joy of the Lord is your strength.
— Nehemiah 8:10

Read Philippians 4:4-13

How does joy make a person strong as today's verse says? Here are a few ideas:

1. *Joy brings strength in times of temptation.* A Christian doesn't want guilt to destroy the peace and joy of a right relationship with God. Therefore, joy can strengthen his spiritual backbone against temptation to sin.

After David's sin with Bathsheba, he had a dry, joyless, guilt-driven experience. He tells of his feelings in Psalm 32:4: "Day and night thy hand was heavy upon me: my moisture is turned into the drought of summer." After he repented and confessed his sin, he prayed, "Make me to hear joy and gladness; that the bones which thou hast broken may rejoice. . . . Restore unto me the joy of thy salvation" (Psalm 51:8, 12).

2. *Joy brings strength in pain and sorrow.* You may become ill. You may lose a son or a spouse to an accident or cancer. You may face financial reverses. You may have chronic pain. Your best friend may forsake you. Yet the joy of knowing that Jesus cares and will walk beside you through your difficulties gives you strength. The joy of trusting that "all things work together for good to them that love God, to them who are the called according to his purpose" (Romans 8:28) gives the Christian fortitude.

3. *Joy brings strength in times of prosperity.* There is real danger that you may be overpowered by materialism. Joy expressed in gratitude to God can provide spiritual power in a culture of covetousness and forgetting God. See Deuteronomy 8:10-14 to be warned of wealth's peril.

4. *Joy makes a strong witness.* Norman Grubb in his biography of C. T. Studd, a missionary who traveled by ship to China, tells of Studd's witness of joy. The captain didn't love the Lord and opposed those who did. The only reason he studied the Bible was so he could argue more knowledgeably with Christians. Hearing about a missionary on board, he encountered Studd and lit into him. Studd didn't argue. He put his arm around the captain and said, "But my friend, I have a peace that passeth all understanding, and a joy that nothing can take away."

   The captain listened and observed him; finally he walked away, saying, "You're a lucky dog." Before the voyage ended, the captain had found joy in Jesus too.

Joyful George

by Janelle (Erb) Kuepfer

It was a cold and starless night in southern Germany. Even the moon hid behind thick clouds. A lone man hurried through empty fields in the inky darkness. He hesitated as he neared a grove of trees. Suddenly he disappeared into the forest. The tall trees with their bare limbs seemed to have swallowed him.

In the shelter of the forest, George dodged from tree to tree. He walked farther and deeper into the forest until he came upon a small clearing, where a few lanterns gave a weak light. He counted about twenty other people sitting on logs and stumps. Even as he watched, others emerged from the shadows.

Silently slipping into the gathering, George seated himself on a log. His lanky legs felt cramped, and the log was no soft seat after a hard day's work. *Wouldn't it be wonderful to have a real church to worship in?* George thought. *I would love to be the one chosen to craft chairs and benches for the church.* His hands, so clever at carpentry, twitched at the thought.

Someone started a song, and the rest of the group joined in. One song led to another. Then George saw two more figures appear from the darkness of the forest. They sat in front of the group of people with their heads bowed.

As the song died out, one of the two new arrivals stood up. "Greetings, brothers and sisters, in Jesus' name. Several of you have been waiting for this night for several weeks. Tonight we will baptize those who desire to be obedient to God's Word and who want to follow the true church."

George leaned forward on the log as the man preached. If only he could remember everything the man said!

The night wore on, deep and cold, but still the people listened. George took his turn watching in the shadows for unwanted guests. He was glad when his turn was over and he could once more listen to the Word of God. At last the preacher invited, "Those who wish to be baptized in the name of Jesus, come forward."

George jumped up from the log and hurried to the front with five others. For a moment, his eyes flicked over those standing with him: an older couple holding hands beside him, two other young men, and an even younger girl. He could only imagine that his face shone just like theirs. The irony of the moment left him breathless. *How amazing that we can be so happy about doing such a dangerous thing! It's like writing our own death sentences!* But George knew he had made the right decision.

"Do you promise to remain true and faithful to Jesus as long as you live?" The minister directed the first question to George.

"Yes, I do." George's strong voice carried through the cold night air. *Nothing* would cause him to betray his Lord! Not even the imprisonment or severe torture that so many other brethren faced. He would rather die! There was no way he could betray His Lord, the One who gave him this peace! George knelt with the others and was baptized into the church of Jesus Christ.

George had just picked up his hammer in his workshop several weeks later when he heard a quiet knock on his back door. He laid the hammer down, brushed sawdust off his trousers, and hurried to see who had come. A boy, well known to George, about eleven years old, handed him a warm loaf of bread wrapped in a cloth.

"Ah," George smiled down at the child and nodded, "just what I wished for. Tell your mother I am grateful." He paused, and then asked, "Do you know of anyone around here who could use some wood scraps?" His eyes twinkled.

The boy played the game well. "I'm sure I do, Brother George." He watched as George reached below his table and picked up scraps of wood. Together they stuffed his pockets, and the boy headed home, whistling, with his hands full of wood chunks.

Meanwhile, George picked up the bread, still wrapped in the cloth, and carried it to his bedroom. Carefully he unfolded the cloth and laid the bread on his bed. He held the cloth up to the window and then reached for a knife in his trouser pocket. Slitting the hem open in one corner, he pulled out a tiny piece of paper. He read the note twice; then he carried the paper to the fireplace in his workshop and watched as flames licked hungrily at it until it was gone. Satisfied, he took the bread to his kitchen and returned to his work.

That evening after dark, when the streets were silent and still, George stepped from his workshop into the cold night air. A bitter wind caused him to shudder inside his well-worn cloak. Clinging to the shadows, he left the streets of town behind, crossing over ditches and fields toward the meadow where tonight's meeting would be held. When he was sure no light from the town could betray him, he broke into a run.

At last he reached the meadow and spied a group of men huddled together. A lantern shone dimly from their circle, and as George hurried to them, he noticed they were reading from a book.

The men shifted when they saw him, inviting him to join their circle. George peered closely at the book. "A Bible!" he whispered in awe. "Praise the Lord!"

He didn't bother to ask who had brought it or where they had found it. Reading a Bible, even owning one, was a crime. The Catholic Church forbade Bibles—even the priests were not allowed to read them. A lump formed in George's throat. *Thank You, Father!* he praised.

As he reached out and gently touched the worn pages, a shout from nearby made him jump. He heard the sound of ancient paper tearing as his fingers jerked. Startled at the commotion, the men looked up from the Bible. Horses thundered across the meadow, their riders carrying lanterns and swords.

Men and women from the secret meeting fled in every direction. In the chaos that followed, the precious Bible fell to the ground.

George spotted the Bible on the ground and snatched it up. *I cannot let the enemy find this precious Book! Oh, God, please help me to reach safety with Your Word!* he breathed. Never had he been so glad for his long legs as he raced for the nearest tree. The air shook with the thunderous sound of hooves.

But the few seconds it had taken him to stoop and sweep up the Bible were costly. A horse plunged to a stop beside him and its rider dismounted. Pouncing on George, he pinned him to the ground, yelling and cursing. George dropped the Bible behind his back as subtly as he could, hoping the man would not see it. But the hunter caught the gleam in the lantern light as the Bible fell to the ground. Snatching it up with an ugly grin of triumph, he hissed, "It will not be well for you, you crazy Anabaptist. We will kill you because we found you with this book." Leering at George, he grabbed a strong rope from his pocket and bound George's hands together.

For a moment, George trembled. Would they torture him? Would they burn him at the stake or put him into a barrel and drown him? Would his friends ever know what had happened to him? *I am so young in the faith, Father!*

A still small voice replied, "Remember My own suffering and death! I know exactly what you are experiencing!"

From deep within him, a joy flooded his being. *I know You'll be with me always, Father, even in death!*

No path led out of the meadow, and George stumbled on the uneven ground. "Keep moving," his captor barked, prodding him with the edge of his sword. George stumbled on, tired and weak. A verse he had memorized days before flashed through his mind: "The joy of the Lord is your strength." Despite the cold and uneven ground, a smile crossed George's lips. *My Father is with me! I have nothing to fear!* His steps gained confidence.

At last they reached the prison. The smell was worse than George had ever imagined. In the darkness, moans and yells echoed in the corridors, and he heard vermin scuttling about. He slipped and nearly fell on the slimy floor.

Shoving him into a cell, his captor slammed and locked the door behind him. George, dreadfully cold and tired, fell into an exhausted sleep.

He awoke the next morning to the sound of a key grating in the lock. Without a word, a guard advanced into the cell. He grabbed George's shoulder, pulled him to his feet, and shoved him out the door and down the hall. Their footsteps echoed in the dark corridors. Ahead of them loomed a large metal door. The guard took a key from his pocket and shoved it into the keyhole. Protesting loudly, the massive door swung open.

George could see what appeared to be a prison courtroom. Still not saying a word, the guard shoved him to a post to which he tied George's hands and feet. Then he sat in a chair beside George and promptly fell asleep.

Give me strength, Lord, George prayed as they waited. *I don't know what my enemies will do to me, but my life is in Your hands.* He continued to pray even when he heard a door slam. He could tell several people had entered the room. Raising his head, he saw a priest of the Catholic Church. Beside him were several other important men.

"What is your name?" began the priest.

"George Bauman."

"How old are you?" the priest questioned. He barely gave George time to answer before he fired more questions. "Are you rebaptized? Do you attend the Catholic Church?"

"I have been baptized once, according to the teachings of God," George answered, "and am a member of the true church of God."

The priest and his men had many more questions for George, arguing with him for hours. They accused him of leaving their church, the Catholic Church. They wanted to know who had baptized him, where the believers met, who attended the meetings, and where they had gotten the Bible. Every word George spoke was copied down by one of the lords. The priests tried their best to convince George to recant, or give up his faith, but George refused. "My Father has done so much for me. I cannot betray Him," he testified.

Defeated, the priest dismissed him and the guard led him back to his prison cell. For several weeks they left him in that horrible place.

Then one day, the guard reappeared. This time, he led George to a room in the basement of the prison. Here he saw many devices used for torture. He began to sweat. Stories swirled in his mind of other believers who had nearly died in torture chambers like this one.

Several men entered the room, one of them a priest. The air about him reeked of craftiness. "We won't torture you if you confess, George! Please, make it easy for yourself and us by confessing your wrongs. Just think, you could go home and never come back to this prison!"

But George replied, "I will remain true to God and will not confess wrong that I have not done."

The priest turned to his companion. "He will confess when he feels the racks! Now!" he ordered.

A rough-looking man grabbed George and bellowed, "Take off your clothes." Meekly, George obeyed. The man laid him on the rack and bound him to it. "I won't hurt you if you tell me who baptized you," the man sneered down at George.

George didn't say anything. He knew these men did not keep their promises. Even if they did, he would not recant. Staying faithful to God was all that mattered.

"If you won't tell me, I will make you!" The man cranked a wheel on the rack, pulling tight the ropes. The more he cranked, the more the ropes stretched George's body. Extreme pain coursed through his body as his joints stretched and muscles and tendons ripped.

The man paused for a moment. "Tell us who you met with, and we will set you free."

George didn't answer even though he was in tremendous pain. He would not betray his friends.

"More! More!" the priest cried.

Again George felt his body being pulled to its limits. Surely he could not bear this much longer. He would soon die! Next the men stopped the rack and poured cold water in George's mouth and over his nose. George gasped for air; he felt as if he were drowning!

At last he couldn't bear it anymore. His body screamed for air. "Stop!" he cried out. "I confess!"

"If you promise to return to our holy Catholic Church, we will quit," the priest vowed.

George hurt all over. He could hardly think, but he knew he could not bear any more torture. Between moans, he managed to say, "I was wrong!" before he fell unconscious.

The priest smirked evilly, and within hours George was released from prison. He hurt everywhere, especially his legs and arms that had almost been torn from his body. The fingers that had been so clever at carpentry now lay swollen and useless.

Often he thought of his fellow brethren and a guilty feeling swept over him. He tried to forget about them, to clear his conscience, but a nagging feeling remained. He still felt as though he were in prison. He was depressed, and nothing could cheer him.

When George recovered enough to hobble, the priests marched him to the Catholic Church. There, George confessed to the wrong he had done by being rebaptized. But deep in his heart he knew the real wrong was not his rebaptism. He had betrayed his heavenly Father. But the priests made sure that he kept his promise. They made him confess a second time. George didn't want to do it, but he was too ashamed to speak to his brethren again. He felt like a traitor, wretched and vile.

Finally, one night after wrestling with his conscience, George came to his senses. What had he done? He remembered the night of his baptism and the joy in his heart that night. He didn't have that joy now. He felt so empty! How foolish he had been to betray the Lord! How he must have hurt his Father when he chose to disobey Him!

Slowly George crawled out of bed, kneeling as carefully as he could. "Father, forgive me!" he wept. "Oh, that I could die for Your sake! If they torture me now till I die, it will be worth the pain and suffering! I would rather live forever with You than to live without peace in my heart! I want Your joy in my life again!"

George slept better that night than he had for weeks.

The next morning George awoke to the sound of rain. But it didn't dampen his mood. He knew spring was coming. And with spring came new life! Maybe his body was worn and tired, but his heart was fresh and new! He burst into song.

Just then a knock sounded on the door. George opened it and saw the priest standing outside. "Time for Mass," he announced. "You must confess your wrongs once more. After this time, we can forgive your sin."

George said nothing even though he was nearly bursting with his news. He followed the priest to the enormous church. He couldn't help but smile at the soft, warm rain. He had made up his mind, and there was no turning back.

For the third time George stood in front of the priest. But instead of confessing, George announced, "You arrested me for becoming an Anabaptist. I recanted and chose to follow you when my pain became too great. But now I am sorry that I recanted and I choose, once again, to follow the true church of Christ."

The priest stepped back, startled.

George continued, "What you teach in the Catholic Church is false. You are worshiping idols and living life for yourself. And if you torture me again, I will not betray my Lord. He has given me a joy in my heart that you cannot take away! If this means dying for the sake of my Father, I am willing," he finished with a smile.

The priest and his helper looked at each other. "Well, what more evidence do we need than what he has just said?" declared the priest. "Bind him," he ordered.

"You *will* die this time," the priest hissed to George. Then he ordered, "Take him to the courts. I will have him sentenced to death immediately! How dare he speak out against the holy Catholic Church!"

George wasn't afraid—in fact, he felt like singing! He had been faithful! He felt no regrets when the judge sentenced him to die the next day.

The following morning, George awoke refreshed and at peace with himself and God. He couldn't stop the songs that burst from his heart. Another prisoner growled at him to stop singing, but George kept on.

When he heard the dull thud of footsteps coming down the corridor, George knew his time had come. "Be faithful, brethren!" he called out to his fellow Christians as he walked out the doors for the last time. Several men and a woman called back, encouraging George to be steadfast to the end. He knew, without a doubt, that he would be faithful to God.

The guard led him out onto the street. They followed the crowd heading to the executioner's block. The rain had stopped in the night, and the streets had lots of gooey mud. George hardly noticed the mud as a song burst from his heart. He had so much to look forward to today. Before long, he would be in Heaven with Jesus! Briskly, he walked through the village.

The guard looked at George strangely, but didn't say anything. *His singing won't last long. He'll be dead in a few minutes. I might as well let him sing as long as he wants.*

The guard noticed George pick up his pace; then for a moment he thought George had stumbled. But George kept right on walking, singing as he went. The guard looked back to see what George had stumbled over. A look of surprise flickered across his face. The mud had sucked both shoes right off George's feet! But he hurried on, barefoot in the mud. And he hadn't stopped singing!

For the first time the guard listened to what George was singing. It sounded like a song of thanksgiving. Listening more closely, he heard George sing the phrase, "The joy of the Lord is my strength" over and over.

The two men stepped up to the executioner's block. A crowd of curious people had gathered around to watch. George continued to sing until the executioner ended his life.

Questions for Review

1. In what country did the story take place?
2. In which two places did the Anabaptist believers meet?
3. Why did they meet in secret places?
4. How did George feel when he knew he was following Jesus?
5. What happened when George was walking as he was thinking of soon seeing Jesus?

Questions for Discussion

1. This story is based on an account in *Martyrs Mirror* (page 438). Do you have a copy in your home, and has anyone in your family read any of it?
2. Why did George lose his joy and happiness for awhile?
3. How did George get his happiness back again?

4. Why were the Anabaptists (who mostly are called Mennonites now) persecuted and put to death?
5. How do Christians feel when they put Jesus ahead of everything else?

PEACE

JESUS, PRINCE OF PEACE

But now in Christ Jesus ye who sometimes
were far off are made nigh by the blood of Christ.
For he is our peace.
— Ephesians 2:13, 14

READ ISAIAH 9:1-7

I love the names ascribed to Jesus in verse 6 of our daily reading—Wonderful, Counsellor, Mighty God, Everlasting Father, and Prince of Peace. How wonderful that we can experience the blessed reality of these names in God's relating to us.

Jesus was Prince of Peace before He was born in Bethlehem. Not only in Isaiah 9:6, but also in Isaiah 32 the prophet tells of royalty. Verse 17 mentions that the King's "work of righteousness shall be peace; and the effect of righteousness quietness and assurance for ever."

Jesus was Prince of Peace at His birth. The angels proclaimed, "Glory to God in the highest, and on earth peace, good will toward men" (Luke 2:14).

Jesus was Prince of Peace in His life. He was able to calm the storms on the Sea of Galilee as He said to the waves beating against the disciples' ship, "Peace, be still. And the wind ceased, and there was a great calm" (Mark 4:39). He was also able to calm the storms of guilt and anxiety as He related to those who put their trust in Him.

Jesus was Prince of Peace in His death. As Colossians 1:20, 21 says, "And, having made peace through the blood of his cross, by him to reconcile all things unto himself; by him, I say, whether they be things in earth, or things in heaven. And you, that were sometime alienated and enemies in your mind by wicked works, yet now hath he reconciled."

He was Prince of Peace in His resurrection. After arising from the dead, He appeared to His peace-deprived disciples with the words, "Peace be unto you" (John 20:19).

He is Prince of Peace to His followers today. Christians testify to the truth of His words, "Peace I leave with you, my peace I give unto you: not as the world giveth, give I unto you. Let not your heart be troubled, neither let it be afraid" (John 14:27). Therefore, as messengers of Christ, we go forth with the word of peace on our lips, the gift of peace in our hands, and the light of peace upon our faces.

Peace From the Prince of Peace

For to be carnally minded is death; but to be spiritually minded is life and peace.
— Romans 8:6

Read John 14:23-29

What is peace? I like one boy's explanation. He said, "Peace is when you feel all smooth inside."

I remember before I became a Christian I didn't feel all smooth inside. I felt rough and unsettled with guilt because I knew I had done wrong things, thought sinful thoughts, said ungodly words, and held carnal attitudes. I felt dread because I knew God would judge me and I would end up in Hell if I didn't repent. I felt conviction because I knew I should repent and surrender to Jesus, but I was unwilling. I felt fear because I knew if Christ would return, I was not prepared for eternity. I felt uncomfortable because several people had encouraged me to yield to God and I didn't want to talk about it. From the time I sensed my accountability to God until I became a Christian when I was about seventeen, I didn't have peace.

But the evening I repented of my sinful way and believed in Jesus as my Saviour and took Him as my Pattern, I knew the blessed reality of "peace with God through our Lord Jesus Christ" (Romans 5:1). I experienced a peace unlike that found in the world, as our daily reading says. I knew there was nothing between my soul and the Saviour. I was ready to die. I was ready for life with Jesus in my heart. I felt so free, so joyful, so smooth inside. It was genuine peace because it was rooted in the reality of Christ's atonement and my response to His promises.

I have never forgotten the peace that comes from sins forgiven and a readiness to do whatever God showed me. I continue to appreciate "the peace of God, which passeth all understanding" (Philippians 4:7). I have lost it sometimes when I have wandered from His commandments and felt guilty. But as I have followed 1 John 1:9, it has returned. "If we confess our sins, he is faithful and just to forgive us our sins, and to cleanse us from all unrighteousness."

Go where you will—your soul will find no peace but in the bosom of Christ. He, the Prince of Peace, is the source of spiritual peace.

PEACE IN SPITE OF GRIEF

The LORD will give strength unto his people;
the LORD will bless his people with peace.
— Psalm 29:11

READ PSALM 119:161-176

A favorite story that left a deep impression on me in my younger years is the book *Stand By, Boys!* It tells of a destructive flood in the Netherlands in 1953. As the water rose, residents climbed into attics and onto the rooftops of their houses, and some even floated on doors and furniture. All of the family featured in the book were eventually rescued except the godly mother, who drowned during the rescue attempt. What especially struck me was the attitude of the father, who reported to his son Art that "We are all safe," meaning that although his wife had drowned, she was safe in Jesus, and so all was well in the ultimate sense. He had peace even in the midst of great loss. He let "the peace of God rule" in his heart (Colossians 3:15). And Art recalled the words of his mother the day before, when rescue looked uncertain: "If we should not see each other again, I want you to know that all is well with Mother. Jesus has made all things well."

A few years before, during World War II, a British missionary in Portugal, Eric Barker, had faced great danger. He had preached the

Gospel there for many years. His family was in such peril during the war that he accepted advice to send his wife and eight children to Britain for safety. His sister and her three children were evacuated on the same ship. Eric remained in Portugal to conclude some mission matters.

The Sunday after Barker's loved ones sailed, he stood before his congregation in Portugal and announced, "I have just received word that all my family have arrived safely home." He then went on with the service as usual.

It wasn't until later that the full meaning of his words became known to his congregation. Prior to the service, he had received word that a submarine had torpedoed the ship and everyone on board had drowned. Because his family members were all believers, he believed they all arrived in their heavenly home.

As verse 165 of our daily reading indicates, nothing need destroy our peace. In the most extreme and painful situations, God can give peace so that the believer doesn't go to pieces.

PEACE AT HOME

Depart from evil,
and do good;
seek peace, and pursue it.
— Psalm 34:14

READ COLOSSIANS 3:12-21

During the Vietnam era in American history, 58,000 U.S. military personnel lost their lives. During the same years, 54,000 women in the U.S. were killed by husbands, ex-husbands, or boyfriends. Policemen called to a home where there is a domestic dispute know they are facing one of their most dangerous assignments. God intends for the home to be a place of harmony and peace, but many homes resemble war zones.

As Christians, we do not kill one another. But if looks could kill, if verbal shots could assassinate more than character, or if hostile attitudes could snuff out more than happiness at home, there would be many casualties.

Whether we relate at home as husbands and wives or parents and children or brothers and sisters, we have been called to peace. I love the words of the song by Henry Ware, "Happy the Home Where God Is There."

"Lord, let us in our homes agree
This blessed peace to gain;
Unite our hearts in love to Thee,
And love to all will reign."

As nonresistant Christians we realize it's not right to go to war. But do we understand that it's not right to quarrel, bicker, seek revenge, and fight in our homes? When husbands and wives are combative, children are often the casualties. Just as in warfare, innocent people often suffer.

Our daily reading mentions valuable attitudes that generate harmony if all family members demonstrate them. Kindness, humility, meekness, patience, forbearance, forgiveness, charity (12-14) all contribute to peace (v. 15). Let's look at the different elements of a family:

Husbands have an important peacekeeping mission. Love your wives. Don't be bitter against them (v. 20).

Wives have an important responsibility. They are to submit graciously (v. 19). This will avoid conflict.

Some children are hostile toward their parents. Teenagers can turn a house into a demilitarized zone by complete obedience. This will please your parents and your heavenly Father (v. 20).

Fathers must avoid frustrating their offspring (v. 21).

Let each member of your family live in harmony. Remember: family peace is homemade.

Restoring Peace

Confess your faults one to another,
and pray one for another, that ye may be healed.
The effectual fervent prayer of a righteous man availeth much.
—James 5:16

Read Genesis 33:1-11

A manager of a restaurant in California, Thomas Martin (now the former manager), reported that a robbery took place just as the eatery was closing. He called the police. Martin provided the police sketch-artist a detailed description of the thief. Before the artist had finished his sketch, he commented on how his picture resembled Martin. Investigators also noted the striking similarity and interrogated Martin. Martin then confessed that he was the wrongdoer.

Jacob engaged in deception and stole his brother's birthright. After being away from home for twenty years, he desired to return and make peace with his brother. Learn some lessons from his experiences:

1. Admit that you were wrong. Jacob's generous gift to Esau indicates his acknowledgment that he cheated his brother. A wag who was familiar with preserving produce in jars and who liked puns said, "A family jar is no good for preserving the peace."

2. Be at peace with God. Just prior to meeting his brother, as shown in the daily reading, Jacob made peace with God and received divine blessing (Genesis 32:24-30). Making peace is best lubricated by prayer.
3. Be humble. As Jacob approached his brother, he bowed seven times. Humble pie is not tasty, but it contains much nourishment.
4. Make restitution. Jacob offered Esau "two hundred she goats, and twenty he goats, two hundred ewes, and twenty rams, thirty milch camels with their colts, forty kine, and ten bulls, twenty she asses, and ten foals" (Genesis 32:14, 15). How much do you think this would be worth in our money?
5. Desire favor with the offended. Jacob's gift was to "find grace in the sight of my lord" (Genesis 33:8).
6. Be thoughtful. Jacob had thought things through. A little of the oil of thoughtfulness will save a lot of friction.
7. Be courteous. Jacob's speech was polite and respectful. He even called Esau his "lord." Courtesy costs nothing, but it gives you things that are priceless.
8. Be complimentary. Jacob told Esau, "I have seen thy face, as though I had seen the face of God" (Genesis 33:10). Don't forget that appreciation is always appreciated.

Confession is good for the soul. It also is good for relationships. Do you know the best way to have the last word in an argument? Apologize!

Making Peace, Not Pieces

Blessed are the peacemakers:
for they shall be called the children of God.
— Matthew 5:9

Read Joshua 22:10-34

Had you known before you read the daily reading about the role Ed played in maintaining peace between two factions in Israel? Conflict and misunderstandings can easily arise in the twenty-first century among God's people. Take a few lessons from Israel's experience:

- *Don't jump to conclusions from hearsay.* The children of Israel heard (v. 11) that the two and one-half tribes east of the Jordan were building their own altar. They assumed they were rebelling and prepared to attack them. Instead of jumping to conclusions, love gives the benefit of the doubt. Don't judge a man's actions until you know his motives.

- *The people involved should talk directly rather than relying on secondhand reports.* The western tribes sent representatives to make investigation (vv. 13-15). This is much better than taking the "grapevine" route to find out "information."

- *Refrain from accusations based on supposition* (vv. 16-19). The western tribes accused the eastern ones of rebelling. This would bring dire consequences (v. 20). Jesus said, "Judge not, that ye be not judged" (Matthew 7:1). Suppositions are like a pair of tinted glasses—they make all the world look dark.
- *Give an opportunity for explanation.* The eastern tribes explained that the construction of their altar arose not from rebellion but from a desire to give witness to future generations that they were part of Israel. When wrongly accused, it is important to remember the Biblical proverb, "A soft answer turneth away wrath: but grievous words stir up anger" (Proverbs 15:1). If you experience a slip of the foot you may soon recover, but a slip of the tongue you may never get over.
- *Accept your brother's sincerity.* Verse 30 says, "When Phinehas the priest, and the princes of the congregation and heads of the thousands of Israel which were with him, heard the words that the children of Reuben and the children of Gad and the children of Manasseh spake, it pleased them." Practice the Golden Rule and have a frame of mind that tends to believe your brother.
- *Communicate accurately.* Upon returning home, the representatives "brought them word again" (v. 32). We should not give a slanted version of events by selective reporting. Thus the misunderstanding among the tribes was eliminated. They called the big altar *Ed* as a witness of their peace (v. 34).

Though Trials Should Come

Run now, I pray thee, to meet her,
and say unto her, Is it well with thee?
is it well with thy husband?
is it well with the child?
And she answered, It is well.
— 2 Kings 4:26

READ PSALM 46

A favorite song of many Christians is "It Is Well With My Soul." One verse begins with the words, "Though Satan should buffet, though trials should come." The author, Horatio G. Spafford, certainly had trials.

Horatio lived in Chicago, where he had very profitable real estate holdings. But then came the Great Chicago Fire of 1871. Many of the buildings he owned were destroyed. He was thankful that he, his wife, and their four daughters had escaped the fire.

In 1873, he experienced another loss. A son was born who lived only a short time.

In view of all the trials they had experienced, Horatio decided a vacation in Europe would be good for his family. A main motive behind the trip was to assist D. L. Moody and Ira Sankey in one of their evangelistic campaigns in England. In November, Horatio put his wife and four daughters on a ship, *Ville de Havre.* He planned to set sail for Europe a few days later after taking care of a few business details.

Halfway across the Atlantic ocean, the *Ville de Havre* was struck by another vessel. Twelve minutes later it sank. All of the Spaffords' daughters—Maggie, Annie, Tanetta, and Bessie—drowned. Mrs. Spafford, rescued from a floating plank, and a few others survived. On December 1, Horatio got a telegram from his wife from England, "Saved alone."

Horatio boarded the next ship to Europe. When the ship sailed over the area where his daughters had drowned, the captain called Horatio to the deck. When Horatio returned to his cabin, he wrote these words:

"When peace like a river attendeth my way,
When sorrows like sea billows roll,
Whatever my lot, Thou has taught me to say,
It is well, it is well with my soul.

Though Satan should buffet, though trials should come,
Let this blest assurance control,
That Christ hath regarded my helpless estate,
And hath shed His own blood for my soul."

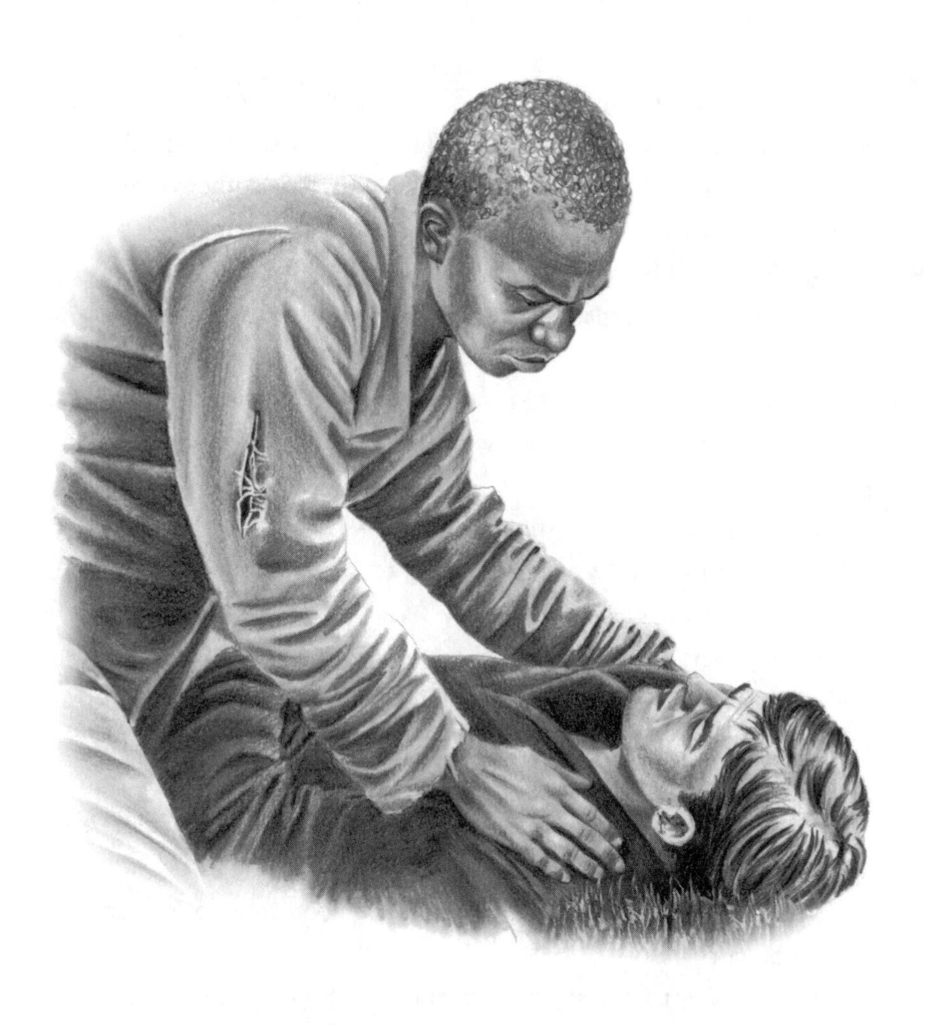

Zeke's Revenge

by Juliann Ropp Good

"Where are you going with that, girlie?" Grandpa asked, catching Hannah's arm as she hurried past his chair.

"I'm in a hurry, Grandpa!" Hannah protested, trying to wriggle free of his grasp.

"Not so fast, young lady, not so fast," Grandpa returned, drawing his arm about Hannah's waist and pulling her close enough that she couldn't escape. "When I see a young lady hurrying somewhere with a hammer in her hand and anger in her face, I need to know where she's going. Now, where are you going?"

"Nowhere, Grandpa, just lemme go!" Hannah was still trying to squirm herself free.

"Hannah!" Grandpa spoke sternly now. "You need to tell me exactly what you plan on doing with that hammer before I will let you go."

Hannah hung her head sheepishly. She was caught, fair and square. "Grandpa, I won't do what I was going to do. I'll go put the hammer away if you let me go."

Grandpa shook his head. "So you were up to no good, I see," he said, "just as I thought. Well, you're in for it now, girlie. You need to tell me what you were going to do with that hammer."

Hannah groaned. She liked having Grandpa live with them, but sometimes it was quite unhandy to have another pair of adult eyes around.

"Well?" Grandpa prodded. "The sooner you tell me, the sooner I'll let you go."

"I was going to smash the airplane that Joel is making!" Hannah burst out, hot anger returning to her face.

"You were . . . you were . . . *what?*" Grandpa was stunned.

"You see," Hannah continued, her eyes flashing, "I was outside having a tea party with Teddy Boy and my dolls, and we were just starting our tea and cookies when that Joel came around. He said he thought Teddy Boy looked miserable sitting with all those girls, and that he'd put him out of his misery. Then he threw Teddy Boy high up in the tree, and his poor little trousers got caught in a branch high up, and he's still hanging there! Joel thought it was the funniest thing ever and ran away laughing. I can't climb the tree because the first branch is too high up, and I was so mad that I decided to smash Joel's airplane and teach him a lesson!"

Grandpa sagged in his chair and raised his eyes to the ceiling. "Children, children," he said, shaking his head. Then he looked back at Hannah. "You ought to know by now that two wrongs never make a right, Hannah. Smashing Joel's airplane wouldn't have resolved anything, and furthermore, it would have showed your actions to be as bad as Joel's. Listen, I know a good story to tell you. I want you to go call Joel. Tell him I want to talk with him. When you're both here, I'll tell you the story."

A few minutes later, Hannah and Joel sat in front of Grandpa, Joel looking a little shamefaced and Hannah still looking sullen.

"This story happened a long time ago," Grandpa began. "I always think of it when someone does me wrong and I'm tempted to do them wrong in return. It makes me feel ashamed of my revengeful feelings, believe me." He looked pointedly at Hannah, who fidgeted a little on her chair.

Grandpa continued with his story. "Zeke was a slave who lived on a big cotton plantation in Mississippi many years ago. He was probably no older than your father, Hannah and Joel, but already he had the body of an old man. His back was stooped from hard labor and his hair was gray. He was a hard worker, dependable, and well liked by everyone.

"Zeke's master, Mr. Cobbs, was not the worst of his kind, but he was not always a good master. He made his slaves work very hard, and his overseers beat anyone they thought too lazy. The slaves lived in crude huts that were difficult to keep clean and got just enough food to keep them alive.

"There came a time when a restlessness crept over Mr. Cobbs' slaves. They were tired of working themselves to death and tired of being hungry all the time. There were whispers of a rebellion: killing Mr. Cobbs and his overseers and taking over his plantation.

"Every Sunday the slaves walked far into the forest to have a church service, for Mr. Cobbs had forbade them to sing within his hearing.

"One Sunday, when the slaves gathered for their worship service, Zeke was surprised to see a white man slip out from behind some bushes and stand in their midst. 'Friends,' said the white man, 'my name is Carl Wilson, and I have come to tell you that there is a better way to freedom than rebelling against your master.' Mr. Wilson told them about a plan for getting slaves to Canada and freedom. Zeke felt some of the tension and restlessness in the air change to excitement and hope.

"Somehow Mr. Cobbs found out about Mr. Wilson, and he gathered the slaves together for a talk. Mr. Cobbs' face was dark and stern as he faced the crowd. His overseers stood beside him, whips in hand, their eyes glittering at all the black faces.

"Mr. Cobbs marched back and forth, shouting, 'I have heard a report about a white man helping slaves escape from their masters. Now, I want all of you to know something. If any one of my slaves runs away from me, he'll get caught. Do you get that? We'll use dogs and horses and catch him. He'll be dragged back here and whipped within an inch of his life.' The veins on Mr. Cobbs' forehead stood out and his face was red. 'Do you hear me?' he yelled.

" 'And now,' he snarled, his voice dropping as he leaned toward them, 'I want something to be very, very clear to you. Zeke, come here.' He motioned toward Zeke. 'Yes, YOU!' he hollered impatiently as Zeke hesitated. 'Now, everyone look at Zeke here,' he continued when Zeke was standing beside him. 'This is what I want you to understand. If any one of you attempts to escape from this place, you will not only be putting yourself in danger, but you'll be putting good ole Zeke here in danger too. Hear that? Now, you wouldn't want poor old Zeke to get a whipping, would ya? Y'all like Zeke, don't ya? He's a good man and a good worker, and you wouldn't want to see him hurt, right? But let me tell you something.' Here Mr. Cobbs lowered his voice some more and his eyes sparked in his reddened face. 'The minute one of you runs off, I will hold Zeke responsible. Yes, you heard me. I'll hold Zeke responsible for the runaway. That means he'll get whipped within an inch of his life!'

"A shudder went through the crowd of slaves, and no one spoke as they went to their work.

"Zeke spent a lot of time praying that day. 'Oh, Lawd, help us,' he prayed over and over.

"A few days later, four slaves ran away. Zeke had heard they were going to, and they had begged him to go with them. 'No,' Zeke had said, shaking his head. 'If I runs away, then someone else'll get my whippin'. I stay.'

"As soon as the runaways were missed, Mr. Cobbs sent men on horses with dogs after them. Then he called all the slaves in from the fields to watch Zeke get the promised punishment. He took Zeke's shirt from him and chained him to a post. Again and again the cruel lash came down across his back. It whistled through the air and sliced into his flesh until Zeke lay unconscious and bleeding. 'Now let that be a lesson to the rest of you,' Mr. Cobbs shouted."

Here Grandpa paused in the story. "What do you suppose Zeke did in revenge for the unjust whipping he had received from Mr. Cobbs?" he questioned. "Do you think he took a hammer and smashed something?" Grandpa's eyes twinkled at Hannah.

"Probably not," she returned thoughtfully.

"You're right," Grandpa said. "A few weeks after Zeke had recovered from his whipping, Mr. Cobbs was out for a walk when he was bitten by a pit viper, a poisonous snake. No one heard his calls for help. His leg swelled horribly, and he almost fainted from the pain. Eventually he became so weak and dizzy that he fell to the ground, no longer able to walk. Zeke, too, was out for a walk, and he happened upon his master lying on the ground. You know, Zeke had a choice to make. He could walk away from the man and let him die. No one would ever know that he had been nearby. He would have been avenged for the mistreatment he had received from his master.

"But you can guess what Zeke did. He rushed to the stricken man's aid. He took Mr. Cobbs' pocketknife and made a cut on the place where the snake had bitten. Then he put his mouth on the cut and sucked up a mouthful of blood. He spat the blood out on the ground and sucked out another mouthful." *

"Oh, Grandpa!" exclaimed Hannah. "Why did he do that? Yuck!"

"He was sucking the poison out of the wound so that Mr. Cobbs would not die," Grandpa replied. "This he continued until he was quite sure he had sucked out as much poison as he could. And Mr. Cobbs did not die."

Grandpa looked first at Joel and then at Hannah. "How do you suppose that made Mr. Cobbs feel?"

"I would think it should have made him ashamed," declared Joel. "But he sounds like such a nasty man that I don't know."

* Though Zeke's method for treating a poisonous snake bite has long been accepted, it is now considered ineffective.

"I guess he did feel ashamed," said Grandpa, "because the story goes on to say that he eventually became a Christian, and I think a big part of the reason was the way Zeke showed him love. And after he became a Christian, he freed all of his slaves."

Hannah heaved a big sigh. "That was a very good story, Grandpa," she said, "and I will try to remember it the next time I want to return evil for evil."

Joel stood up and held out his hand to his sister. "I'm sorry for throwing Teddy Boy in the tree," he said, "and if you'll come with me, I'll get him down for you now."

Grandpa watched them go, and a smile played across his face.

Questions for Review

1. What had Joel done to destroy peace between his sister and him?
2. What had Hannah been planning to do when Grandpa stopped her?
3. Why was Hannah going to smash Joel's airplane?
4. How was Zeke kind to Mr. Cobbs?
5. How did Mr. Cobbs change?

Questions for Discussion

1. If Hannah had smashed the plane with her hammer, what do you think would have happened next?
2. How did Grandpa's story about Zeke help Hannah?
3. What things did Joel do as a result of hearing Grandpa's story?
4. What should you do (or not do) to make your home a place of peace?
5. What Bible verses or principles did Zeke apply?

LONG-SUFFERING

I WANT IT *NOW*

But let patience have her perfect work,
that ye may be perfect and entire, wanting nothing.
—James 1:4

READ ROMANS 15:1-7

Most North Americans don't like to wait—not at a grocery store checkout, nor at a doctor's office, nor for a traffic light, nor for a meal. We expect things to be ready quickly, if not instantly. So we have instant potatoes, instant coffee, instant cereals, and instant relief for headaches. Buying on credit allows people to buy things before they have the money to pay for them.

As a teacher, I've had lots of opportunity to exercise patience. But I never had the experience of one teacher who was putting on the boots of thirty-two first graders. As she was putting on the last pair, a little girl said, "You know what, teacher? These aren't my boots."

The teacher removed them. Then the girl continued, "They are my sister's, and she let me wear them." The teacher quietly put the boots back on her pupil's feet.

Teachers need patience. Parents need patience. Employers need patience. Siblings need patience with each other. Everyone needs patience.

Impatience is a temptation common to man. It means a feeling of restlessness arising from a desire for change. It is an intolerance of something that postpones one's goal. It implies an irritable or testy attitude. A child's definition of impatience: waiting in a hurry.

But impatience is not only a modern problem. It goes back thousands of years. For example, after Esau returned home from a hunting foray, he got into quite a stew because he was so hungry. His brother Jacob made a deal with him. Esau in his impatience and shortsightedness gave Jacob his birthright, and Esau got his stew.

Aaron and the Israelites grew impatient when Moses delayed his return from Mount Sinai where he was meeting with God. The people said, "Make us gods, which shall go before us: for as for this Moses, the man that brought us up out of the land of Egypt, we wot not what is become of him" (Exodus 32:23). So Aaron called for gold items, threw them into a fire, and, according to Aaron's story, out came a calf—an idol, which they then worshiped.

Impatience is and always has been a human problem. "Ye have need of patience" (Hebrews 10:36). God makes a promise—faith believes it, hope anticipates it, patience quietly awaits it. So cultivate the Spirit fruit of patience. If you pluck the blossoms, you must do without the fruit.

Patience of God

Now the God of patience and consolation grant you to be likeminded one toward another according to Christ Jesus.
— Romans 15:5

Read Psalm 86

Praise God for His patience. If He were not longsuffering, we wouldn't have a second chance to repent and receive pardon for our sin. Because He longs for us to repent, He patiently gives us opportunity. "The Lord is . . . longsuffering to us-ward, not willing that any should perish, but that all should come to repentance" (2 Peter 3:9). This merciful attribute of longsuffering is part of His goodness toward man that we dare not despise. Romans 2:4 says: "Despisest thou the riches of his goodness and forbearance and longsuffering; not knowing that the goodness of God leadeth thee to repentance?"

God in three persons is patient. In the Old Testament, Moses viewed God as longsuffering. "And the Lord passed by before him, and proclaimed, The Lord, The Lord God, merciful and gracious, longsuffering, and abundant in goodness and truth" (Exodus 34:6). David saw God's longsuffering. "The Lord is merciful and gracious, slow to anger, and plenteous in mercy" (Psalm 103:8). See verse 15 of the daily reading too.

God the Son demonstrated patience repeatedly. He patiently taught His group of slow learners—the twelve disciples—about servanthood when they wanted to be chief (see Mark 10:35-45). He was patient with the jostling crowds. He was longsuffering toward His enemies. One of His slow learners wrote, "If, when ye do well, and suffer for it, ye take it patiently, this is acceptable with God. For even hereunto were ye called: because Christ also suffered for us, leaving us an example, that ye should follow his steps" (1 Peter 2:20, 21).

God the Spirit is longsuffering. Take, for instance, His dealings with mankind before the Flood. Notice His patience and also the fact that it has its limits, ultimately. Peter tells us that "the longsuffering of God waited in the days of Noah" (1 Peter 3:20). Yet take warning from Genesis 6:3: "My spirit shall not always strive with man."

God's patience is reflected even in creation. An unknown writer said:

> Did the leaves of the trees say something to you as you passed them today?
> They were not created this spring, but months ago.
> (And right now, others are being fashioned for another year.)
> At the bottom of every leaf is a cradle, and in it is an infant germ:
> The winds will rock it and the birds will sing to it all summer long, and next spring it will unfold.

Learn Patience From James and Job

Behold, we count them happy which endure.
Ye have heard of the patience of Job,
and have seen the end of the Lord;
that the Lord is very pitiful, and of tender mercy.
—James 5:11

Read James 5:1-11

A friend told me his version of the golden rule: Whoever has the gold makes the rules. Although it may sometimes seem that way, ultimately the rich who oppress the poor will face miseries, as today's Scripture says. James tells oppressed Christians to take a long-range view. Riches acquired wrongly and used selfishly will lead to a day of slaughter (v. 6). Ill-gotten gain is always great loss.

Wait for Jesus to come. He will put things in order and give us treasure in Heaven. Be like a farmer who plants the seed—he doesn't expect to harvest the grain within a week. Rather, he has long patience (v. 7). In Palestine the early rain in autumn softened the soil and helped the seeds to germinate. The latter rain of February and March helped to mature the grain. James tells us to patiently hang in there (v. 8) for what may seem a long time. After all, patience is a virtue that carries a lot of "wait."

Not only should we patiently wait for the Lord's return, we should be patient when we face trouble and patient with those who have problems. James points to the example of Job. He lost his wealth (thousands of animals) to a natural disaster. He lost his children in a turbulent tempest. He lost his health as blistering boils caused pain from "the sole of his foot unto his crown" (Job 2:7). He lost the support of his wife, who said, "Curse God, and die." Yet he patiently persevered.

Job's friends did not have patience with Job. They forgot that patience is an ointment for all sores. After a period of silence, they launched their verbal assaults, questioning Job's integrity, and philosophizing about why Job was in trouble (and they weren't).

Be understanding to those in difficulty. A man's car stalled in heavy traffic as the light turned green. All his efforts to start the engine failed, and a chorus of honking began. He finally walked back to the first driver and said, "I'm sorry, but I can't seem to get my car started. If you'll go up there and give it a try, I'll stay here and blow your horn for you."

It's not only trials like Job's that demand longsuffering. It's the little things that may strain our patience. We can sit on a mountain, but not on a tack.

Causes of Impatience

For ye have need of patience, that,
after ye have done the will of God,
ye might receive the promise.
— Hebrews 10:36

Read Acts 27:1-25

I struggle with impatience when my expectations or goals are not met. A slow driver jeopardizes my prompt arrival for an appointment. Or I'm on time, but the other two people are late.

A person usually is free from impatience when relaxing on Sunday afternoon, when curled up in front of the fire with a good book on a winter evening, or on a relaxing fishing trip. It's different when there are schedules, appointments, or deadlines (self-imposed or otherwise). Impatience can be a problem especially for individuals who are time-conscious, who see the importance of promptness, who are goal-oriented, who are well organized, or who are strict.

Impatience will increase where there are unrealistic expectations from others—a spouse, a child, an employee, a motorist. Or the weather may not mesh with our plans. Julius, the centurion mentioned in our daily reading, had a goal to sail to Italy or at least to Phenice, but the winds were uncooperative, and Julius became impatient.

Another cause of impatience is self-centeredness. I may feel impatient because circumstances or the decisions of others interfere with my plans. *Hurry and get done talking—I've got something to say,* we think. Or we may think, *I've got things to do.*

A lack of sleep affects one's ability to wait patiently amidst delays and frustration. It definitely affects children, but many adults are powerfully impacted by sleep loss too.

Anger is another cause of, or at least a close cousin to, impatience. It is virtually impossible to be impatient without being somewhat angry.

Impatience can be brought on by being pressured by others or by the exigencies of a situation. For example, when King Saul was waiting for seven days for Samuel to arrive and formally plead for God's blessing on Israel by offering a sacrifice, he got edgy. The enemy was approaching, the men of Israel were going into hiding in a demoralized state, and still the prophet didn't come. "I can't understand what is taking him so long," we may say in similar circumstances. The pressure builds up and we vent our impatience in words or body language.

We may try to accomplish too much and pack our schedule too tightly; therefore, we look for shortcuts. When they don't work out, our blood pressure rises and we easily become curt or snappy. We forget that we get the chicken by hatching the egg, not by smashing it open.

Developing Patience

Rejoicing in hope; patient in tribulation;
continuing instant in prayer.
— Romans 12:12

Read Romans 5:1-8

I admire the patience of Sir Isaac Newton, a notable scientist and a Christian. He spent eight years writing a major work. His pet dog, Diamond, completely destroyed the papers on his desk. Without any sign of anger or impatience, Newton quietly said, "Diamond, little do you know the labor and trouble to which you have put your master." And then he sat down at his desk to begin again.

How can a person develop longsuffering? Abide in Jesus and yield to the Spirit—it's the Spirit's fruit. Consider seriously and prayerfully the Biblical commands to be patient. For example, 1 Thessalonians 5:14 says, "Be patient toward all men." Ephesians 4:2 tells us to walk "with longsuffering, forbearing one another in love." Colossians 1:11 states Paul's prayer for his friends that they would be "strengthened with all might, according to his glorious power, unto all patience and longsuffering with joyfulness." 1 Peter 1:5, 6 tells the believer to add patience to the other virtues of a growing Christian.

Face tribulations with trust. Our daily reading links peace with God arising from faith to patience. “Therefore being justified by faith, we have peace with God. . . . We glory in tribulations also: knowing that tribulation worketh patience” (vv. 1, 3). The missionary physician David Livingstone faced numerous trials in Africa. When Henry Stanley, an American journalist, was sent to see if he was still alive, Stanley stayed with him for several months, marveling at his patience with the Africans. For Christ’s sake, Livingstone was untiring, long-suffering, and zealous. Stanley writes, “When I saw that unwearied patience, that unflagging zeal, I became a Christian at his side, though he never spoke a word to me about it.”

Practice patience. H. W. Beecher suggested, “There is no such thing as preaching patience unto people unless the sermon is so long that they have to practice it while they hear. No man can learn patience except by going out into the hurly-burly world and taking life just as it blows.”

Keep your sense of perspective. Does the long lineup ahead of you, the item broken by a child, the procrastination of a friend, merit getting all steamed up and impatient? Many a parent has undone many hours of teaching and years of example by impatiently yelling hurtful words at a child. Don’t sacrifice the permanent on the altar of the immediate.

SWEET FRUIT OF PATIENCE

Better is the end of a thing
than the beginning thereof:
and the patient in spirit is better
than the proud in spirit.
— Ecclesiastes 7:8

READ PSALM 37:1-11

Your next helping of Jell-O may help you to remember a benefit of patience. In 1897 a man called Pearl Wait invented Jell-O. In addition to being a construction worker, he dabbled in making things like cough medicines and selling them door-to-door. In his experiments he tried mixing fruit flavoring with granulated gelatin. His wife dubbed it Jell-O. But sales weren't very strong, so two years later he sold his Jell-O rights for $450 to a neighbor who knew how to market a product. Within eight years Wait's neighbor had turned it into a million-dollar business. Now over one million boxes of Jell-O are sold every day. But the Wait relatives get no royalties. Wait just couldn't wait.

When I think of the benefits of patience, I recall a story I heard of a missionary who didn't receive her monthly allowance. She was seriously ill and because of the lack of money had to live on oatmeal and canned milk. She received her check thirty days late.

Later, on furlough, she mentioned the experience to her doctor. After describing to him the digestive trouble she had had, he said, "If your allowance had arrived on time, you would now be dead. The best treatment for your illness was a thirty-day oatmeal diet."

Living patiently allows God to work in ways often unknown to us at the time. "We know that all things work together for good to them that love God" (Romans 8:28). Patience is waiting without worrying. Verse 7 of the daily reading says, "Rest in the LORD, and wait patiently for him: fret not." John Newton wrote, "Be patient enough to live one day at a time as Jesus taught us, letting yesterday go, and leaving tomorrow till it arrives."

Another spiritual benefit of patience is maturity. James 1:3, 4 says, "The trying of your faith worketh patience. But let patience have her perfect work, that ye may be perfect and entire."

Another blessing of patience is progress toward our destination. Hebrews 12:1 instructs us to "run with patience the race that is set before us." A runner of a race is not going to win if he doesn't continue to run to the finish line.

Patience contributes greatly to successful parenting. I have heard the opinion that nothing prejudices children against accepting their parents' beliefs and spiritual truth as much as parental impatience.

Patience in Daily Life

Be patient toward all men.
— 1 Thessalonians 5:14

Read Genesis 40:1-15, 20-23; 41:1

Patience is something you admire greatly in the driver behind you, but not in the one ahead of you. We so easily forget that patience on the highway may often prevent patients in the hospital. But it's not only on the road that patience is needed—it's on the job, at school, and especially at home. Patience is the ability to keep your motor idling when you feel like stripping the gears.

Longsuffering is needed on the job. The habits and idiosyncrasies of fellow employees may demand patience and forbearance. The wonderful thing about patience is that it goes a long way, and yet the more we use it, the more we have.

Patience is needed in the classroom. Students sometimes need to wait in line. Slow learners demand patience from fellow students and teachers.

Patience is needed with children in the home. John Wesley's behavior as an adolescent often displeased his dad. His mother was more forbearing. Once, when she had just instructed John for the twentieth time on a particular subject, the elder Wesley exploded, "How can you have the patience?"

"Why," replied Mrs. Wesley, "if I had told him but nineteen times, I had wasted my breath."

Even when husband and wife appreciate and love each other, tones of impatience can easily slip into daily conversation. Many marriages could be improved if a husband was as patient with his wife as he is when he is waiting for a fish to bite.

Patience is needed when a person is ill or injured. A doctor was asked by a patient who had experienced a serious accident, "Doctor, how long do I have to lie here?"

"Only one day at a time," was his answer.

Joseph, as shown in the daily reading, demonstrated great patience and perseverance. Given an indefinite prison sentence on a false charge after doing what was right, he nonetheless patiently waited for the Lord to intervene. Then when he saw an opportunity to be released, the butler forgot him and Joseph had to wait another seven hundred days.

Patience is related to faith, hope, and charity. Be patient with God—that is faith. Be patient with self—that is hope. Be patient with others—that is love.

Patience Is a Virtue

by Danette Schrock Martin

"Ouch!" Thomas clutched his stinging right earlobe. That little green strawberry had packed a lot of power for its size.

Up the next row of berries, his brother Lyle was bent over, working diligently, but even his back looked guilty.

"Lyle! That hurt!" Thomas rubbed his ear again.

Lyle stood, a plant stem dangling from the scissors he held in one hand. "I just needed to put some life into this job. You didn't want a break?"

"What I really want is a break from this whole strawberry business. So far it's been all work and no money."

"I could have told you we were in for 'all work' way back when Mom came home with that van load of strawberry plants." Lyle lifted his cap slightly and worked one corner of his mouth. "What's it been, two years now?"

Thomas nodded, remembering the beginnings of a Ropp family dream. He recalled one meeting in particular, after Dad and Mom got serious about a Trip Out West, or the TOW, as the boys began to call it.

A trip, especially one long enough to take a family of seven to the Pacific Ocean and back, required money. The Ropps didn't have dollar trees growing in their tiny orchard. How could they earn the money?

Suggestions had bounced around like Sunday evening popcorn out of Dad's kettle. Should they answer the ad in the Grant County *Tribune* asking for worm-pickers? Thomas's fifteen-year-old sister, Sarah, shuddered. "Ew-w, no!" His younger brother Dexter said, "Hey, Thomas, you can use my headgear flashlight! You need both hands to grab those fast night crawlers, you know." Dexter's pupils were wide with excitement.

Or maybe Mom and Sarah could bake cookies and pies to sell at the Rockwood Market. "Folks would love that stuff," we assured Mom.

Dad looked at Mom with that mushy look. "But there are all those ingredients and the rental fees. Too much overhead."

Thomas was about to look up, but at that moment Lyle hooted. He pointed at Dexter, squinting at the ceiling.

"Overhead means things that eat up your money in a business, like electricity and heating costs," Dad explained.

Perhaps they should pick up pop cans in the ditches for the aluminum recyclers? assemble toys for the leather crafter uptown? cut firewood? The ideas rolled by Thomas before he could properly sample them all. Three-year-old Missy fell asleep against Susan's arm.

Finally, Mom had said, "Well, we'll just need to keep praying about it." Mom was like that. She talked to God about everything from stray cats to leaky refrigerators.

The words were scarcely out of her mouth when Dad suggested raising strawberries. Somehow, that felt just right.

"Well, Harry Watson is getting rid of his pick-your-own-strawberries business. I heard anyone who wants strawberry runners can have them." Mom stood and stretched.

"Free plants would be no overhead." Thomas was pleased to be able to use the business word properly.

Soon afterward, Mom and Sarah went out the lane armed with spades and came home with over 2,000 starter bundles.

That had been last fall. Now Lyle was thirteen, Thomas was ten, and the strawberry patch as real as the ache in his back.

"We're getting closer to the money part every season, you know." Lyle bent over again, his scissors poised. "I have to keep that in mind when I get tired of this snipping."

Thomas slowly stuck his fingers into the holes of his scissors. Easy for Lyle to say. He liked work so much, he'd fit right in with an ant colony. Thomas could hear Mom behind him, coaching Dexter. "Cut off the plant stems with white flowers on them, like this," she said. "That way the energy will go into the plant instead of the berries." Thomas knew all that by heart now. He knew bigger plants meant bigger strawberries next year, but this still seemed to him like a senseless amount of work.

Thomas snipped blossoms until he felt like a cutting machine. In his opinion, his family had put too much work into this strawberry project already. Since the evening Mom had hauled the 2,400 plants home, they had dug, set, tamped, strawed, watered, and weeded. The weeding had been the worst. Those "established" plants had come with weeds firmly grounded too.

Thomas's thoughts kept pace with his shears. The watering had been quite a chore too. Couldn't God have told them right away that maybe the strawberry idea should wait; that the next year would be dry? They had hauled bucket after bucket of water, but still the plants had seemed thirsty.

Just when Thomas thought he might collapse from too much work, Susan called from the picnic table. "Lemonade! Get your ice-cold lemonade here!" Thomas jabbed his scissors into the dirt and dashed to the yard.

Thomas took a tall glass from the tray as the others gathered around the wooden table. The sweet-sour coolness slid down his throat and soothed his weariness. But it didn't do much for his frustration. "I'm sick of strawberry plants!" he blurted. "What's the use of working so hard for nothing?"

"All good things take time." Mom wiped her freckled forehead with the back of her hand. "Growing a garden builds character. I think God is growing patience in all of us."

Patience. What was that saying Thomas sometimes heard Mom and Dad say to each other? Something about a man, a woman, and patience. "Always" and "never" were in there too. Depending on which parent chanted it, the words got switched around.

Hearing about patience must have jogged Lyle's memory too. "That patience verse you quote to Dad sometimes—how does it go?" he asked.

"Oh, that. It's not a verse from the Bible." A little chuckle escaped Mom. "It's just a saying Dad and I picked up one time. 'Patience is a virtue—possess it if you can: seldom found in women, never found in men.' But if Dad wants to tease me about my impatience, he says, 'never found in women, always found in men.' "

Susan sucked in her breath. "Doesn't that bother you?"

"No, because he grins as he says it." Mom smiled into her glass of lemonade. "And sometimes I change the words for him when he gets impatient. But that's not very often. Patience really is one of your father's virtues."

"What's virtue?" asked Dexter. "It sounds like something you eat."

"No, virtue is something strong inside your heart that helps you act right," Mom said. "It could be called fruit, but not the kind you eat. In Galatians 5 there's a list of virtues called Spirit-fruit. The virtue of patience is called *longsuffering* in that list. You could think of patience as a product and Fruit of the Spirit as the brand name."

Susan set her empty glass back on the tray. "Then that saying isn't quite right, is it? I mean, women don't automatically have patience, and men automatically not, or the other way around."

"You're right. When God's Spirit is working in us, patience is one of the results. God uses our circumstances, the things that happen to us, to help us develop patience."

"So God is growing patience in us while we grow strawberries in the garden," said Lyle.

Thomas touched the mark his scissors had made on his thumb. "You got that right!"

"We should change the saying," said Dexter.

"Patience is a virtue, possess it if you can; seldom found in . . ." Susan's voice trailed off. "Hmm, it should end with something about 'God's man.' That would mean the women, too, of course."

"How about this?" asked Mom. "Patience is a virtue—possess it if you can; but it won't start to grow in you until you are God's man."

The Ropps needed the new saying frequently over the next months. Thinking ahead to the TOW was sometimes the only thing that kept the children plugging through their strawberry chores.

Little rain fell the following spring. "We can water and water," Mom sighed, "but what those plants really need is God's liquid sunshine." Nevertheless, the end of June brought sizable berries for the first real picking.

Thomas squatted beside the row and parted the bushy leaves in search of the bright red fruit. What if each berry would be a dollar? Wouldn't it be neat to pick quarts of money? When his two green plastic boxes were full, he gripped them carefully and headed for the end of the row.

He met Lyle at the rectangular cardboard crate near the edge of the patch. Thomas set his quarts beside the others in the box and wiped his hands on his pants. Lyle squeezed his quart into the remaining space and whistled. "Look—one whole flat already!"

"Problem is, we have to sell loads of flats to make enough money for the TOW. And I'd be ready to head out there tomorrow."

Lyle looked at Thomas and grinned. "Patience—"

"Oh, hush," cut in Thomas. "I could say that in my sleep." He frowned and lowered his voice. "Not sure it's working, though."

Susan walked up to the boys. In one hand she cupped a few berries she had taken from the full quart she held in the other. "Did you notice any berries like this? See these green knots?"

"Hmm, I didn't think about it on mine." Lyle bent over and peered into the flat. "Yes, there are some in here." He held up a berry by the stem. "This one has a hard, seedy part. Looks like it didn't finish growing at the tip."

"I wonder why that is." Susan frowned. "Too many seedy tips could affect sales."

"You don't think so!" Thomas felt his stomach lurch. "Not when we're this far!"

"At any rate," Susan answered, "we should tell Mom and Dad."

Several weeks later the Ropps sat around the picnic table. "Rolls, please," called Lyle. "I need another one for more jam."

"This strawberry jam is so-o-o good," said Dexter, spooning out a generous mound.

"You may just get your fill of it this year," said Mom. "I've made so many batches, I've lost track."

Susan used her knife to scrape a few green bits onto the edge of her plate. "It's not easy to hide those seedy tips, but I suppose you've found the best way."

"Well, maybe, but I think if we were to do it again, I'd have you children remove the seedy tips before making the jam," replied Mother.

Thomas watched the jam jar circulate, a lump in his throat. "I'd rather add to the TOW fund than stock up on jars of jam."

"Why couldn't we just sell the jam?" Missy twirled her blond braid. "I could help make a sign: For sale, seedy tip jam, only twenty-five cents."

Dad patted her head as everyone laughed. "Do you know what Sam told me today? When I described our strawberries to him, he said no, it's not a dry-weather problem. It's actually insects that cause the hard ends. There's a special spray for it." Dad glanced at Mom and shrugged his shoulders. "I figured with his produce experience, he should know."

Because of the seedy-tip problem, it took another year and another strawberry crop before the TOW plans materialized.

Thomas looked around at his family, sitting at a picnic table miles from their own backyard. A stiff breeze rattled a loose piece of tin on the shelter overhead. Gulls screeched as they skimmed the nearby surf.

"I keep thinking, 'This is the best place on our TOW,' " Dexter declared, his eyes shining. "And then we get to the next thing, and I think, 'No, this is!' "

Mom nodded. "I know what you mean. I love seeing the variety and creativity in God's world."

"The redwoods were my favorite," said Susan. "I felt so small, and God seemed so big."

Lyle gazed out over the ocean. He sighed. "Sometimes I still can hardly believe we're here. It's everything I'd hoped for and more."

"That reminds me of waiting on God," Dad mused. "We wait—sometimes a while—for Him. Then He comes, and He's always more than we longed for."

"There's sand in my bread!" wailed Missy.

Dad's eyes crinkled at the edges. "Didn't you know that's why they're called 'sand'wiches, dearie?"

"At least this time the sandwiches have the right shape, Dexter," said Thomas. "At our last picnic, I couldn't tell exactly what I was eating, the bread was so squished."

Dexter quickly swallowed his bite of cookie. "How was I supposed to know, when it was as soft as a pillow?"

"Oh, the look on your face when you realized you were sitting on our loaf of bread!" Susan gave Dexter a gentle nudge with her elbow.

"I thought you did fine in that crisis," said Mom. "Really, you all have been quite patient on this trip."

"Even at the railroad crossing?" asked Dad.

Mom wrinkled her forehead. "I couldn't imagine one more thing delaying us that night, but it did."

Thomas could almost feel the impatience gnaw inside him again, as it had when they sat there in the dark van, waiting in front of the railway crossbars. He could almost hear the incessant warning bell replaying.

"All that annoying ding-dinging." Missy rolled her eyes. "And here it wasn't even a train! Something had its wires crossed!"

"I wouldn't be surprised," said Mom, "if the strawberry project earned you more than just money for this trip."

"It wasn't a strawberry patch," said Thomas, "as much as it was a patience patch!"

Lyle, gathering up the trash from the table, grinned at his brother. "Dare I say it?"

"Aw, sure. Why not?"

"Patience is a virtue—possess it if you can; but it won't start to grow in you . . ." Thomas's voice rose above the rest, ". . . until you are God's man!"

Questions for Review

1. Why did the Ropp children want to make money?
2. What did the children need to develop?
3. Is virtue something that you eat?
4. Were the Ropp children glad that they had patiently kept on with the strawberry project?
5. What is the saying about patience that the family members often said?

Questions for Discussion

1. What were the obstacles that the family needed to overcome to be able to sell strawberries?
2. How did the Ropp family handle the disappointment of seedy tips on some of their strawberries?
3. Which family member needed to have the most patience?
4. How was patience rewarded?
5. When has your family needed to exercise patience and perseverance?

GENTLENESS

God's Kindness

Hear me, O Lord;
for thy lovingkindness is good:
turn unto me according to the
multitude of thy tender mercies.
— Psalm 69:16

Read Isaiah 63:7-16

I like the title of a small book: *Little Pillows*. It consists of 365 of God's promises in the Bible to be read when retiring for the night. Whether we experience night because of physical darkness or because of dark circumstances, God gently gives us rest as we trust in Him.

The word *lovingkindness* that appears in the Bible is a combination of two ideas—love and faithfulness. God's gentle love toward us is steadfast and constant. No wonder the psalmist describes God's lovingkindness as marvelous. "Shew thy marvellous lovingkindness, O thou that savest by thy right hand them which put their trust in thee" (Psalm 17:7). No wonder he says it is the best. "Because thy lovingkindness is better than life, my lips shall praise thee" (Psalm 63:3). No wonder he keeps it in focus. "For thy lovingkindness is before mine eyes: and

I have walked in thy truth" (Psalm 26:3). No wonder he describes it as great. "For his merciful kindness is great toward us" (Psalm 117:2).

Jeremiah wrote of the attractiveness of God's lovingkindness. "The Lord hath appeared of old unto me, saying, Yea, I have loved thee with an everlasting love: therefore with lovingkindness have I drawn thee" (Jeremiah 31:3). Hosea wrote of the permanence of God's lovingkindness. "I will betroth thee unto me for ever; yea, I will betroth thee unto me in righteousness, and in judgment, and in lovingkindness, and in mercies" (Hosea 2:19). Isaiah was impressed with the "multitude of his lovingkindnesses" (verse 7 of our daily reading).

The Spirit's fruit of gentleness has its origin in God. Gentleness means kindness. As King David praised God, he said, "Thy gentleness hath made me great" (2 Samuel 22:36). The same principle is true of us. All of our abilities and opportunities arise from God's kindness and grace. All people are the recipients of God's kindness. Jesus said, "He is kind unto the unthankful and to the evil" (Luke 6:35).

As songwriter Samuel Medley says, we should wake up to the fact of God's lovingkindness.

Awake my soul, to joyful lays,
And sing thy great Redeemer's praise;
He justly claims a song from me,
His lovingkindness, oh, how free!
Lovingkindness, lovingkindness,
His lovingkindness, oh, how free!

Medley goes on to describe God's lovingkindness as great, strong, and good.

God's grace is immeasurable, His kindness inexhaustible, His peace inexpressible.

Kindness of Christ

Who can have compassion on the ignorant,
and on them that are out of the way;
for that he himself also is compassed with infirmity.
— Hebrews 5:2

Read Matthew 20:29-34

Two missionaries to the East Indies found it next to impossible to learn the native language. But they were able to communicate in the universal language—kindness. They reported, "The natives do not understand our theology, but they understand our kindness, and let themselves be won by it."

Someone has observed, "Kindness has converted more sinners than zeal, eloquence, or learning."

Jesus' ministry on earth was characterized by compassion, moving Him to kind deeds. He had compassion on multitudes. Sometimes He kindly healed them. For example, Matthew 14:14 says, "Jesus went forth, and saw a great multitude, and was moved with compassion toward them, and he healed their sick." Sometimes He kindly taught them. For example, Mark 6:34 says, "Jesus, when he came out, saw much people, and was moved with compassion toward them, because they were as sheep not having a shepherd: and he began to teach them many things." Sometimes He kindly provided food. For example, Matthew 15:32 says, "Then Jesus called his disciples unto him, and said, I have compassion on the multitude, because they continue with me now three days, and have nothing to eat: and I will not send them away fasting, lest they faint in the way." He then fed over five thousand using five loaves and two fish.

He also showed gentle kindness to individuals. He was kind to the handicapped, healing blind Bartimaeus, the sick man at the Pool of Siloam, the man with the withered hand, the mute, the deaf, the lame. He was kind to the outcast, befriending Zacchaeus. He was kind to women such as the Samaritan woman at Jacob's well and the widow of Nain who was bereaved of her son. "When the Lord saw her, he had compassion on her. . . . And he came and touched the bier. . . . And he said, Young man, I say unto thee, Arise. And he that was dead sat up, and began to speak. And he delivered him to his mother" (Luke 7:13-15). He was kind to children. Although His disciples wanted to send the mother and children away, Jesus "took them up in his arms, put his hands upon them, and blessed them" (Mark 10:16).

Interestingly, the Greek words for Christ and kindness are very similar. *Christos* means "Christ" and *chrestos* means "kindness." I have read that some Romans would get the two words confused, appropriately so, because Christ and kindness and Christian are inseparable.

Kindness at Home

And be ye kind one to another, tenderhearted,
forgiving one another,
even as God for Christ's sake hath forgiven you.
— Ephesians 4:32

Read Matthew 1:18-25

A mother evidently had a kindness switch that she could turn off and on. Away from home, it was on. At home, it was often in the off position, as she was irritable and faultfinding. One night she heard her daughter pray, "Dear God, make Mommy be kind to us like she is to people we visit."

Somewhat amused, she told her husband. He turned to her with a serious expression, saying, "You do not treat us with the courtesy you show to business people and our friends." She determined to keep her kindness switch always on.

As the virtuous woman of Proverbs 31 related to her family, "In her tongue is the law of kindness." A husband should give honor to his wife by gentle words. As 1 Peter 3:7 says, "Ye husbands, dwell with them according to knowledge, giving honour unto the wife, as unto the weaker vessel, and as being heirs together of the grace of life; that your prayers be not hindered."

Kind deeds should prevail at home. Joseph was gentle and sensitive to Mary, as indicated in our daily reading. Moses experienced kindness from Pharaoh's daughter, from his mother Jochebed, and from Jethro, who showed him hospitality prior to becoming Moses' father-in-law (Exodus 2) and helpful advice after (Exodus 18).

Kind mothers will reap tremendous rewards. Matthew 10:42 says, "Whosoever shall give to drink unto one of these little ones a cup of cold water only in the name of a disciple, verily I say unto you, he shall in no wise lose his reward." A cup of cold water was a proverbial expression for a small kindness. When our children were small, my wife probably gave hundreds of such "cups" in a week.

Kindness, like seeds, can be planted in a child's heart to bear fruit in future years.

The word the Greek writers used for gentleness characterizes the attitude of parents toward offspring, a nurse with trying children, or a teacher with difficult pupils.

The world wants smash hits at the box office, home runs on the ball field, movie stars on stage, and record profits on Wall Street. The Lord wants gentleness at home—gracious words and deeds of kindness. You cannot do a kindness too soon because you never know how soon it will be too late.

Kindness to Siblings

Put on therefore, as the elect of God,
holy and beloved, bowels of mercies, kindness,
humbleness of mind, meekness, longsuffering.
— Colossians 3:12

Read Genesis 50:15-21

I like the Hebrew legend of two brothers who lived on adjoining farms. The older one had a large family; the other was single. One night the older brother lay awake and thought, *My brother lives alone; he has not the companionship of wife and children to cheer his heart as I have. While he sleeps, I will carry some of my sheaves into his field.*

At the same hour, the younger brother reasoned, *My brother has a large family, and his financial needs are greater than mine. As he sleeps I will put some of my sheaves on his side of the field.*

Thus the two brothers went out, each laden with sheaves—and met at the dividing line. There they embraced. The legend goes on to say that years later, at this very place stood the Jerusalem temple, and on the very spot of their meeting stood the temple's altar.

These siblings expressed the truth of Romans 12:10, "Be kindly affectioned one to another with brotherly love; in honour preferring one another." The only ones you should try to get even with are the ones who have helped you.

In fact, as shown in our daily reading, kindness should be returned for bad treatment. Siblings can be very mean to each other, as Joseph's brothers demonstrated. How gentle and noble of Joseph as "he comforted them, and spake kindly unto them" (v. 21).

A songwriter said:

Little deeds of kindness, little words of love,
Make our earth an Eden like the Heaven above.

Siblings, in practical terms, can show kindness in the home by helping with dishes, listening to each other's frustrations, playing games with siblings, or doing the work of a sibling who has a big test the next day.

An anonymous poet wrote:

Forget each kindness that you do
As soon as you have done it,
Forget the praise that falls on you
The moment you have won it;
Forget the slander that you hear
Before you can repeat it;
Forget each slight, each spite, each sneer,
Wherever you may meet it.

Remember every kindness done
To you, whate'er its measure;
Remember praise by others won
And pass it on with pleasure;
Remember those who lend you aid
And be a grateful debtor;
Remember every promise made
And keep it to the letter.

Kindness to the Handicapped

Now we exhort you,
brethren, . . . comfort the feebleminded,
support the weak.
— 1 Thessalonians 5:14

Read 2 Samuel 9:1-13

During a thunderstorm one night, a large branch broke from a tree in a campground where my brother's family was camping in a tent trailer. My sister-in-law had sat up to check on their infant son and was struck by the falling branch. It broke her neck and made her a quadriplegic for the rest of her life.

I was impressed with the kindness of my brother to her over the next ten years until she died, doing wheelchair transfers, giving personal care, etc.

I am also impressed with the kindness and consideration of David toward lame Mephibosheth as shown in the daily reading. The reason for his disability is given in 2 Samuel 4:4: "Jonathan, Saul's son, had a son that was lame of his feet. He was five years old when the tidings came of Saul and Jonathan out of Jezreel, and his nurse took him up, and fled: and it came to pass, as she made haste to flee, that he fell, and became lame."

I also appreciate Job's attitude. He testified, "I was eyes to the blind, and feet was I to the lame. I was a father to the poor: and the cause which I knew not I searched out" (Job 29:15, 16).

From my sister-in-law, I learned some guidelines for wheelchair etiquette:

1. Always ask the wheelchair user if he or she would like assistance before you help. Your help may not be needed or wanted.
2. Don't lean on a person's wheelchair. It is part of the wheelchair user's personal body space.
3. Speak directly to the person in the wheelchair, not to someone nearby as if the wheelchair user does not exist or is mentally defective.
4. If the conversation lasts more than a few minutes, consider sitting down or kneeling to get yourself on the same level as the wheelchair user.
5. Don't discourage children from asking questions about the wheelchair. Open communication helps overcome fear and misleading attitudes.
6. Don't be patronizing or condescending.
7. Don't assume that using a wheelchair is in itself a tragedy. It provides freedom to move about independently.
8. It is all right to use expressions like "running along" when speaking to the wheelchair user. It is likely the wheelchair user expresses things the same way.

Be gentle to those who are disadvantaged. Kindness is a language the deaf can hear and the blind can see.

Kindness in the Community

But whoso hath this world's good,
and seeth his brother have need,
and shutteth up his bowels of compassion from him,
how dwelleth the love of God in him?
— 1 John 3:17

Read Acts 28:1-10

Recently some friends and I were travelling on a side street in an Ontario town. "What is that on the road?" I asked. An overturned box of tools, with wrenches and sockets, was scattered on the snowy road. We picked them up and took them to an acquaintance who lived on the street, hoping he would be able to find the owner.

The Israelites were instructed to try to return what was lost to the owner. Deuteronomy 22:1-3 says that oxen, sheep, asses, raiment, and "all lost thing[s] of thy brother's" were to be returned.

Kindness can also be shown in lending. "A good man sheweth favour, and lendeth" (Psalm 112:5). Kindness should be shown to the poor. Proverbs 14:21 says, "He that despiseth his neighbour sinneth: but he that hath mercy on the poor, happy is he."

One day Gandhi boarded a train in India. In doing so, one of his shoes slipped off. He was unable to retrieve it as the train began moving. To the amazement of his companions, Gandhi calmly took off his other shoe and threw it back along the track to land close to the first. Asked by a fellow passenger why he did so, Gandhi smiled. "The poor man who finds the shoe lying on the track," he replied, "will now have a pair he can use."

We can show kindness in a community in various ways. Matthew 25:34-36 gives this commendation: "Come, ye blessed of my Father, inherit the kingdom prepared for you from the foundation of the world: for I was an hungred, and ye gave me meat: I was thirsty, and ye gave me drink: I was a stranger, and ye took me in: naked, and ye clothed me: I was sick, and ye visited me: I was in prison, and ye came unto me." Whoever is in need, as shown by the daily reading, should be treated gently.

Proverbs 19:22 says, "The desire of a man is his kindness: and a poor man is better than a liar." I like the Amplified version, "That which is desired in a man is loyalty and kindness."

An Irish blessing urges us to show kindness while we have opportunity:

'Tis better to buy a small bouquet,
    And give to your friend this very day,
Than a bushel of roses white and red,
    To lay on his coffin after he's dead.

Kindness at Church

And beside this, giving all diligence,
add to your faith virtue; and to virtue knowledge;
and to knowledge temperance; and to temperance patience;
and to patience godliness;
and to godliness brotherly kindness;
and to brotherly kindness charity.
— 2 Peter 1:5-7

READ JEREMIAH 38:6-13

I can never get out of debt, even if you give me millions of dollars. At least, according to a Malayan proverb, "One can pay back the loan of gold, but one dies forever in debt to those who are kind." Jeremiah, as shown in our daily reading, was forever in debt to Ebedmelech. The imprisoned Paul was indebted to Onesiphorus. He wrote: "The Lord give mercy unto the house of Onesiphorus; for he oft refreshed me, and was not ashamed of my chain" (2 Timothy 1:16). The Philippian jailer and Paul were in debt to each other. Paul kept him from harming himself and led him to faith in Jesus, and the jailer then washed his whipping wounds.

One aspect of the tri-part summary of a life pleasing to God is kindness. "He hath shewed thee, O man, what is good; and what doth the Lord require of thee, but to do justly, and to love mercy, and to walk humbly with thy God?" (Micah 6:8). The phrase *love mercy* is sometimes translated as *love kindness*. The Shunammite woman loved kindness as she and her husband prepared a room for the itinerant Prophet Elisha.

An unknown poet wrote:

If you have a friend worth loving,
  Love him. Yes, and let him know
That you love him, ere life's evening
  Tinge his brow with sunset glow.
Why should good words ne'er be said
  Of a friend—till he is dead?

If you hear a song that thrills you,
  Sung by any child of song,
Praise it. Do not let the singer
  Wait deserved praises long.
Why should one who thrills your heart
  Lack the joy you may impart?

If you hear a prayer that moves you
  By its humble, pleading tone,
Join it. Do not let the seeker
  Bow before his God alone.
Why should not your brother share
  The strength of "two or three" in prayer?

If you see the hot tears falling
  From a brother's weeping eyes,
Share them. And by kindly sharing
  Own your kinship in the skies.
Why should anyone be glad
  When another's heart is sad?

Gentleness Comes Back

by Katrina Hoover

Brooke is ten years old. She knows how to make her own eggs for breakfast. She loves language class, but she does not like math. She loves to talk, and she loves to talk on paper. Someday, she wants to write a book. She makes really good chocolate chip cookies. She has beautiful thick brown hair; sometimes her friends are jealous of it. In the winter, she likes to ice skate or go sledding. In the summer, she goes on long bike rides.

Well, she *used* to go on long bike rides in the summer. This summer, Brooke found out that she had cancer, a terrible disease that ruins parts of the body. Brooke had to go to the big clinic on the hill. The doctors and nurses at the clinic spoke kindly to Brooke and her parents. The doctor said that Brooke would have to come to the clinic more times to take special treatments. The medicine in the treatments would make Brooke feel sick. It would make her feel tired. It would make her hair come out. But hopefully it would kill the cancer.

"We'll get books on CD for you to listen to," Mom said. "You like to read anyway, and that would be even better than reading."

"I'll make your eggs for you in the morning if you can't make your own," said her older sister Angie.

"I'll take you on drives in the evenings if you feel like it," Dad offered.

Brooke was glad they were so kind, but she wished she would not have ever gotten cancer. She wanted to make her *own* scrambled eggs.

Brooke did not get very sick after her first treatment, but she didn't feel like doing anything. She lay on the couch all day long. Brooke turned her pillow and moved her head to a different spot. Nothing was comfortable. The couch scratched her through the blanket. Her tongue clung to the roof of her mouth. She sat up and took a drink from the glass of ice water on the coffee table. That was too much work. She fell back on the pillow. The voice on the CD player kept talking, but she had forgotten the beginning of the story.

"How are you feeling?" Mom asked. She paused the player.

"Okay," Brooke sighed. "I just don't feel like doing anything. I don't even want to listen to the story anymore."

"Shall I comb your hair a little?" Mom asked. "It looks hot and uncomfortable."

"I don't care," Brooke said. "Do you think my hair will come out soon?"

"I don't know," Mom said as she helped Brooke sit up and began combing her hair out of her eyes. "The doctor said everyone is different. Some people don't lose their hair."

"Do you think I'm going to die, Mom?" Brooke asked. "If I die, I'll never get to be a writer. I want to write books and newspapers and all sorts of things. Do you think I'll be able to do that someday?"

Mom did not say anything right away. When she did begin to talk, Brooke could tell that Mom was about to cry. Brooke started to cry a little bit too.

"I don't know, Brooke," Mom said. "The doctor thinks these treatments might kill the cancer completely. But do you know what I read in the Bible last night, Brooke?" Mom got up and went across the room for her Bible. She opened it to a place in Psalms.

"In this verse, the writer says to God, 'Thy gentleness hath made me great.' Imagine that, Brooke! Most people think they will be great if they are famous and everyone likes them or because they did something special like write a book. But this verse says that God's gentleness can make a person great."

"Gentleness . . . does that mean like being kind?" Brooke asked.

"I think that's what it means," said Mom. "God can be really gentle with us, because He knows what we're going through, and He can teach us things and make us great even if we're sick. God will make a beautiful story with your life, no matter what happens, Brooke."

"How can it be beautiful or great if my hair falls out?" Brooke asked. She knew her friends would not be jealous of her hair after it all fell out. "What if my friends laugh at me?"

"Your friends won't laugh at you," Mom said. "Of course, people might stare a little if you have to wear a wig or bandanna, but they'll get used to it."

On Sunday Brooke got out of bed early. She went to her window. The sunrise, the birch tree outside her window, and the long road dipping through the fields were all so beautiful. Brooke wished she could write a poem or a story about them. They made her feel strong and healthy. She was tired of staying in the house all the time.

"Are you sure you feel well enough to go to church?" Mom asked.

"I think so," said Brooke.

But Brooke had forgotten about all the questions people might ask her.

"How are you doing, Brooke?" an old lady asked as soon as Brooke walked through the door. She was a stooped grandma who did many kind things for others, but she was also very nosy.

"Okay," said Brooke. She didn't know what else to say.

"I always went to visit my neighbor girl when she got her cancer treatments," the lady went on. "Well, I didn't go at the end when she was really sick. After she died, I missed visiting her." The lady gave Brooke a warm smile and walked away.

She must think I'm going to die, Brooke thought. *I wish I would have stayed home.*

More people asked Brooke questions. No one else talked about dying, but Brooke was tired of all the questions. She didn't mind her friends asking her. But some of these other people never used to talk to her. Now they were all paying close attention to her.

Brooke wished she didn't have to go to Sunday school class. She was afraid her teacher would ask her all the same questions again and her friends would stare at her while she tried to answer.

Brooke's friends liked her. They had more fun when Brooke was with them, because Brooke talked a lot and told funny stories. They loved Brooke's chocolate chip cookies. Tonya liked to study math with Brooke. Still, Brooke's friends did not know what it was like to have cancer. They could chatter and talk about clothes or shoes or restaurants or homework, but they did not know what to say about treatments and clinics.

The girls' Sunday school teacher was a lady named Sara. Sara's daughter Emily came to class too. But Emily was not like the other girls. Emily had a condition called Down syndrome. Emily could not learn very fast. She couldn't talk very well. Her mouth was always open and her eyes squinted.

Brooke liked Emily. When they were little girls, they had played together. Today Emily sat between her mother and Brooke. Brooke was glad to sit beside Emily because she knew Emily would not ask questions or stare at her.

Brooke sighed with relief when Sara asked for prayer requests. Sara did not look at Brooke or ask any questions. She taught the class just the same as always.

After the class was over, Brooke stayed to help Emily pick up her books and pencil and put away her chair.

"Thanks, Brooke," Sara said. "I really appreciate how you help Emily. I hope people aren't asking you lots of tiring questions today about your treatments."

Brooke looked at Sara in surprise. "Yes, actually they are," Brooke said. "I don't mind if my friends ask, but *everybody* is asking me how I feel, like I'm some strange person."

"Just smile at them and say you're okay," Sara said with a laugh. "They're trying to be nice, and they don't know how tired you get of all the questions."

Brooke felt much better after that. More people asked her questions after church, but she did just what Sara had said. She just grinned at them and said, "Okay."

That afternoon Brooke sat on the wooden glider in her mom's flower garden, thinking of Sara. Mom sat on a patio chair nearby, reading a book.

How did Sara know that everyone would ask me questions? Brooke wondered. Maybe Sara had had cancer when she was a girl. Brooke leaned her head back against the smooth slats of wood and let the sun fall on her whole face. Could it be that Sara knew what it was like to go to a big clinic with colorful pictures and get treatments that made a person sick and tired? Could it be that she had lost her hair?

"Mom, did Sara ever have cancer?" Brooke asked.

Mom marked her place in the book she was reading and looked up at Brooke. "Cancer? I don't think so," Mom said. "Why do you wonder?"

Brooke told Mom what Sara had said. "You said that God is gentle with us because He knows what we're going through. So I thought maybe Sara is gentle because she knows what I'm going through."

"Well, I guess she's just a gentle person," Mom said. "Some people just have a gentle touch and know what to say."

That evening Brooke could barely sit at the table to eat popcorn. She knew she could not go to church. Mom stayed home with her. The rest of Brooke's family went to church without them.

Later that night, Mom and Brooke heard a knock on the door. It was Sara and Emily. Mom invited them up to Brooke's bedroom where Brooke had just crawled between the sheets.

"I'm sorry to interrupt you, Brooke," Sara said. "But I brought something for you that I thought you might like."

Sara reached into her tote and pulled something out.

"A computer?" Brooke asked. Her eyes opened wide.

"It's just an old laptop," Sara said, "but I thought you might like to write stories on it while you have to be in bed. It was my sister's, and she got a new one. So I asked her if you could have this one."

Brooke didn't know how to type, but she loved to mess around on Dad's computer. This would be her own! She could have this computer in bed with her!

"Thank you so much!" Brooke said. "I'm so excited. Did you ever have cancer, Sara? You seem to know just what it's like. You think of just the right things."

Sara looked surprised. "No, I didn't. I don't know what it's like to have cancer. But my mom died of cancer when I was twelve."

"Oh!" said Brooke.

"Yes, it was a hard time because I had two little sisters. I had to take care of them a lot until my dad married again. After that I didn't have to work as much, but I did have to try to learn how to get along with my new mom, and that was really hard."

"Your mom died when you were just a little older than me?" Brooke said. She tried to imagine her mom dying. It seemed impossible.

After Sara and Emily left, Brooke stared at the glowing stars on her bedroom ceiling. No wonder Sara was such a kind, gentle person! She knew just what it was like to feel terrible. She remembered standing beside her mom's grave when she was only twelve.

The next week Brooke had great fun with her new computer. She tried to teach herself to type without looking at the keys. She wrote stories and letters. In the evenings, Dad helped her print them out on his printer.

Then, at the end of the week, Brooke's beautiful hair fell out. First, it just came out in wisps when she combed it. Soon it came out in huge clumps. Brooke looked sadly at the haystack of hair Mom collected in a plastic Wal-Mart bag.

On Sunday Brooke had to go to church with a scarf on her head. Mom had told her she could have a wig if she wanted, but Brooke didn't want fake hair. She just wanted her real hair back again.

She stepped inside the church door feeling almost angry. Why did she have to be the one to lose her hair when all the other girls had nice hair? What if the nosy grandma asked her questions again? She looked at the floor.

"Good morning, Brooke." It was Sara's gentle voice. Brooke raised her eyes.

There stood Sara and Emily, smiling at her. On her head, Emily wore a scarf exactly like Brooke's. Of course, she still had hair. But Brooke felt so much better because someone else was wearing a "weird" scarf.

Emily pointed at Brooke's scarf, and then at her own. Emily's mouth opened and she laughed and laughed. She was happy she could wear a scarf like Brooke's. Brooke laughed back.

"May I sit with Emily?" Brooke asked Mom.

"Sure," said Mom. Brooke was surprised to see tears in Mom's eyes again.

In their chatter after church, none of the girls in Brooke's Sunday school class made fun of her scarf.

"It's cute," said Tonya.

"I wouldn't have even thought about it that your hair is gone," said another girl.

"Isn't that cute that Emily wore a scarf too?" said Tonya. "Her mom must have thought of it."

In September, the doctor at the clinic told Brooke and her parents good news. The cancer was gone! He said that Brooke would need to come back for checkups just to make sure; the cancer might come back. But if the cancer did not come back, she would not have any more treatments.

Everyone in Brooke's family was happy. Dad laughed more. Angie teased Brooke again like she used to before Brooke had cancer. Mom sang while she made supper. Brooke told stories while she made her own scrambled eggs.

Brooke still had to wear her scarf to school, but her hair was coming back. Brooke's hair had always been straight, but it grew back in gentle waves. First it peeked out from beneath her scarf. In a few weeks, she got rid of the scarf altogether.

By November, Brooke's hair was still a bit short, but her life was back to normal. She studied math and told secrets with Tonya. She made chocolate chip cookies and went on bike rides.

Whenever Brooke saw Sara, she remembered her gentle spirit and how she knew just what to do to help someone feel happy. She still used the computer that Sara had given her. Brooke hoped she would remember to be a gentle person like Sara, but she was afraid she would forget.

It was almost Christmastime. Every year Brooke's church planned a big Christmas meal for church people and their friends and neighbors. The supper took up the whole gym at the school, and lots and lots of people came. Every year several children Brooke's age stood at the door and said "hello" to all the guests and gave them a piece of paper called a program. The program told the guests what would happen that night. It was a fun job; the children got to meet all the guests. After they finished handing out programs, they got to sit at a special table to eat supper.

This year, Mom helped plan the meal, and Brooke was chosen to pass out programs.

"Oh, good!" said Brooke. "I always thought that job looked like so much fun."

"You need to pick a friend to help you," said Mom. "If you decide soon enough, maybe the two of you can have matching dresses."

"Oh, Tonya and I already have matching dresses," said Brooke.

"Is that who you want to help you?" Mom asked.

"Probably," Brooke said. "I'll think about it."

Brooke went to her closet to look at her clothes. She wanted something really nice.

When she opened her closet door, something fell from a top shelf—the scarf she had worn when she lost her hair. The scarf reminded her of Emily's scarf; Emily had been so happy to wear a scarf like Brooke's. Brooke picked up the scarf and ran her fingers along the hem. Her eyes stared at the scarf, but she was not really seeing it. She was thinking.

The next day, Brooke and Tonya worked on math problems together at school. After several problems, Brooke dropped her pencil.

"Tonya, I'm going to ask Emily to help me pass out programs at the Christmas supper. I hope you don't mind." Brooke's voice felt dry. Would Tonya be angry that Brooke was not asking her?

Tonya looked sad for a moment. Then she smiled. "That's a good idea. Remember how Emily wore a scarf when you had to?"

"I know; that's why I thought of asking her. Plus, her mom is so nice to me."

Tonya nodded.

"I'm glad you don't care too much," Brooke said. "It would be more fun for me to do it with you. But I think Emily would really like it."

There was no snow the night of the Christmas supper, but it was still a beautiful, clear night. Sara had made matching dresses for Emily and Brooke. Brooke was sure it was the most beautiful dress she had ever worn.

Emily stood in the entryway at school, waiting for Brooke. Her mother stood beside her.

"Hi, Emily," Brooke said. "Hi, Sara. Thanks so much for making this dress. I love it!"

"You're welcome, Brooke," Sara said. Her eyes looked as if she were about to cry.

Moms are strange, Brooke thought. *You never know when they are going to cry about something!*

Brooke and Emily stood inside the gym door at the beginning of the candlelit path that led to the tables. Emily held the basket of programs; Brooke passed them out to the guests. Both girls smiled merrily at each person who came in.

Tonya gave a hug to both Brooke and Emily when she came through. "You girls look so nice!" she said.

Brooke and Emily posed for pictures all night long. Everyone wanted a picture of the girl who had cancer with the girl who had Down syndrome.

"Did you hear?" people whispered to each other. "Brooke chose Emily to be her friend to help pass out the programs. Isn't that neat?"

One of the visitors at the Christmas banquet was a writer. After the meal and program, this lady talked to Brooke. "Would you mind if I wrote a story about you for the newspaper?" she asked.

Brooke didn't know what to say. "I don't care," she finally stammered. "But maybe you should ask my mom and dad. They're over there."

The writer got permission from Brooke's parents to write a story. She told them she would come to their house the next day to talk to Brooke and her mom and dad. Brooke was excited! She had never talked to a newspaper writer before.

The writer asked Brooke a lot of questions the next day. She wanted to know how long Brooke and Emily had known each other. She wanted to know why Brooke had chosen Emily to be her program friend at the banquet.

"That's really kind that you thought of including Emily," the lady said to Brooke.

"Oh, but it wasn't really my idea," Brooke said. "It was Emily's mom who was kind to me first. She was such a gentle person when I was getting my treatments."

"I see." The writer smiled thoughtfully and wrote on her notepad.

One day, when Brooke came home from school, Mom met her at the door with a smile.

"Remember when we talked about God's gentleness last summer?" Mom asked. "I told you that it's God's gentleness that makes us great and teaches us, and that He will make a beautiful story out of your life. Remember that?"

"Yes," said Brooke. "What's that in your hand?"

"It's part of your beautiful story," Mom said, "and how God used your cancer to teach you to be gentle." She handed Brooke the newspaper.

There was the picture of Emily and Brooke! In big letters, the newspaper said "GENTLENESS COMES BACK." Underneath the big letters was the story about Emily and Brooke.

"I'm going to keep this newspaper," Brooke said after she read the story. "And someday I'll write a story myself."

Questions for Review

1. This story about Brooke and Emily is based on an account of some students in Wisconsin, one of which had Hodgkin's lymphoma and the other had Down syndrome. Do you know anyone who has cancer or Down syndrome?
2. During her treatment, what did Brooke wish the people at church would not do?
3. What did Emily do that was thoughtful to Brooke?
4. What did Brooke do that was kind to Emily in return?
5. How did gentleness come back?

Questions for Discussion

1. In what way was Brooke's mother kind and gentle to Brooke?
2. How was Sara kind to Brooke?
3. In what way was Sara prepared to gently help Brooke with understanding and advice?
4. How can you be gentle and kind to those who have cancer?
5. How can your family be kind to those who have physical or mental challenges?

GOODNESS

Barnabas: A Good Man

Remembering without ceasing your work of faith,
and labour of love,
and patience of hope in our Lord Jesus Christ,
in the sight of God and our Father.
— 1 Thessalonians 1:3

Read Acts 11:22-30

The words *good* and *God* are closely related. God is good and His children under the influence of the Holy Spirit are good. Goodness means godliness pervading the Christian's life. The Spirit fruit of goodness is a natural outgrowth of a close relationship with God.

According to a legend, an angel offered a godly bishop a choice of special powers such as healing the sick. His reply? "The thing I most desire is that God would bestow upon me the gift of doing a great deal of good without knowing it myself."

A British nobleman was known for his good works and benevolence. A stranger to the city asked how he might identify him. He was told, "Look for a tall gentleman helping somebody."

Barnabas was like that: wherever we see him in Scripture he is helping someone. No wonder Acts 11:24 describes him as "a good man." What are the characteristics of this good man?

- *Generous.* When we are introduced to Barnabas, he is selling land and bringing the money to the apostles for the purpose of helping the needy (Acts 4:36, 37).
- *Encouraging.* The apostles gave Joses the name Barnabas, meaning *son of encouragement.* As verse 23 of our daily reading says, he exhorted them all to cling to Christ.
- *Sympathetic.* He introduced the newly converted Saul to the church leaders that he had recently been trying to kill. Acts 9:27, 28 says, "Barnabas took him, and brought him to the apostles, and declared unto them how he had seen the Lord in the way, and that he had spoken to him, and how he had preached boldly at Damascus in the name of Jesus. And he was with them coming in and going out at Jerusalem."
- *Hardworking.* He was an instructor in a yearlong Bible school at Antioch.
- *Dependable.* When the first-century Christians in Antioch wanted to send financial help to the famine-stricken believers of Judaea, Barnabas and Saul took it (v. 30).
- *Evangelistic.* He was part of the very successful mission team on Paul's first missionary journey.
- *Merciful.* He wanted to give John Mark another chance on the second missionary journey.
- *Humble.* He, who was the leader, graciously let Paul become the lead person. The man who humbly bows before God will walk uprightly before man.

BRAVE ESTHER

Have not I commanded thee?
Be strong and of a good courage;
be not afraid, neither be thou dismayed:
for the LORD *thy God is with thee whithersoever thou goest.*
—Joshua 1:9

READ ESTHER 4:5-16

A little church in Texas used a large collection basket for taking up the offering. When it reached a Native American who was poor in possessions and finances, the man said to the usher, "Please put it down a little lower."

The usher lowered the basket. The man said, "Still lower, please."

When the collection basket reached the floor, the Native American stepped into it. It was his way of saying he wanted to give *himself* to Christ. With good insight into what it means to be a Christian, he was offering his total self to God.

Esther also in a sense placed her life in the offering basket. She was willing to die for the people of God. She was dedicated to do God's will. Are you?

What was noteworthy about Esther?

- Esther recognized the predicament that faced the Jews after Mordecai saw to it that she received the information about the danger to all Jews (Esther 4:7-9).
- Esther was reluctant to go to the king and beg him to save the Jews. King Ahasuerus had not called for Esther for thirty days. Execution was certain if the king did not feel like holding out his golden scepter (v. 11). Secular history shows us that Ahasuerus was a cruel, unpredictable man.
- Esther requested fasting by all the Jews in Shushan, and after three days she would risk her life.
- Esther was resigned to God's will. She was a committed queen, prepared to perish in her attempt to save the Jews. Mordecai believed that if Esther failed in her duty, God would provide deliverance in some other way for the Jews through whom the Messiah would come.
- Mordecai asked a question of Esther that we do well to ponder: "Who knoweth whether thou art come to the kingdom for such a time as this?" God has a definite purpose and wonderful plan for you! There is a reason you are alive at the present time and in your particular situation. Be faithful in your duties now. God, no doubt, plans to use you to help others find deliverance.

HELPFUL AARON

And the anger of the LORD was kindled against Moses,
and he said, Is not Aaron the Levite thy brother?
I know that he can speak well.
And also, behold, he cometh forth to meet thee:
and when he seeth thee, he will be glad in his heart.
— Exodus 4:14

READ EXODUS 4:27-30; 17:9-13

A sea captain and his chief engineer were arguing over who was most important to the ship. To prove their points to each other, they decided to swap places. The chief engineer ascended to the bridge, and the captain descended to the engine room.

Several hours later, the captain suddenly appeared on deck covered with oil and dirt. "Chief!" he yelled, waving aloft a monkey wrench. "You have to get down there: I can't make her go!"

"Of course you can't," replied the chief. "She's aground!"

Aaron had an important role to fill, working alongside Moses. In contrast to Moses, who was "not eloquent . . . and of a slow tongue" (Exodus 4:10), Aaron could "speak well" (v. 14). Together, Moses and Aaron made an effective team as God directed them. God's message was channeled through Moses to Aaron, who then spoke the truth to the Israelites.

Consider a comparison. A friend of yours is hospitalized. You think Philippians 4:4-13 would encourage him. So you phone your friend. God has a message for your friend, which He channels through you, using the telephone to convey the message to the patient. Aaron served as a "telephone."

- Aaron was a valuable help to Moses. What characteristics did he reveal that are examples for us?
- He had enthusiasm and love for his brother rather than jealousy or indifference. Upon meeting Moses after forty years of separation, he was glad in his heart and kissed his brother. In your family, do you eagerly support your leader?
- He listened (v. 28). Do you listen attentively to all your spiritual leaders say to you?
- He cooperated with Moses and accepted God's plan (v. 29). Do you show a spirit of cooperation with God and those in authority over you?
- He faithfully spoke God's message. Do you speak for the Lord?

Aaron had a supporting role—literally! He with Hur held up Moses' weary arms, contributing to victory.

How often in the battles of life leaders need the support of godly friends and family. What a difference obvious, strong support makes when the enemy threatens to prevail. Will you be a faithful supporter of your leaders?

Although Aaron was a dismal failure as a temporary leader in Moses' absence (see Exodus 32), he did serve God and Moses many years as a valuable helper.

Lydia: A Good Businesswoman

Being confident of this very thing,
that he which hath begun a good work in you
will perform it until the day of Jesus Christ.
— Philippians 1:6

Read Acts 16:9-16

A small, quiet man who was a vendor of fruits and vegetables regularly walked by a Christian's home. One day as he walked past the house he happened to drop a small notebook. The Christian homeowner was about to hand him the notebook when he noticed the words on the front page: "For His body's sake which is the church." More curious than courteous, his eyes scrolled down the page. He read:

- "The following were absent from church last Sunday—be sure to visit them."
- "Ask about the sick baby."
- "Leave fruit for the blind lady."
- "Speak a word of cheer to the old crippled man."

The peddler took the book modestly from the homeowner's hand. "You see," he said, "this is my book of reminders." Pointing to the first page, he continued, "That is why I do these things."

Our daily reading tells of a woman who exemplified goodness and a heart for worship and the church. She was the first person to become a Christian in Europe under Paul's ministry. She showed the Spirit's fruit of goodness both in her response to God and in her desire to serve others. Lydia knew some things that please God—regular prayer, a day of rest, worship. She was open to the truth Paul presented in that outdoor worship service. She responded to Paul's message of salvation through Jesus Christ and became a Christian.

How should we follow the good example of Lydia? We should worship, pray, and keep the Lord's Day. We should listen to God's spokesmen. We should be receptive to new truth. If we have not allowed the Lord to open our hearts and convert us, we should be ready to respond when the Lord calls us.

Like Lydia, God's work of conversion will be evident in us. She was baptized, indicating a change of heart, a public testimony of her yielding to the lordship of Jesus. Her love to God was shown, as it always is, by an expression of love to God's children. She courteously invited Paul and company to accept her hospitality. That she besought and constrained indicated her sincerity and eagerness to express brotherly love and possibly learn more of the Gospel.

Goodness consists not so much in the outward things we do, as the inward things we are. Lydia was good at heart, and she did good.

JETHRO: A WISE ADVISOR

The way of a fool is right in his own eyes:
but he that hearkeneth unto counsel is wise.
— Proverbs 12:15

READ EXODUS 18:7-26

After a day of travel through the hot, dusty plains, everyone on the train coach was weary. Now in the evening, all hoped to enjoy a refreshing sleep. However, at the end of the coach a tiny baby kept crying and fussing. As it became dark, the baby, held by his father, became more restless and noisy.

After some time, a big, husky man gave the father some advice. "Why don't you take that baby to his mother?"

After a moment of silence, the father replied, "I'm sorry. I'm doing my best. The baby's mother is in a casket in the baggage car ahead."

Wisely, the big, husky spokesman gave some additional advice with more understanding. Apologizing, he said, "Give me the baby. I'll rock him. You get some sleep." All night he cared for the little one.

Advice—so easy to give, so hard to give properly.

Parents are frequently best qualified to give advice. Such was the case with Jethro and his son-in-law Moses. Jethro, like Christian parents today, was well suited to give helpful advice.

- Jethro had previously shown kindness to Moses and enjoyed a good relationship with him (Exodus 2:20, 21, and 4:18). Christian parents show much kindness to their children.
- He was interested in Moses' well-being before he saw the need for advice (Exodus 18:7). Christian parents today show genuine concern for the happiness of their children.
- He observed at some length first; then asked questions to make sure he understood the situation before he gave his counsel (vv. 13, 14). Parents also have opportunities for understanding their children's situations.
- He was concerned about Moses' health and the welfare of God's people (v. 18). This concern for youth and the church is shared by godly parents today.

Jethro spoke his counsel courteously, clearly, and with good insight.

Jethro presented his personal evaluation of the situation. He was not trying to force Moses to accept his plan. He could see great benefit for both Moses and the multitude of Israelites.

Jethro wisely mentioned one condition. The plan would need to meet with God's approval. Moses would need to talk it over with the Lord and receive His directions.

It has been pointed out that "the willingness of the ordinary man to give advice is equaled only by his unwillingness to take advice." Moses was no ordinary man. He gladly listened and learned from an in-law.

President of the Dorcas Society

Pure religion and undefiled before God and the Father is this,
To visit the fatherless and widows in their affliction,
and to keep himself unspotted from the world.
—James 1:27

READ ACTS 9:36-43

Some women who sew for the needy in their communities and across the globe call themselves the Dorcas Society. This is appropriate because a godly woman at Joppa called Dorcas was known for her sewing.

Not only did she sew, she shared. When she got sick and died, the widows she had given clothes to were heartbroken. It must have been a very moving scene when Peter entered the upper chamber where her body lay. As our daily reading says, "All the widows stood by him weeping, and shewing the coats and garments which Dorcas made."

The Spirit fruit of goodness will try to provide clothing for those who are destitute. It's not enough to feel sorry for them and pray God's blessing on them. "If a brother or sister be naked, and destitute of daily food, and one of you say unto them, Depart in peace, be ye warmed and filled; notwithstanding ye give them not those things which are needful to the body; what doth it profit? Even so faith, if it hath not works, is dead, being alone" (James 2:15-17).

Our family is glad to regularly pack clothes via Christian Aid Ministries for those without suitable durable clothing. I am pleased that several former students of mine have been involved in "Dorcas activities" in mission settings. Jesus commends those who respond to the needs of those who are destitute of clothing (Matthew 25:34-40).

Menno Simons wrote about what true evangelical faith will do. "True evangelical faith . . . cannot lay dormant; but manifests itself in all righteousness and works of love; it . . . clothes the naked; feeds the hungry; consoles the afflicted; shelters the miserable; aids and consoles all the oppressed; returns good for evil; serves those that injure it; prays for those that persecute it" (Menno Simons, *Why I Do Not Cease Teaching and Writing, 1539).*

It wasn't only Dorcas who was involved in meeting the needs of the poor. Aristides wrote to the emperor Hadrian about Christians: "They love one another. They never fail to help widows; they save orphans from those who would hurt them. If they have something, they give freely to the man who has nothing; if they see a stranger, they take him home, and are happy, as though he were a real brother. They don't consider themselves brothers in the usual sense, but brothers instead through the Spirit, in God."

Jonathan: A True Friend

A friend loveth at all times,
and a brother is born for adversity.
— *Proverbs 17:17*

Read 1 Samuel 18:1-4; 23:14-18

Damon and Pythias were good friends who lived in Greece. King Dionysius heard that Pythias had criticized him and so threw Pythias into prison and condemned him to die in three days. Pythias asked permission to visit his wife and child some distance away, promising to return by sunset the third day. Damon, who had gone with his friend to the king to beg this favor, said to the king, "I will stay in prison in his absence, and if he is not back in time, I will die in his place." The king agreed, thinking, *Pythias will not return to die, so Damon will be put to death, and so I will be rid of both my enemies.*

Pythias stayed with his wife and child a little while, kissed them, and said good-bye. However, he faced many obstacles, including the death of his horse by his servant who did not want him to return to the king.

Sunset of the third day had almost come. Great crowds gathered, for it was known that Pythias had not returned and Damon must die for his friend. When Damon was led out of prison, King Dionysius sneered, "Your friend has not returned to die. You were foolish to think he would keep his promise. I knew better. Do not plead for mercy, for none will be granted."

"I ask no mercy," said Damon. "Something has prevented Pythias. He would be as faithful to me as I am to him."

As the sun sank in the western sky, Damon was led onto the platform where he was to die. Suddenly a shout rose from the crowd. A horse borrowed by Pythias burst through the crowd.

"Forgive me, Damon," Pythias cried. "I could not come sooner, but I am yet in time."

A long, loud cry to the king went up from the crowd, "Pardon, pardon for Pythias."

King Dionysius, astounded by the friendship of the two men, said, "Free the prisoner."

A similar loyalty of two friends is evident in today's reading.

What a blessing to have a friend like Jonathan in times of difficulty and discouragement! Like Jonathan, we can strengthen the hands of our friends by our words, our encouragement not to fear, our compassion, our interest, and our very presence.

In prosperity, our friends know us; in adversity, we know our friends. Friendship is like arithmetic—it doubles our joy and divides our grief.

Envious Ben

by Juliann Ropp Good

"I have something to tell you," Miss Roth announced. The fifth graders straightened in their seats. "Have you noticed the paper ladder that I've stuck on the wall?" their teacher continued. Heads nodded across the room. "The ladder has one hundred rungs, and here is a cat to climb it," said Miss Roth. "Now, here is the plan.

Whenever someone gets 100 percent on a spelling test, he may move the cat up one step on the ladder. When the cat has climbed to the very top, you will all be treated to a special prize."

Ben frowned slightly as he listened. Spelling was definitely not his favorite subject. Why did Miss Roth need to choose spelling for this project? Ben decided that he would probably never be able to move the cat, because he rarely got 100 percent in spelling.

Miss Roth placed Ben's spelling test on his desk, and he looked at the grade inked in red on the top: 67 percent. It certainly was better than the 50 percent he had gotten last week, but it still wasn't a very good mark. He sighed. Then he glanced across the aisle at his friend Carter. Carter's face was glowing and his eyes sparkled. Ben glared at him. Probably he had received 100 percent. It seemed Carter was good at everything, and especially at spelling.

"Now," Miss Roth said, "if you had 100 percent, come to the front, please, and you may move the cat up the ladder."

Sure enough, Carter got up and walked to the front of the room along with three others. "We're off to a good start," Miss Roth encouraged, "and I'm sure if we all try hard, we'll be able to reach our goal before the end of the school year."

What's the use in trying? Ben thought to himself. *If only I had brains like Carter has. Look at him, strutting back to his seat. He thinks he's so smart. I just wish I was that smart.*

All the rest of the day, Ben thought about that spelling chart. And he thought about Carter. It seemed Carter was so happy, so pleased with himself, and Ben resented him for it. When Carter offered him his apple at recess, Ben turned his back and walked away. Carter stared after him, puzzled. What was wrong with Ben?

The next week, eight students received 100 percent in spelling, and Carter was one of them. Ben was not. He scowled at the pleased expression on Carter's face. *Why can't I spell as well as he can?* he thought. *I wish I had brains like he has.* The more he thought about it, the more dissatisfied Ben became with his own abilities, and the more jealous he became of Carter. At recess, when Carter wanted to walk with him out to the ball field, Ben stalked away from him. And he laughed very loudly when Carter struck out. *Serves you right,* he thought. *If you're so smart in spelling, I'm glad you're dumb at something else.*

The next week Ben studied very hard for his spelling test. But when he got it back, he saw that he had only received an 86 percent. *Why, oh why, can't I be as good as Carter?* he thought as he watched Carter move the cat up the chart again. *It seems he always gets 100 percent, and I don't think he studies much at all! And I study a lot and can't even get a 90 percent.*

Then a plan began to form in Ben's mind. *Ah-ha,* he mused, *perhaps I CAN be as good as Carter. A simple little plan is all I need to help me.* And he smiled to himself.

The next week Ben put his plan into action. Just before spelling class, he opened his textbook and decided which words were the hardest ones. Then he took a pen and carefully wrote the hard words on the palm of his hand. Now, when he didn't know how to spell a word during the test, he would only need to look in his hand to see the answer.

That's cheating! Ben's conscience screamed at him, but he ignored it. He wanted to be as good as Carter, just for once.

The spelling test began. The first few words were easy. Then Miss Roth called, "*Sleigh.* The horses pulled the sleigh over the snowy hills. *Sleigh.*"

Ben could never remember how to spell *sleigh.* Was it *s-l-a-y?* No, there was a g in it somewhere. He looked down at his lap and discreetly opened his hand. There it was, spelled out for him: *s-l-e-i-g-h.* Quickly he copied it down on his paper and then looked up to see if anyone had noticed. No one had. Ben did that several more times throughout the test. *Now,* he thought to himself, *perhaps Carter will be surprised to see me up there with him on Monday.*

On Monday when Ben received his test back, he was pleased to see a big 100 percent written across the top. A little tinge of guilt nagged at him, but he brushed it aside. "All those with 100 percent come to the front, please," said Miss Roth. Ben puffed out his chest a little as he marched to the front. "There are nine of you today," their teacher went on. "That's almost half the class, and I'm very pleased with your effort. Good work."

Ben stood beside Carter. His friend turned to look at him, and surprise flashed across his face. *Yeah,* Ben thought, *take a good look at me. From now on, I will be up here with you every time. You're surprised I got 100 percent, aren't you?*

Then a big smile lit up Carter's face. "Good for you," he whispered. Ben smiled back, suddenly a little ashamed of all the nasty thoughts he had been thinking about his friend.

For the next several weeks, Ben continued to cheat in spelling. At first he was so glad to be as good as Carter that he didn't think about anything else. But after a while, he began to feel guilty. Miserably guilty. He wasn't as good a speller as Carter, and he knew it.

Ben became so miserable that people began to notice it. Carter, of course, noticed it. So did some other boys at school, and Ben's parents wondered what was wrong with him. Miss Roth also noticed, and being the wise teacher she was, she made some guesses.

One Monday after Ben had received another 100 percent on his spelling test, Miss Roth asked him to stay in at recess time.

Ben squirmed in his chair. Did Miss Roth know all about his cheating? He knew he would be in big trouble if she did.

"I've been wondering about something," began the teacher after they were alone in the classroom. "You have never been a very good speller. I know you usually try hard, but your marks are not usually very high. But suddenly, a few weeks ago, you started to get 100 percents on your tests. Not just one of them, but all of them! Can you tell me why you have changed so suddenly?"

Ben and Miss Roth stayed inside for the entire recess, and by the time it was over Miss Roth had heard the entire story: how Ben was jealous of Carter's good grades in spelling, how he wanted to be as good as Carter, how he had written spelling words on his hand and cheated on his tests.

Then Ben went to the principal's office to take his punishment for cheating.

And the cat dropped down the ladder several steps on the spelling chart.

After school, Ben and Carter had a little talk. Ben asked Carter to forgive him for all his unkindness, and Carter readily did. "I'm glad we can be friends again," Carter said warmly. "If I'm better than you at spelling, you're better than me in baseball. See? Now we're even!"

A warm feeling flooded Ben's heart as he looked at his friend. "No," he said, shaking his head, "I still say you're better than I am at a lot more things than just spelling. But it doesn't really matter. What matters is that we don't get jealous of each other because of it. Because jealousy makes even more problems. Hey, do you want to play catch for a few minutes?"

And the two boys ran happily to the ball field together.

Questions for Review

1. Is the Spirit fruit of goodness shown by being jealous of others?
2. Why was Ben jealous of Carter?
3. What did he decide to do so he could move the cat up the ladder?
4. Who were some people who noticed that Ben was unhappy?
5. Why did Ben need to stay in at recess?

Questions for Discussion

1. How did Ben's envy affect his relationships?
2. Ben's cheating and getting 100 percent made him happy: true or false? Explain your answer.
3. What other sins developed after Ben allowed envy in his heart?
4. How did Ben become happy again?
5. How can a person guard against becoming jealous?

FAITH

Jesus Is Faithful

Wherefore, holy brethren, partakers of the heavenly calling, consider the Apostle and High Priest of our profession, Christ Jesus; who was faithful to him that appointed him.
— Hebrews 3:1, 2

Read Hebrews 10:12-23

Smelling smoke in the house, Shep began to bark and scratch at bedroom doors in the home where Mrs. D'Angelo and her six children were sleeping. The collie then raced out of the burning house to the factory where Mr. D'Angelo was working the night shift. Rushing to him, Shep whined and pulled repeatedly at his trousers. Deciding that something must be wrong, he followed the dog out of the factory toward home. Soon he saw the glow of the burning house. The father arrived at the house just as the last of his seven family members ran from the burning building. The family was extremely grateful for Shep's faithfulness.

Jesus faithfully warns us to flee from the fire of Hell by trusting in Him. Hebrews 2:17 describes Him as a merciful and faithful high priest who provides salvation. From the beginning of His manhood at age twelve when He said, "I must be about my Father's business" (Luke 2:49) until He died at Calvary, He was the epitome of faithfulness.

"The fruit of the Spirit is . . . faith" (Galatians 5:22). The Greek word has the thought of faithfulness arising from faith.

Jesus was faithful to His Father. He said, "I do always those things that please him" (John 8:29). At Jesus' baptism, the heavenly voice said, "This is my beloved Son, in whom I am well pleased" (Matthew 3:17). He faithfully resisted the temptations that Satan presented. He faithfully taught, preached, and healed the lame, blind, deaf, mute, and emotionally crippled.

He faithfully followed the road to the cross. Sensing the need to fulfill God's plan for providing salvation, He said He "must go unto Jerusalem, and suffer many things of the elders and chief priests and scribes, and be killed, and be raised again the third day" (Matthew 16:21).

Very appropriately, the Book of Revelation calls Him the faithful witness. "Jesus Christ, who is the faithful witness, and the first begotten of the dead, and the prince of the kings of the earth. Unto him that loved us, and washed us from our sins in his own blood" (Revelation 1:5). And as the conquering King on a white horse, He is called "Faithful and True" (Revelation 19:11).

As our daily reading indicates, "He is faithful." Therefore, let us faithfully hold fast to our faith in Him. You can depend on the Lord. Can He depend on you?

FAITH IN ABRAHAM'S SHIELD

Through faith also Sara herself received strength to conceive seed,
and was delivered of a child when she was past age,
because she judged him faithful who had promised.
— Hebrews 11:11

READ GENESIS 15:1-7

A wild storm raged around a prairie home. The windows were blown in, and no lights could be kept burning. The mother, grandmother, and three children sat in darkness in a room on the sheltered side of the house, fearing that any moment it might be swept from its foundation.

Suddenly, they discovered that eleven-year-old Walter was missing. Only minutes before he had been holding a whispered conversation with his grandmother. Frantic with fear, the mother called, but got no answer and started to grope in the darkness to find him. She finally found him in his room fast asleep! And when she asked him how he could go to sleep when they were all in danger, he simply replied, "Why, Grandma told me God would take care of us, and I thought I might as well go to bed again."

Walter believed God would be a shield to him, even as God said He was a shield to Abraham (verse 1 of our daily reading). Abraham's problem wasn't a storm. It was a lack of descendants. How could he be the father of many nations as God had promised, if his wife Sarah bore him no children?

God was the focus of Abraham's faith. He believed in God and God took note of Abraham's right attitude (v. 6).

What did the word of the Lord to Abraham include?

- *Fear not.* This is first of many comforting reassurances from God to fear not.
- *I am.* This is the first *I am* of Scripture. Since Jesus is the Word (John 1:1), we may think of this vision as Christ appearing to Abram. See John 8:56-58 also.
- *Thy shield.* This is the first use of the word *shield* in the Bible. The Lord provides "the shield of faith" (Ephesians 6:16). In fact, "The Lord God is a sun and shield" (Psalm 84:11).
- *Great reward.* This is the first instance of the word *reward* in Scriptures.
- *You shall yet have a son.* Not the servant, Eliezer, but Abraham's own son would be his heir.
- *Your descendants will be beyond number.* To a childless man this was beyond logic, yet Abraham accepted it by faith.

God will reward our faith in Him. As an early church writer put it, "Faith is to believe what we do not see; the reward of faith is to see what we believe."

Holy and Wholly Committed

Save Caleb the son of Jephunneh; he shall see it,
and to him will I give the land that he hath trodden upon,
and to his children, because he hath wholly followed the Lord.
— Deuteronomy 1:36

Read Numbers 13:26-33; 14:1-9

At Sunday school, each student in a class made a plaque with the words "Have faith in God." After class one girl boarded a bus to take her home. As it started to move, she realized she didn't have her motto. She jumped from her seat and shouted to the driver, "Stop the bus. I've lost my 'faith in God'!"

Obviously, Caleb, unlike the ten spies, had not lost his faith.

"Faith is just believing what God said He will do." So said the songwriter, and so demonstrated Caleb. How did Caleb reveal his great faith? Our daily reading shows six ways:

1. He was not afraid to stand up to the majority opinion of the ten spies. He and Joshua alone stood for the Lord. We today need faith to stand up for Jesus even though most people do not have faith in God and His Word.

2. He was not afraid to speak boldly to people who were rapidly becoming upset, discouraged, and rash. He *stilled* the people and tried to *instill* in them confidence toward God. We today need a bold faith to speak to friends, relatives, and neighbors about unpopular teachings of God.
3. He was not afraid of the big walls of the Canaanite cities or the big warriors in those cities (Numbers 13:28). We today should trust God to help us conquer big problems.
4. Caleb was not afraid to urge immediate obedience: "Let us go up at once." We today need to follow promptly as God leads us.
5. Caleb was not afraid to claim the promises of God. That is the only way he could assert, "We are well able to overcome it." Through trust in Christ, we today can be "more than conquerors through him that loved us" (Romans 8:37).
6. Caleb's faith stands in stark contrast to the ten spies' lack of faith. The ten spies did some unfortunate mathematics. They subtracted God from their forces and said, "They are stronger than we." They added to the difficulties of conquering Canaan by saying the land "eateth up the inhabitants thereof." They multiplied the size of the men of Canaan. And they divided the spies into two groups—faithless and faithful.

"Dare to be a Daniel"—and a Caleb! Faith is dead to doubts, dumb to discouragement, and blind to impossibilities.

A Dying Leader's Challenge: Be Faithful

And Israel served the Lord all the days of Joshua,
and all the days of the elders that overlived Joshua,
and which had known all the works of the Lord,
that he had done for Israel.
—Joshua 24:31

READ JOSHUA 24:1, 11-27

Consider the prayer of Jim Elliot, a dedicated missionary martyred by the Auca Indians of Ecuador in 1956: "Father, make of me a crisis man. Bring those I contact to decision. Let me not be a milepost on a single road; make me a fork, that men must turn one way or another on facing Christ in me."

Joshua was a "crisis man" in calling people to a decision to serve the Lord and in portraying a godly example. Our daily reading shows his faith—the challenge and the choice he gave near the end of his life regarding faith and obedience. His clear words still confront us today: "Choose you this day whom ye will serve."

How did Joshua inspire faith by his final challenge to the Israelites?

- He called everyone together to present themselves before God (v. 1).
- He pointed out to the people God's intervention on their behalf (v. 12).
- He declared God's gracious gifts to man (v. 13).
- He told them to be sincere and truthful in their relationship to the Lord (v. 14).
- He insisted on them putting away any rival to God (v. 14).
- He encouraged them to serve the Lord (v. 14).
- He pointed out the necessity of choosing (v. 15).
- He clarified that there are only two ways (v. 15).
- He gave a good example in forthrightly stating that he and his family would serve the Lord (v. 15).
- After the people stated their decision to serve the Lord, he made sure they understood that their decision must be genuine and permanent (v. 19).
- He made the covenant more official by writing their promises down and setting up a visible reminder (v. 26).

The final words of a person who knows he is dying are usually considered very important. In one case, a family gathered around the deathbed of a man who became rich and famous because of a restaurant chain he had established across the United States and Canada. They heard him whisper the main thought of his life: "Slice the ham thin." Joshua's time of death was near (Joshua 24:29), and he spoke the words closest to his heart. After giving the challenge and receiving a commitment to be faithful, Joshua died.

Diligent Deborah

Then sang Deborah and Barak the son of Abinoam on that day, saying, Praise ye the LORD.
—Judges 5:1, 2

READ JUDGES 4:1-16

On the tombstone of Fanny Crosby, blind writer of six thousand hymns, are the words "She Hath Done What She Could." So it was with Deborah, who diligently served the Lord, as recorded in the daily reading.

God had some very unusual assignments for Deborah at this time of deep need in Israel. She was willing to do what God's plan involved. God has a plan for your life too. Will you accept God's directions even though they may seem difficult or very unusual?

- Deborah judged. A palm tree provided a place for her to give advice and make decisions.
- Deborah spoke God's message. She told Barak that God wanted him to gather and organize an army.
- Deborah showed courage. She willingly placed herself in great danger. She seems to have had more courage than the military commander, Barak.

- Deborah cooperated. When Barak pleaded with her to go with him, she was willing.
- Deborah acted. She arose and accompanied Barak to the battle site.
- Deborah exercised faith. For Deborah and for us today, faith gives the ability to face the present with confidence and the future with courage. She said confidently and with conviction, "Up; for this is the day in which the Lord hath delivered." Her trust was in the Lord and not in her ability. Her life tells us that when we do what we can, God will do what we cannot.

  The Lord "discomfited" (routed or defeated) the enemy. It appears there was a rainstorm (5:20), which changed the Kishon River into a raging torrent (v. 21) that swept some of them away.
- Deborah praised the Lord. She did not take credit for the victory, but called for the important people of Israel to pay attention to her praise so all would know that the victory was due to the Lord's aid. She praised the Lord as did the psalmist in Psalm 98:1: "O sing unto the Lord a new song; for he hath done marvellous things: his right hand, and his holy arm, hath gotten him the victory."

"Will you tell me in a word," said a Christian woman to a minister, "what your idea of consecration is?" Holding out a blank sheet of paper, the pastor replied, "It is to sign your name at the bottom of this blank sheet and let God fill it in as He wills."

Let Your Heart Be Steadfast

And fear not them which kill the body,
but are not able to kill the soul:
but rather fear him which is able to
destroy both soul and body in hell.
— Matthew 10:28

READ PSALM 115:1-13

About 250 years after Christ a godly young man named Symphorian lived in what is now France. One day he met a procession that included an idol on a wagon. Because he refused to worship the idol, he was arrested.

The judge asked, "Why didn't you worship the image?"

Symphorian replied, "I am a Christian and worship only the living God. If you will let me, I will gladly break the idol in pieces with a hammer." He knew, as our daily reading indicates, that an idol is not alive and can do nothing.

The judge had him scourged and cast into prison. Some time later, the judge had him brought to court again. "If you will sacrifice to the gods, I will reward and promote you. Otherwise, we will torture you."

Symphorian replied, "I'm ready to die for Christ. Our treasures are eternal in Christ. Even though you have lots of things, you really possess nothing. The pleasure you enjoy in this world is like fine glass, which, if placed in the heat of the sun, cracks and breaks in two; but God alone is our supreme happiness."

Symphorian thereupon was sentenced to be beheaded. As he was being led out to die, his mother called down from the wall of the city, urging him to be faithful. "Symphorian, my son! My son! Remember the living God; let your heart be steadfast and valiant. We can surely not fear death, which beyond doubt leads us into the true life. Lift up your heart to Heaven, my son, and behold Him who reigns in Heaven! Today your life will not be taken from you, but be changed into a better one. If you remain steadfast today, you shall make a happy exchange: leaving this earthly house, you shall go to dwell in the tabernacle not made with hands."

Symphorian and his mother had grasped the reality of 2 Corinthians 5:1, 8, "We know that if our earthly house of this tabernacle were dissolved, we have a building of God, an house not made with hands, eternal in the heavens. . . . We are confident, I say, and willing rather to be absent from the body, and to be present with the Lord."

The Lord's tomorrow of blessing is only waiting for our today of faithfulness.

FAITHFUL UNTO DEATH

Fear none of those things which thou shalt suffer: behold,
the devil shall cast some of you into prison,
that ye may be tried; and ye shall have tribulation ten days:
be thou faithful unto death, and I will give thee a crown of life.
— Revelation 2:10

READ ACTS 7:54-60

Felix Manz, a single man in his early twenties, was intent on knowing God and doing His will. He joined himself with others at the feet of Zwingli in Zurich, Switzerland, in the 1520s to learn what the Bible taught. By 1525 it became apparent that Zwingli was more loyal to the local government than to the Bible, so Felix, along with men like Conrad Grebel and George Blaurock, met at Felix's mother's house to pray and discuss God's will.

They concluded that, since the Bible taught adult baptism, they should be baptized. Felix took the step of faith, because he wanted to be faithful. Since he didn't hide the fact of his rebaptism but promoted baptism as an outward testimony of conversion, the Swiss authorities arrested and imprisoned him. Amazingly, he escaped and faithfully kept testifying of Jesus, urging people to repent of their sinful ways and go the way of the cross. Several times he was arrested along with other brothers and sisters and put into prison and given a diet of bread and water. Again and again he escaped from prison and kept preaching salvation through Christ.

After about two years as an Anabaptist, he received the death sentence: "Manz shall be delivered to the executioner, who shall tie his hands, put him into a boat, take him to the lower hut, there strip his bound hands down over his knees, place a stick between his knees and arms, and thus push him into the water and let him perish in the water."

As he was taken through the streets of Zurich to the Limmat River, he praised God with a loud voice. He cheerfully testified to the people that he was going to die for the truth.

He was placed in a boat near the fish market at three o'clock in the afternoon. He heard his mother's voice on the shore calling, "Be faithful, Felix."

Like Stephen, told about in the daily reading, he committed himself to God in death. He prayed as did his dying Saviour, "Father, into thy hands I commit my spirit" (in Latin). He died faithful to the end, the first Anabaptist to be put to death at the hands of the Protestants.

A Dog's Last Name

by Danette Schrock Martin

Lyle yanked at the sweaty neck of his shirt and bent over the drinking fountain. Behind him, he heard a snicker.

"Hey, guzzler, leave some for the rest of us." The voice was that of his good friend Roger, pretending to be Mr. Shantz, the principal.

Lyle wiped his mouth with the back of his hand and turned toward the gym. He saw Roger's smack coming and braced himself, but even so he almost lost his last mouthful of water when Roger connected with his shoulder. "Nice spiking in there!" Roger boomed.

"Thanks." Lyle tried to abbreviate his smile but half a grin sneaked out. That volleyball victory had made him feel good.

"Say, could you do something for me?" Roger asked.

Lyle paused, his hand on the gym door. Sure, he could take the volleyball to the equipment room. No problem.

"We're going to Rice Lake over the weekend. Mom's got an uncle and aunt there." Roger pulled on his ear in that nervous gesture he had. "Could you look after Napoleon for me? He'll be in his crate Friday night, but Saturday, he'll need some exercise, and food and water. Food's in the garden shed. You know where the key is."

Dog-sit. Would he? "Sure!" Lyle grabbed a breath. He couldn't believe he hadn't told Roger his own good news yet. "Guess what – we're probably getting a dog too. Dad gave half his consent anyway."

"Serious? What kind of dog?"

"A wolfhound, if we listen to Dexter – the bigger, the better, you know. Thomas is dead-set on a collie but I'm okay with any kind, I think; I've wanted a dog for so long."

Roger nodded. "Full-grown?"

"Likely a puppy, so we can train him easier. Not a house dog. Mom doesn't want a live-in."

"Try calling a farm. I see ads for farm puppies all over."

Ha. Roger had no idea how he sat, poring over the classifieds, every evening. "That's what we're aiming to do."

Roger headed toward the lockers. "Got to go – my ride's probably here. I hope you find a dog soon." He grabbed his book bag. "Don't forget Napoleon this weekend!"

In the driveway at home, Lyle unfolded his legs from the narrow backseat of Mrs. Troyer's car. "Thanks for the ride. See ya tomorrow." He bounded toward the house, pausing long enough at the basketball net to toss his lunch pail through for a clean shot. He was so happy he could almost put himself through the net. Volleyball and a dog!

On Saturday morning Lyle ran his finger down the *Pets for Sale* column in the *Grant County Tribune.* Poodles. Too ugly. Shih tzus. Too yappy. Terriers. Too pedigreed. Why were even the Jack Russels' and Blue Heelers' price tags in the hundreds of dollars?

Then, there it was – "Farm puppies, collie cross, first shots, $50." This ad would impress the most skeptical in the Ropp family. Then again, it didn't say anything about the dogs' trainability. His fingers shook as he picked up the newspaper. Would he be able to convince Dad?

Lyle found Dad in the shop, and thrust the paper under his nose. Dad pushed up his glasses, squinting at the newsprint. "Hmm, sounds a lot like the pup you've been hankering for. Not a bad price." He looked up. "If you're still paying half."

Lyle thrust his hands in his pockets. "Sure am."

Dad picked up a pencil from the workbench and doodled in the column's margin. "An 882 number . . . they must live in the Rockwood area . . ." Dad's voice trailed off, and Lyle held his breath. "Maybe we could check it out this afternoon," Dad mused.

Lyle let his breath out. "Suits me! Can Thomas and Dexter come, too?"

On Sunday morning at breakfast, the boys were still recounting the successful visit to the farm. "Oh, the puppy we're getting is so cute." Dexter happily licked a spot of jam off his thumb.

Susan rolled her eyes. "You've said that how many times already? And use a napkin, please."

Thomas stopped sipping his juice. "When you see that pup, you'll talk too!"

"Just two more weeks to wait." Lyle spread a healthy layer of peanut butter on his toast. "That'll give us plenty of time to come up with the perfect name."

Dad poured Cheerios into his bowl. "And enough time to enter Dog Training 101." He sounded serious, but his eyes crinkled at the corners.

Lyle swallowed. Dad thought responsibility was a dog's last name. He'd heard Dad so many times, he could give the lecture himself. You had to be patient. You had to be firm but gentle; always, always, consistent, to earn their trust. You had to do the messy stuff, too, like clean up messes and feed them and water . . .

No! He couldn't have forgotten, he just couldn't have! Shame wrenched his stomach and pushed at his eyelids. He threw his scrap of toast on the table.

Mom gasped. "What's wrong?"

Lyle shoved his chair away from the table, half rose, then slumped back on the seat. "Roger's dog, Napoleon. I was supposed to let him out and feed him yesterday morning already." He tried to shore up his voice. "He's probably dead by now."

Dexter's eyes grew wide. "Oh, Lyle."

Lyle got up. He might as well clear away his dishes, or something, but what was the use? His arms flopped to his sides. "I'm never doing chores for anybody again!"

"Now isn't the time to decide that," Dad said briskly. "Hop on your bike and go check things out. You have time before church to do what you promised to do."

Lyle wrestled his ten-speed out of the tangle of bikes in the shop. Maybe it was better to bike over to Roger's than to have Dad drive him. This way he wouldn't have to face the dog he'd murdered quite so soon. The wind in his face might dry his eyes too.

At Roger's place, Lyle fished the key out from under the metal turtle on the porch. Dread mushroomed in his chest, squeezing against his lungs. Choking, he turned the key in the lock. Wait. Was that a bark?

He shoved the door open and almost tripped over the mat. Kneeling at the crate, he fumbled at the latch while Napoleon went crazy inside. As soon as his prison opened, Napoleon streaked to the front door. Lyle ran after him.

Once outside and business finished, Napoleon plunged his nose into his outdoor water bowl. Alternately he slurped, barked, and danced around his food bowl. Lyle glanced at the dog. "Stay right here." Then he grinned as he sprinted toward the house. As if a starved dog would leave his food bowl!

Inside the breezeway, Lyle checked around Napoleon's crate for dog food. There wasn't even a speck of kibbles dust at the bottom of his indoor food bowl, much less a bagful sitting nearby.

Where did these people keep their dog food anyway? It wasn't on the counter, where Roger might have put it out for Lyle's convenience. He poked his head into the storage closet. Not there, either. He opened the door leading to the basement. No food for dogs among the empty jars perched on the stairs.

Lyle kicked at a squeak toy on the floor. Depending on him was about as nourishing for Napoleon as gnawing on that rubber bone. See if he'd ever promise to look after someone else's pet again. He'd have to slink home and tell Dad he couldn't do a simple thing like find a bag of dog food. Dad would cancel the puppy order for sure.

He shook his head. Disappointment welled up his throat and pricked his eyelids. Through a blur, he caught sight of the garden shed through the breezeway window. Of course. If his head hadn't been so full of dog when Roger was handing out instructions, it might have come to him sooner. Food's in the garden shed.

Weeks later, Lyle rode in the front seat of Mrs. Troyer's car, watching impatiently for the first sight of home and his beloved pet. He drummed his fingers on the door handle. The ride home from school seemed to take twice as long as usual these days. Mrs. Troyer signaled at the Ropp mailbox, and Lyle's eyes swept the laneway to the curve. Good. No pup in sight – yet. Maybe his training session with Patches last night had worked.

The car eased around the bend. Lyle's shoulders drooped. His brown and white trainee dashed toward them, stomach to the ground and his feet a determined blur. Mrs. Troyer gripped the steering wheel. Patches ran at the tires, barking madly while the car crept along. Lyle licked his lips. Mrs. Troyer was cautious, but seeing her white knuckles made his stomach tighten. He would tell that dog! Patches had to listen! He was going to get tough this time!

He stepped out of the car and was instantly attacked by a furry armful of exuberance. While he drew in a breath to lecture Patches, his feet became tangled in the dog's loving attentions and he tumbled to the grass. Patches frantically washed his face, burrowed into his belly, and ended with a thorough nipping of his ears.

Lyle cuffed him, trying to dig out his roughest voice. "Know what?" He growled, "You're a problem." The dog jerked away, then crawled back, laying his head sorrowfully on his paws and rolling his eyes upward at Lyle. Lyle laughed at the puppy's penitence. "The best problem I've ever had," he relented.

The next day, the phone rang at lunch. Dad answered. When he hung up, he turned back to the table, his lips in a firm line. "Jack Brown says Patches is over there running around with their dog. Couple times he was close to the road. Didn't even faze him—too young to have a clue." Dad looked straight at Lyle. "Like I've been telling you, he'd better be tied up."

"I have been." Lyle jammed his hands in his pockets. "I thought he's been doing better lately. It's hard to keep him chained all the time."

"It's okay to let him run loose while you're out with him, but otherwise, I think you ought to keep him tied up. It's not safe for him to run around. You'd better scoot over to Browns and get your dog before he makes too much of a nuisance."

Lyle sighed and headed for the door. He hated to have Patches whining at the end of a long chain. It wasn't his idea of a carefree farm dog's life.

On a rainy Sunday in May, the family arrived home after church. Lyle tumbled out the van doors after the others and scanned the yard for Patches. He whistled before going into the house, but no dog appeared.

Lyle went to his bedroom and hung up his suit. The phone rang. That was strange, on a Sunday noon. Mom answered it. Her taut voice and clipped sentences pulled him out into the hall. By the time he reached the kitchen, she had hung up and turned to Dad. "That was Jack. Patches was hit on the road in front of their place this morning."

Lyle felt like he'd been shot. He clutched his side. "Wha-what happened?"

"Patches was romping with Jack's dog this morning and Jack saw when he headed back over here. Patches didn't even look when he crossed the road. A car came and the lady braked hard but she couldn't stop in time—it was wet and slippery. Jack saw the whole thing happen." Mom's voice quavered. "He could barely tell me."

By now the children had gathered around, wide-eyed and pale. Mom gathered herself as she looked at them. "The poor lady driving the car was beside herself. She thought maybe she saw a bit of life in Patches, so she offered to take him to her dog's vet. It's on Lakeshore in Rockwood. Jack has the number."

Dexter sniffled and Missy burst into tears, but Lyle raised his head. "You mean he's not dead? I mean, I thought . . ." He stopped mid-sentence, the picture too graphic for his own composure. If only he'd tied up Patches before going to church!

Dad reached for the phone. "I'll get that number from Jack."

Soon Dad was on the line with someone at the vet clinic. Mom pulled a large pan from the oven and poked at its contents, but the children had their eyes on Dad. His eyebrows went up as he listened. "Doing well? Sure, I'll hold." He cupped his hand over the mouthpiece and whispered, "The receptionist says the initial report sounded good. She's going to let me talk directly to the vet."

Lyle's flicker of hope flared. He looked at Thomas, whose eyes sparked with sudden promise. Missy smiled through her tears. Then Lyle saw Dad's face fall. "He's gone? Oh, I see. I should come there to get the body? Thanks for everything you've done."

Dad gently replaced the receiver. Without a word, he walked over and squeezed Lyle's shoulders. Lyle bowed his head. Pain nearly choked him. Wouldn't it be easier if Dad just said, "I told you so"?

Half an hour later, Mom and the children were on their way to visit their friends, the Gingerichs, who had invited them for Sunday dinner and to stay overnight. While Dad went to Rockwood to pick up what remained of Patches, the rest of the family would carry on with their previous plans. He would join them when he could. Burying Patches would need to wait until the next day.

Daylight was fading when the Ropps returned home Monday evening. While Mom and the girls emptied the van, Dad and the boys headed toward the burial site at the edge of the woods. When they neared the spot, Lyle's steps lagged. Would he recognize his pet?

Lyle knelt and gazed at the still form lying on a sheet of cardboard. It looked like Patches, all right, more than he thought it would. The dog could be taken for sleeping, his eyes closed the way they were, and his fur unruffled. Lyle reached out a timid hand. The body was cold and stiff. He stood slowly, his eyes stinging. Dad handed him a shovel.

Lyle jammed it into the rectangle of dirt Dad had already marked out with his digging. Maybe he should have stayed away from this.

The grave was almost done when Mom and the girls came out. They stood, hunched together, Missy's mittened hand tight in Mom's glove. Lyle couldn't tell if their tears were from cold or grief.

Dad stuck his shovel into the mound. "Give me a hand here, boys." Shivering, they each lifted a corner of the cardboard and slid Patches into the hole. Dad took the shovel again and began covering the dog. Lyle looked away and coughed, pushing against the "no!" that rose in his throat.

Dad finished his somber task, and glanced around the silent circle. "Let's have a little prayer," he said. Lyle looked up. Pray? Maybe his hearing was as blurred as his vision.

Dad walked over, laid an arm across Lyle's shoulders and bowed his head. "Dear God, Thank You that You care about everything in our lives. We're all sad right now, but especially Lyle. Thank You that he could enjoy having Patches for the time that he did. Help him to know that You care. In Jesus' name. Amen."

On the way back to the house, Lyle trailed behind the rest. The sun slipped below the horizon. Lyle looked up the hill at his family, dark-framed in the red sky. He stopped briefly when his eyes rested on his father.

A surge of appreciation filled his heart as he thought of his dad. One word came to his mind—dependable. That was Dad—dependable with advice, dependable with helping with problems. Dependable in caring for the needs of his family.

I want to be like Dad he thought to himself. His dad had learned responsibility. He was as dependable as the sun each morning. Lyle knew he had a long way to go but he committed himself to develop personal responsibility.

Questions for Review

1. What did Roger want Lyle to do on the weekend?
2. How did Lyle show a lack of faithfulness and responsibility in his care of Napoleon?
3. Why didn't Lyle know where Napoleon's food was stored?
4. How did Patches die?
5. Who was at fault for Patches' death?

Questions for Discussion

1. Why did Lyle forget about Napoleon?
2. What should Lyle have done differently in his training of Patches?
3. How did Lyle's dad try to teach him responsibility?
4. What do you think of Lyle's dad praying after Patches was buried?
5. How could you (and your siblings) show more responsibility and faithfulness?

MEEKNESS

Meekness of Jesus

Even as the Son of man came not to be ministered unto, but to minister, and to give his life a ransom for many.
— Matthew 20:28

Read Philippians 2:1-8

It is important to learn to read. It is valuable to learn math. It is beneficial to learn to cook. But far more important is to learn of Jesus. Matthew 11:29 says, "Take my yoke upon you, and learn of me; for I am meek and lowly in heart: and ye shall find rest unto your souls."

Meekness is a wonderful fruit of the Spirit. It is cultivated and expressed in the life of a person who has come to Jesus and is learning of Him. Meekness means a submissive attitude toward God that reveals itself in gentleness toward others. It denotes a controlled strength. In the Greek, the term was used to describe an animal that had been trained by its master. Although a meek person has the power to retaliate, he chooses to be patient and gentle.

Jesus showed meekness throughout His ministry. When the disciples were slow to learn, He was meek. When He was criticized by the Pharisees, He was meek. When He faced the injustices of His trial before the Jews and before the Romans, He was meek. When He was tormented and ridiculed, He was meek. Such was His strength. Meekness is not weakness.

Our daily reading reminds us of two things. First, Jesus left the majestic heights of Heaven and became a lowly servant and went to the cross. Second, we should relate to each other with "lowliness of mind" and meekness.

I appreciate the meek attitude and action of Booker T. Washington, who was born a slave but who became a great educator, founding the Tuskegee Institute. He served as its principal and advised President Roosevelt. After he had become a prominent and influential figure, a woman one day called out to him as he walked down the street. She had not recognized him and yelled, "Hey, you, come in here and chop some wood."

Washington cheerfully turned onto her sidewalk, took off his coat, and chopped the wood. He carried it into the house before leaving.

A servant girl recognized him and told her employer who he was. The woman was dismayed and appalled at how she had treated this great African-American. She immediately went to apologize. "It is quite all right, ma'am," he replied. "I delight to do favors for my friends."

THE NEED FOR MEEKNESS

Seek ye the LORD, all ye meek of the earth,
which have wrought his judgment;
seek righteousness, seek meekness.
— Zephaniah 2:3

READ JOHN 13:1-17

Peter was born to wealthy parents of noble ancestry in the late 1500s in Europe. His family expected that, after college, he would become a high-ranking official and be rich, powerful, and honored.

But Peter decided to go a different direction. He went to the West Indies to help the slaves as they arrived from Africa. The docking of a slave ship sent strong men running, partly because of the sight, but mostly due to the smell. Hundreds of people had been chained together in the ship's hold unable to move. Some had died, some were dying, many were ill, and all were decidedly unclean.

Peter meekly devoted his life to meeting slave ships and going on board to care for the living and to bury the dead.

Not only in service, but also in correction, meekness is needed. As Galatians 6:1 says, "Brethren, if a man be overtaken in a fault, ye which are spiritual, restore such an one in the spirit of meekness; considering thyself, lest thou also be tempted." Without humility and recognition of one's own weakness, attempts to bring an erring brother to repentance are unlikely to succeed. The lessons taught by Jesus in our daily reading are very instructive. In order to help our brother and sister to be clean, we need to have a humble stance.

Meekness is also needed when disagreeing and attempting to lead another person to accept the truth. Second Timothy 2:24, 25 says, "The servant of the Lord must not strive; but be gentle unto all men, apt to teach, patient, in meekness instructing those that oppose themselves."

Meekness is also needed when sitting in church and listening to a sermon. James 1:21 says, "Wherefore lay apart all filthiness and superfluity of naughtiness, and receive with meekness the engrafted word, which is able to save your souls."

Meekness is needed in the presence of condescension. George Washington Carver, great scientist and inventor, was standing along a street in Alabama. A white woman thought he was a poor black laborer looking for work. She called him to paint her fence.

"Sure, I'd be happy to," he said. After several hours, a friend told the woman who he was. She was horrified at her mistake and apologized for her attitude. He replied, "That's okay. I didn't have much to do today. I'm very happy to paint your fence."

Meekness in Relation to God

The meek shall eat and be satisfied:
they shall praise the Lord that seek him:
your heart shall live for ever.
— Psalm 22:26

Read Isaiah 6:1-8

The story is told of a father and son who were walking along a downtown street in a large city. Coming upon a construction site, they stopped and looked upward and watched work being done on a skyscraper.

"Dad, what are those little boys doing up there?"

"Oh," his father chuckled, "those aren't boys. They are adult men."

"But why do they look so small?" asked the boy.

"It's because they are so high."

After thinking a moment, the son asked, "So when they get to Heaven, there won't be anything left of them, will there?"

When Isaiah got close to God, he felt very small and inadequate, as shown in the daily reading. The smaller we become, the more room God has for us.

Humility is a vital aspect of meekness. "Humble yourselves in the sight of the Lord" (James 4:10). We are to "walk humbly with our God" (Micah 6:8). Man's natural tendency is to bring glory to himself. A Christian is to "do all to the glory of God" (1 Corinthians 10:31).

A girl who stood in church to give a testimony was excited because a friend was present for the service. She wanted to make a good impression by saying how wonderful God is, but her words came out wrong: "I'm so glad I'm so wonderful." If we're not humble, our words may come out right, but our lives come out wrong.

Meekness is also needed when facing suffering, disappointment, and adversity. Instead of trusting God and submitting to Him, some people become bitter toward God. They forget that God chastens in love. As Hebrews 12:5, 6 says, "Ye have forgotten the exhortation which speaketh unto you as unto children, My son, despise not thou the chastening of the Lord, nor faint when thou art rebuked of him: for whom the Lord loveth he chasteneth, and scourgeth every son whom he receiveth."

God will take care of what you go through; you take care of how you go through it. Let trouble make you better, not bitter. God brings people into deep water not to drown them, but to cleanse them.

THE VALUE OF MEEKNESS

Not rendering evil for evil, or railing for railing:
but contrariwise blessing;
knowing that ye are thereunto called,
that ye should inherit a blessing.
— 1 Peter 3:9

READ LUKE 9:51-56

In ancient Greece, a young soldier wrote to his beloved girl. He said he hoped to give her a special horse as a present, a powerful silver stallion. "He is the most magnificent animal I have ever seen, but he responds obediently to the slightest command. . . . He allows his master to direct him to his full potential. He is truly a meek horse."

Meekness is controlled strength. The Lord wants that control to be evident when we relate to people who are inconsiderate or cruel. Romans 12:19 says, "Dearly beloved, avenge not yourselves, but rather give place unto wrath: for it is written, Vengeance is mine; I will repay, saith the Lord." Our daily reading shows the meekness of Jesus in contrast to the sons of thunder, James and John.

Our culture does not value meekness. It teaches men and women to be assertive, to boldly compete and trample others down, to be manipulative and revengeful. It admires a person who does what he wants and bends others to his will. It takes affront at slights and snubs and aims for payback. It values the macho man, not the meek man. It recognizes the loud woman, not the lowly one.

But the Bible has very significant promises and provisions for the meek. Meekness permits God's guidance. Psalm 25:9 says, "The meek will he guide in judgment: and the meek will he teach his way." Meekness brings fulfillment. Psalm 22:26 says, "The meek shall eat and be satisfied: they shall praise the LORD that seek him: your heart shall live for ever." Meekness brings joy. Isaiah 29:19 says, "The meek also shall increase their joy in the LORD, and the poor among men shall rejoice in the Holy One of Israel." Meekness brings exaltation. Psalm 147:6 says, "The LORD lifteth up the meek: he casteth the wicked down to the ground."

Hudson Taylor was invited to speak to a large church. The moderator introduced the missionary in glowing terms, telling the large congregation of Taylor's accomplishments in China and presenting him as "our illustrious guest."

Taylor stood quietly for a moment and then began to speak. "Dear friends, I am the little servant of an illustrious Master."

Meekness Demonstrated

Blessed are the meek:
for they shall inherit the earth.
— *Matthew 5:5*

Read Ephesians 4:1-13

I like the story of a Bible school principal in Manila. The son of a wealthy Filipino businessman arrived as a student. He soon informed the principal that the bathroom and toilet in the boys' dorm was dirty. The principal said, "I'll take care of it." The student assumed that the principal would send a servant.

A few minutes later, the student heard the sounds of splashing and scrubbing. Some time later he saw the principal emerge, wet with sweat. "Your bath is clean," he said.

"Sir, you didn't," protested the student.

The principal nodded. "We can't afford to have a janitor, so we have to do things for ourselves."

It was a lesson in meekness that the student never forgot. As the daily reading says, we should conduct our lives "with all lowliness and meekness."

Vine explains the meaning of meekness: "It consists not in a person's outward behavior only; nor yet in his relations to his fellowmen.

Rather it is an inwrought grace of the soul; and the exercise of it is first and chiefly toward God. It is the temper of spirit in which we accept His dealings with us as good, and therefore without disputing or resisting; it is closely linked with humility."

Moses demonstrated meekness. In fact, Numbers 12:3 says, "Now the man Moses was very meek, above all the men which were upon the face of the earth." This was spoken in the context of Moses being criticized by his siblings. Other times he faced murmurers who complained about the quality of food, the scarcity of water, and the route of travel. He responded evenhandedly without bitterness or rancor.

Christian wives are to demonstrate meekness, especially if they have unbelieving husbands. Rather than wearing decorative clothing, jewelry, or stylish hairdos, a godly woman's adorning should be of a different sort. "Let it be the hidden man of the heart, in that which is not corruptible, even the ornament of a meek and quiet spirit, which is in the sight of God of great price" (1 Peter 3:4).

God values meekness. He is pleased with Christians who stay cool in hot places, sweet in sour places, and little in big places.

MEEKNESS IN ACTION

If it be possible, as much as lieth in you,
live peaceably with all men.
— Romans 12:18

READ TITUS 3:1-8

The oil can is mightier than the sword. The Bible instructs us to "overcome evil with good" (Romans 12:21).

I remember reading of a Christian Aid Ministries' combine that was kept busy harvesting grain for many small village farmers in Romania in the mid-1990s. The authorities had been keeping a shrewd eye on foreigners. One village mayor had made it hard for CAM workers. Nevertheless, CAM combined the mayor's grain as well as that of the other villagers.

I appreciate this practical nonresistance. Romans 12:20 could be paraphrased, "Therefore if thine enemy hunger, feed him; if he thirst, give him drink; if he has a grain crop, harvest it for him: for in so doing thou shalt heap coals of fire on his head."

What are some other areas of applying principles of love and meekness? Observe six ideas from verses 1 and 2 of the daily reading.

1. Obey the law. We should submit to government rules unless they conflict with God's rules.
2. Be quick and willing to do good deeds. Assist in all things that need assistance; resist all things that need resistance. You will not get dizzy from doing others a good turn.
3. Speak kindly without slander. A gossiper is the devil's postman.
4. Don't be a brawler (literally, "not disposed to fight"), trying to pick a quarrel with anyone and everyone.
5. Be gentle, showing forbearance and consideration.
6. Show courtesy and meekness to all. This includes those within the congregation and among neighboring congregations.

Some time ago, two groups of Mennonites used the same church building on alternate Sundays. They came to a disagreement about erecting a new church building. Neither group was willing to do what the other desired. After a period of strife and contention, the case was taken to court. The judge said, "It is to be regretted that the members of this religious organization should have such differences which they cannot harmonize. The Mennonite Church is world-renowned for peace, brotherly love, and goodwill to all, and for the amicable settlement of all difficulties among themselves in a Christian spirit."

They missed the Spirit fruit of meekness, which was the key to fit the deadlock.

Meekness in Building Relationships

But the meek shall inherit the earth;
and shall delight themselves in the abundance of peace.
— Psalm 37:11

READ PHILEMON 1-21

A man bought a farm and soon his nearest neighbor came over to see him.

"Have you bought this farm?" asked the neighbor.

"Yes."

"Well, we've got a problem. I am planning to sue you. Your fence line is ten feet on my side. I'm going to take the matter to court and prove it."

The new owner said, "Oh, don't do that. If the fence is on your property, we'll just take it up and move it back."

"Do you mean it?" asked the neighbor.

The new owner assured him that he did.

"Well, in that case," said the neighbor, "that fence will stay right where it is."

Sometimes we can make peace on our own, but on some occasions we need the help of a neutral party. Either way, meekness is a helpful attitude.

Paul had two close Christian friends, each at odds with the other. As our daily reading says, Philemon was "dearly beloved" (v. 1) and had noble Christian qualities (vv. 4-7). Paul's other friend, Onesimus, had helped him a lot (v. 13). But before Onesimus had become a Christian, he had run away from his master Philemon, probably stealing money as well.

Our daily reading portrays Paul's attempt to reconcile Philemon and Onesimus. Notice the characteristics of his wise and meek appeal as he presents his plea from various angles.

- Motivated by love (v. 9).
- Presented by Paul the aged, probably about sixty years old (v. 9).
- Made by a prisoner on behalf of a potential prisoner (v. 9).
- Given on behalf of a (spiritual) son (v. 10).
- Offered in anticipation of Onesimus becoming profitable again, thus living up to his name, which means "profitable" (v. 11).
- Recognized that the final decision was Philemon's (v. 14).
- Suggested that Onesimus's running away may have been providential to give him opportunity to meet Paul and Christ (v. 15).
- Declared Onesimus not simply to be a slave but a brother beloved (v. 16).

How do you think Philemon would have received Paul? No doubt with open arms, gladness, appreciation, kindness, and honor. That's how Paul asks that Onesimus be received.

Paul has confidence in Philemon. How much easier Paul's method of appeal has made it for Philemon to receive Onesimus back without harsh punishment!

Picnic Day

by Katrina Hoover

Mr. Yoder had warned them to study hard for the last spelling test. "It's the hardest test of the year," he said. "You want to have a good score on your last report card."

Mr. Yoder helped them study in class. He made flash cards to help them learn the vocabulary words. He played spelling basketball with them to help them learn how to spell the words. But he told them they would still have to study on their own.

As the bell rang, Cody sighed. He dreaded the test. No matter how hard he studied his spelling words, he could never get a good grade. He went to pick up his backpack and lunch box from the hall. Chad came up beside him. Chad was the tallest boy in class, with hair so blond it was almost white. Even though he was tall, he could not run fast. But he was good at spelling and math.

"That spelling test is going to be so easy!" Chad said loudly. "I don't know why Mr. Yoder even wants us to study." He aimed a sly grin down at Cody. "Don't you think it's going to be easy, Cody?"

"No, I don't," Cody snapped. He snatched his lunch box and hurried down the hall. He ran out into the parking lot and jumped into his sister Carla's car.

"What's wrong, Cody?" Carla asked after Cody slammed his door.

"Chad makes me so mad!" he exploded. "He knows he's the best at spelling, so he brags about how easy the test is going to be. He knows I always get C's even if I study, and he always gets A's even if he doesn't study."

Carla started the car and they drove across the gravel lot and onto the road. Cody did not look back at the school. He did not want to see Chad.

"Getting mad won't help you any," Carla told him. "It won't change Chad and it won't make you feel better or spell better. Just accept it and cheerfully do your best. And you know, Cody, even if you can't spell, you can do other things well. You're one of the fastest runners in the whole school."

"Oh, I don't know about that. But running fast doesn't count," Cody said. "School is all about spelling and tests, not running games. Except for Picnic Day, and that only comes once a year."

"Well, it's coming pretty soon," said Carla. "You'll get to do all those running games and races and relays. Those are fun. Just try to be nice to Chad."

Cody felt terrible the morning of the spelling test. He had studied, but there were just too many words, and they got all mixed up in his mind like a bowl of alphabet soup.

He began the test. The first matching section had ten questions. Two were easy, but he had to guess on the other eight. His throat felt dry and pasty. He so badly wanted to do well on this test; he didn't want a bad grade on his report card. Plus, he wanted to please Mr. Yoder. He was a good teacher, and Cody liked him.

Worst of all, Cody saw Chad out of the corner of his eye. Chad's pencil danced up and down the pages as if the test were a game. Even Chad's golden hair seemed to be happy about the easy test. Cody felt angry at Chad all over again.

The last vocabulary word was *meekness*. Cody rubbed his forehead with his hand, trying to remember the definition for meekness. He shifted in his chair and looked out the window, as if he thought he might see the words out on the playground.

Meekness, meekness, he thought to himself. *What does meekness mean? I can't remember!*

Finally he wrote down "not strong." He knew it wasn't quite right, but his head hurt from trying to think too hard and he could not remember.

With a sinking heart, Cody handed the test to Mr. Yoder. He wished he would never have to see it again. He looked out the classroom window again at the clear, sunny day. All he wanted to do was go outside.

Why does school have to be so much about books and studying? Cody wondered. If school were just playing games and sports, he would like it. And then Chad wouldn't make fun of him.

Cody waited with dread to get his test back the next day. He did not want to see his score. As Mr. Yoder began to pass the graded tests back, Cody felt his heart begin to beat strangely. He saw Chad's test, with a big "Good Job!" written across the top. Chad smiled and nodded when he saw the 98 percent on the test.

Mr. Yoder slid the test upside down onto Cody's desk. Cody took a gulp of air and flipped the test over. A bright red 52 percent was written on the top in Mr. Yoder's neat handwriting. Mr. Yoder had not written a letter grade beside it, but Cody knew that was an F. He turned the test back over. He didn't even look to see which questions he had gotten wrong. He didn't care about spelling. He didn't care about this test. He didn't care what meekness meant. He didn't care if he never saw a spelling test again.

Well, at least the test was over. Now he only had one or two more exams and then it would be the last day of school. A softball game, running races, relays, a picnic with lots of good food . . . Picnic Day couldn't come too soon for Cody.

"What did you get on your test?" Carla asked that afternoon.

"I'm not telling you," Cody mumbled. Then he changed the subject. "Did you know I'm old enough to play in the father-son softball game this year?"

"I wouldn't even want to if I were you," said Carla. "Playing with all those big guys? What if one of them runs you over?"

"I'm a good player," said Cody. "I might not be that tall, but I can run fast. No one's going to run me over. I hope I can have at least one good hit, or do something great. I'd really like to be pitcher. I hope it doesn't rain and I hope it's not too hot. I can't stand running when I'm dripping with sweat."

For the next few days, Cody thought a lot about the picnic and the relays and the softball game. He never once thought of spelling words or what meekness meant. He wanted to forget about that test, and the "Good Job" Mr. Yoder had written on Chad's test.

On the morning of the picnic, Cody looked out his window at the birch tree nearby. He could always tell by looking at the birch tree what kind of day it was going to be. On rainy days, of course, the birch tree was dripping wet. On cloudy days, the birch tree was all gray. On bright, sunny, clear days, the birch tree was bright white, striped with its own shadows.

Today the birch tree was bright with sunshine, but the sunshine seemed heavy and sticky. Cody could tell from the way the birch tree wavered now and then in a sluggish breeze that it was going to be a hot, sticky day. Even the sky looked heavy and sticky, as if it were thinking of a thunderstorm.

Oh well, Cody thought, *I'm going to have a good day whether it's hot and sticky or not.* But still, he wished it would be clear and just a little chilly in the morning.

Everyone arrived at the picnic in good spirits and on time. Some of the dads got the grills going for hot dogs and hamburgers. The moms stacked bowls of salads and trays of Jell-O in the school refrigerators. The students grouped together outside on the playground where the running races and relays would be held.

The high school boys had marked off an oval track in the grass for the running races. Most of the races and relays were done on this track. But Cody's favorite, the long race, was run around the entire school playground. The teachers placed orange cones to show where the path turned so that the runners would know where to go.

Cody was delighted to see that Mr. Yoder was in charge of the games and races. He wanted so badly to show Mr. Yoder that he was good at something! And this time he knew he would succeed.

"All right, those in the races, please gather by the track!" Mr. Yoder called. "We are going to start with the four-team relays."

Cody liked the relays a lot. It wasn't quite like running a race by yourself, because you had to depend on teammates too. Three other boys were on Cody's team. Aaron and Kyle were average runners. But

Chad was in their group too. Cody wished Chad were on someone else's team. He was slow and clumsy. But at least that meant Chad didn't brag about running.

Aaron was running first, Kyle second, and Chad third. Because he was the fastest, Cody would run last. Cody looked at the other teams. They all had weak runners too. He thought his team had a good chance of winning.

All the teams got in order and Mr. Yoder shouted, "On your mark, get set, go!"

Cody cheered for Aaron as he ran his stretch of the track. Kyle ran next, and Cody watched as he outran two of the other teams. Now they had only one team to beat. If Chad did a good job, Cody was pretty sure he could pass up the other team too. He watched tensely as Kyle finished his lap and Chad took off.

Then it happened—as he began to pick up speed, Chad stumbled and fell flat into the grass. The runners from the other teams raced past Chad as he scrambled back to his feet. By the time Chad got to where Cody was waiting for him, the other runners were far ahead. Cody was fast, but he was not *that* fast. There was no way he could ever catch up.

Still, Cody figured he might as well do his best anyway. He took off running as fast as he could—faster than he ever remembered running before. He could see nothing but a blur of grass, blurry forms of the other runners ahead of him, and the blurry orange blot of the cone at the end of the race.

Cody strained with all his energy, and right before they reached the orange cone, he passed the runner ahead of him. At least his team was not last. But Cody was still disappointed. If Chad had not fallen, they would have won.

He flopped flat on the grass, gasping for breath. "Good job, Cody," he heard Carla say. He managed to respond.

"Not really," he gasped, "we came in third. That's bad."

"Oh, but you ran faster than anyone," Carla said.

Cody rested for a long time, trying to get his breath back. Mr. Yoder directed other races. Cody watched them dimly. All he wanted to think about was the long race.

Chad came over and flopped on the grass beside him. Cody stiffened. He really didn't feel like talking to Chad right now. It would only remind him of the ruined race, and of the times Chad had made fun of him. Then he remembered what Carla had said. Getting angry wouldn't change anything or help him feel better. Still, he didn't know what to say to Chad.

"Sorry I fell and ruined the race," Chad said.

Cody stared at Chad with surprise. Chad was really disappointed, and Cody could tell he felt bad. Even his golden hair didn't seem to be shining as brightly.

"Hey, that's okay," Cody said. At least Chad wasn't bragging anymore. Cody got up to stretch. He knew he could win the long race.

"Are you ready for the long one, Cody?" asked Mr. Yoder.

"Yes, I am," Cody said with a smile.

Only three boys wanted to run the long race. Aaron was running too, and a boy named Caleb. Cody knew he could outrun Aaron, and he was pretty sure he could outrun Caleb too.

When Mr. Yoder shouted "Go!" the three boys started slowly down the path. They did not want to run fast right away, because they did not want to get too tired. Cody knew just how fast to run so that he would not run out of energy.

Caleb sprinted ahead. He was tall and could run fast. Cody was next. Aaron was last.

About halfway through the long race, Caleb began to get tired because he had tried to run too fast. With a burst of speed, Cody shot past Caleb and followed the orange cones to the finish line and flopped on the grass. Caleb and Aaron panted in behind him.

Mr. Yoder came up to Cody. "Cody, did you notice you missed the last cone?"

Cody stared. He looked at the cone that marked the last turn in the long race. "Oh, I was supposed to go on the other side, wasn't I?" he asked in despair.

"Yes. Of course, we can all see that you were the fastest runner," Mr. Yoder said. "But if a person misses a cone or goes off the track, we can't give him the first prize."

"Okay," was all Cody could think of to say. He knew Mr. Yoder didn't think it was a big deal. But it *was* a big deal to Cody. He went into the school and took a drink at the fountain. He felt like hiding in the classroom and never coming out. He had just lost two races. He remembered the other thing Carla had said: Just accept it and cheerfully do your best. Well, he had done his best, and hiding, like getting angry, wouldn't help. *Maybe Carla should have turned it around,* he thought. *Do your best and cheerfully accept it.* He took anther drink and headed back outside.

When he came back out, he smelled barbecue sauce and saw some dads setting up the soft ice cream machine. Boxes of gloves, bats, and softballs reminded Cody about the softball game coming up. He began to feel better.

Carla was pouring juice at a picnic table. "Did you win the long race?" she asked.

"No," Cody said. "I missed a cone."

Even though the food smelled good, Cody did not want to eat too much. He knew he would not be able to play softball very well if he was too full of lunch. Cody ate a grilled hamburger, a square of Jell-O, and a bowl of ice cream. As he licked up the last ice cream in the bowl, he thought about the softball game. Usually when they played at school he was the pitcher for his team. He hoped he could pitch, but he was afraid he was too young.

Mr. Yoder asked two high school boys to arrange the teams. Chad offered to keep score. He didn't want to play.

Derrick, the high school captain of Cody's team, looked the team over and asked people where they wanted to play.

"Who's going to be pitcher?" Cody heard someone ask.

"I don't know," Derrick said. He looked around the group. "Cody, you pitch sometimes, don't you?"

"Yes, I do," said Cody. "I like to pitch, but I don't have to if someone else wants to."

"He's a pretty good pitcher," another high school boy said. "I say, let's let him pitch."

"I don't think anyone else wants to," Derrick said. "The job's all yours."

Cody could hardly keep from grinning. He loved to pitch. He liked seeing how many perfect pitches he could pitch in a row. He liked to catch the fly balls that popped up to the infield. He liked to throw to first base. Plus, Mr. Yoder would be the umpire. Cody couldn't wait to throw a strike into Mr. Yoder's glove.

Cody's first-inning pitching wasn't really dramatic. Most of the batters hit the first pitch, and all of the hits went past him, so Cody didn't get a chance to do anything.

The first batter for the second inning was Aaron's dad. Aaron's dad was big and tall. Cody pitched him a nice fast pitch. It was just a little low, but he struck.

It happened in a split second. The softball shot through the air straight for Cody's head. Cody instinctively swung up his glove to protect his face, but the ball was moving too fast. It hit Cody's face with a crack, right above the eye. The next thing anyone knew, Cody was lying on the ground, blood dripping down his face from the gash over his eye.

Cody's parents and teachers hurried to the pitcher's mound. Someone grabbed the first aid kit. Mr. Yoder put a cold pack against the wound.

Cody's brain was foggy. He tried to sit up, but he felt dizzy. The only thought he could really think was that he might not be able to pitch for a few innings. He could barely remember what had happened. He could not even remember who had hit the ball.

Then he heard the word "stitches."

"I don't want to go to the hospital," he managed to mumble.

"You won't have to go to the hospital," his dad said, "just to the doctor. It won't take long."

Cody could not argue; his head felt heavy and thick, and he could not stand on his own. Still, he couldn't help feeling really, really sad on the way to the doctor. *Why did everything have to go wrong today?* he asked himself. *I lost every race I tried, and now I can't even play softball. Mr. Yoder is going to think I'm just as useless in sports as I am in spelling.*

The friendly doctor tried to make Cody feel better about his accident. He told stories as he numbed the injury and stitched the gash shut.

"You're a lucky boy to have someone bring you in for stitches," the doctor said. "When I was your age I got hit by a softball too. But my parents didn't take me to the doctor; we just bandaged it up. It healed okay, but look at my eyebrow now . . . . I still have a scar there."

Cody looked at the narrow white line in the doctor's eyebrow. The scar didn't look that bad to him. In fact, it might be neat to have one!

After stitching Cody's scar, the doctor gave him some pills to help him feel better, and Cody and his parents left the doctor's office. Cody looked at himself in the mirror and groaned. The neat row of stitches above his eye looked like a zipper. His eye and forehead were puffy and red.

"Do you want to go home?" asked Dad.

"Oh, no," Cody said. "I want to go back to the game."

"You can't play!" said Mom.

"Well, I can watch," Cody said.

The game had reached the seventh inning when Cody and his parents got back. Aaron's dad came over and apologized to Cody. Cody laughed. He hadn't even remembered that Aaron's dad had been the batter.

Cody's friends crowded around to see his stitches and got him a camp chair so he could sit and watch the game.

"Do you want to keep score?" Chad asked. "I've been doing it for a while anyway."

"Sure," Cody said. He was glad to at least do something.

Mr. Yoder was up to bat.

"Go, Mr. Yoder!" Cody and Chad yelled.

There were two runners on base. Mr. Yoder hit a powerful drive to left field. Both runners made it to home base. Mr. Yoder stopped at third base, but then the catcher missed the ball, and Mr. Yoder ran home.

"A home run for Mr. Yoder!" Cody cheered, and marked a diamond in Mr. Yoder's box on the score sheet.

Mr. Yoder sat down beside Cody. "How's your eye feeling?" he asked.

"Not too bad. The doctor gave me some stuff to make it feel better for a while."

"That's good," said Mr. Yoder. "You know, Cody, I've been impressed with you today."

Cody almost jumped with surprise. "Why?" he asked.

"Well, you lost two races that you could have won. Then you got hit in the face with the softball. But instead of being angry, you're back again, keeping score and cheering for my home run!"

"Well, it wouldn't help to be angry," said Cody. "It wouldn't change anything." He remembered how angry he had been at Chad. Just like Carla said, that had not helped him feel any better. Plus, Chad wasn't too bad!

"That's right," said Mr. Yoder. "It reminds me of the word *meekness* that we had on that vocabulary test."

Cody sighed. "I couldn't remember what that word meant," he said. "I put down 'being weak' or something dumb like that."

"Actually, a lot of people have that idea of meekness," Mr. Yoder said, "but really being meek takes a lot of strength. The right definition of meekness for the test was 'patiently enduring injury.' A meek person patiently accepts bad things that happen or bad treatment from other people and doesn't get angry about it. You showed me today what it means to be meek."

Cody wanted to do a cartwheel. Mr. Yoder thought he had done a good job! But Cody knew he still had a lot to learn.

That night Carla asked Cody a question. "Did this Picnic Day get spoiled for you because of all the bad things?"

"No," said Cody. "I had a good day."

Questions for Review

1. What test did Cody hate to take?
2. What word means "patiently enduring injury"?
3. Why did Cody's team lose the relay race?
4. Why did Cody lose the long race?
5. What did Cody do during the last part of the softball game?

Questions for Discussion

1. Is the definition of meekness that Cody wrote down a common misunderstanding?
2. What problems did Cody face on the day of the picnic that could have upset him?
3. Why did Mr. Yoder think highly of Cody by the end of the picnic day?
4. When have you seen someone display meekness?
5. What do you admire about Cody?

TEMPERANCE

Be Temperate

Thou therefore endure hardness,
as a good soldier of Jesus Christ.
— 2 Timothy 2:3

Read 1 Corinthians 9:24-27

When I was in fifth and sixth grades I took a course each year about temperance from the Christian Women's Temperance Union. Although I attended a public school, the dangers and evils of alcohol and substance abuse were presented to me from a Christian point of view. I learned a lot in those years, but I've found that learning temperance is a lifelong enterprise.

The root word of *temperance* (Galatians 5:23) is *strength.* In 1 Corinthians 9:25 the word is used to refer to the control of an athlete over his body and its desires as he trains for competition like the Olympics. It means a balanced life characterized by self-restraint. I read that an American swimming champion, in preparation for the Olympics, swam the equivalent of several times around the world.

In contrast to the Spirit fruit of self-control, the works of the flesh include many things that are out of control. For example, the desire for pleasure is out of control, resulting in drunkenness, wild partying, fornication, uncleanness, adultery, and shameless immorality.

Likewise, relationships show a lack of temperance and restraint leading to contention, hatred, wrath, and strife.

Jesus is a model of self-control. His disciples were frustratingly slow to catch on, yet He patiently taught them. His critics goaded Him with tricky questions, and He responded with temperance, balance, and truth.

When falsely accused before Pilate, He was silent, much to the governor's annoyance. When brought before King Herod and expected to perform a miracle for Herod's entertainment, He was quiet. When ridiculed and mocked on Calvary, He prayed.

Some religious folk think that when a person is full of the Spirit he or she will show bizarre, uncontrolled behavior—falling over backward in church services, bellowing like a bull, roaring like a bear, rolling on the floor, laughing uncontrollably. They don't realize that the fruit of the Spirit is self-control. By God's grace, discipline yourself so others won't have to.

Developing Self-Control

But Daniel purposed in his heart that he would not defile himself with the portion of the king's meat, nor with the wine which he drank: therefore he requested of the prince of the eunuchs that he might not defile himself.
— Daniel 1:8

Read 2 Timothy 1:1-10

A car out of control is quite a problem. If you had been in West Haven, Connecticut, on November 9, 1994, you could have seen a car go backward in circles for two hours. According to Reuters News Service, a man had pulled up to a busy intersection and shifted the car into park so he could get out to check on his vehicle. He thought perhaps he had a problem with his brakes. With no one at the wheel, the automobile abruptly slipped into reverse and took off at a high speed. The steering wheel spun, and the car circled around and around in the middle of the intersection.

Police and emergency vehicles were called. After about two hours they got three front-end pay loaders normally used for earth moving. They drove them simultaneously into the circling car and stopped the vehicle. Finally the ignition was turned off.

Christians dare not be out of control. We need to be self-controlled. As our daily reading (v. 7) says, God has given us a spirit "of power and of love and of a sound mind." Sound mind has the idea of self-control, and "of a calm and well-balanced mind and discipline." It keeps life in balance instead of becoming extreme in action or attitude. This fruit of temperance comes from God: it is not getting hold of oneself by human effort or sheer determination, nor is it asceticism.

The Bible declares the importance of temperance. Second Peter 1:6 says it should be added to faith as well as qualities like virtue, patience, kindness, and charity. A lack of temperance caused the Roman ruler, Felix, to tremble as Paul witnessed to him. "As he reasoned of righteousness, temperance, and judgment to come, Felix trembled, and answered, Go thy way for this time; when I have a convenient season, I will call for thee" (Acts 24:25).

Temperance is a sign of Christian maturity. Paul wrote to Titus that the aged men should be "sober, grave, temperate, sound in faith, in charity, in patience" (Titus 2:2). Temperance is a qualification for ordination. Titus 1:8 says, "But a lover of hospitality, a lover of good men, sober, just, holy, temperate."

Whether or not we are in the ministry, we do well to pray, "O Lord, help us to be masters of ourselves that we may be servants of others."

How to Grow the Fruit of Temperance

If we live in the Spirit,
let us also walk in the Spirit.
— Galatians 5:25

Read Ephesians 5:8-20

Some people have an obvious lack of temperance. Take, for instance, a thirty-two-year-old man who died of overeating. He weighed over 650 pounds. Five days before he died, he ate an entire piglet for dinner. As a result he was admitted to the intensive care unit of a local hospital. Extreme eating led to extreme health issues.

While our need for self-control may not be as pronounced, it is as real. How can we develop the fruit of temperance?

1. *Yield to God the Holy Spirit.* As shown in the daily reading, we are to walk as children of light so that we can bear Spirit fruit. Galatians 5:16 puts it this way: "This I say then, Walk in the Spirit, and ye shall not fulfil the lust of the flesh." And verse 18 of Ephesians 5 tells us to be filled with the Spirit, that is, be controlled by the Spirit, under His influence.

2. *Put on Christ.* Romans 13:13, 14 commands the Christian to renounce a life of intemperance and take Christ's way instead. "Let us walk honestly, as in the day; not in rioting and drunkenness, not in chambering and wantonness, not in strife and envying. But put ye on the Lord Jesus Christ, and make not provision for the flesh, to fulfil the lusts thereof."

   If you would learn self-mastery, give self over to the Master. Look to Christ's example of self-control. His calmness and silence astounded Pilate. In the face of ridicule, insult, and lies, He had remarkable restraint. "Christ also suffered for us, leaving us an example, that ye should follow his steps: . . . Who, when he was reviled, reviled not again" (1 Peter 2:21, 23).

3. *Abstain from all wrong.* Don't experiment with sin. Flee temptation. Live a life of self-denial by God's grace.

4. *Exercise discernment.* Paul prayed that the Philippian believers "may approve things that are excellent" (Philippians 1:10). Temperance requires determining what is good and what is bad. It relinquishes all that is questionable. It avoids activities that could hinder a fellow Christian. It senses what is not necessarily a sin, but is a "weight" which we should "lay aside" (Hebrews 12:1).

To be the master of myself, I must be the servant of Christ.

What Esau Saw

Lest there be any fornicator, or profane person, as Esau,
who for one morsel of meat sold his birthright.
For ye know how that afterward,
when he would have inherited the blessing,
he was rejected: for he found no place of repentance,
though he sought it carefully with tears.
— Hebrews 12:16, 17

READ GENESIS 25:27-34

I*'m starved!* Esau thought. *Plus, I'm just plain worn out. What a day it has been! Here I am, known as a famous hunter, bringing nothing home—nothing but an empty stomach. I'm so famished I can hardly make it. Ah, what's that smell? Stew! I've got to have some, quick.*

"May I have some of that delicious stew, please?" Esau begged his brother, who was stirring the soup temptingly.

A crafty look came over the face of the soup-maker. "I'll make you a deal. You can help yourself to my stew if I can have your birthright."

"I'm dying of hunger," the hunter said recklessly. "What good is a birthright to me?"

"Swear to me now that the birthright is mine, and I'll give you this tasty stew."

"I'll swear before God it is yours. Now give me that stew and some bread."

A costly meal, that was. Decide in haste, repent at leisure.

Esau lacked the self-control that the Apostle Paul had, who said, "I keep under my body, and bring it into subjection" (1 Corinthians 9:27).

It is doubtful, since Esau had the strength to return from hunting, that he wouldn't have had the strength to prepare some food or wait at home until someone prepared some food for him. But he was governed by his appetites and cared little about putting first things first.

The birthright gave a number of privileges and responsibilities:

- The right to lead the household. Isaac told Jacob (who he thought was Esau), "Be lord over thy brethren, and let thy mother's sons bow down to thee."
- The responsibility of giving spiritual leadership. This involved building an altar and leading in worship (Genesis 35:1-3). Probably it also involved passing on God's Word and His promises.
- The eldest son usually received double the inheritance (see Deuteronomy 21:17).

Esau was not interested in spiritual things. He was a *profane* person (Hebrews 12:16), meaning "godless." He married two heathen wives (Genesis 26:34, 35). He was shortsighted, for he thought present food was preferable to future blessing.

Someone defined self-control as the capacity to break a chocolate bar into four pieces with your bare hands and then eat just one of the pieces. How do you think Esau would have fared with a chocolate bar?

IMPORTANCE OF SELF-CONTROL

And every man that striveth for the mastery is temperate in all things. Now they do it to obtain a corruptible crown; but we an incorruptible.
— 1 Corinthians 9:25

READ HEBREWS 11:23-28

An interesting study of the benefits of temperance was made with a group of children. As told in his book *Emotional Intelligence,* Daniel Goleman researched the link between self-control and quality of life.

In a test, four-year-old children were brought into a room one at a time and offered a marshmallow. Each was told that he or she could eat the marshmallow "right now" or, if they waited until the researcher got back from completing another task (in about fifteen minutes), they could get a second marshmallow.

Researchers followed these children as they grew up. Parents and teachers found that the children who exercised self-control and delayed gratification were generally better adjusted. They were more dependable, confident, adventurous, and better-liked teenagers. The children who chose not to wait for a future reward tended to be easily frustrated and lonely. They showed stubbornness, couldn't handle stress well, avoided challenges, and did more poorly in school.

Instead of short-term gratification, Moses chose true and eternal riches, as indicated in our daily reading.

Jesus taught His disciples to forgo present ease and riches and popularity for future blessings and rewards. "And every one that hath forsaken houses, or brethren, or sisters, or father, or mother, or wife, or children, or lands, for my name's sake, shall receive an hundredfold, and shall inherit everlasting life" (Matthew 19:29).

He Himself had a future joy that He kept in view. Hebrews 12:2 tells us to be "looking unto Jesus the author and finisher of our faith; who for the joy that was set before him endured the cross, despising the shame, and is set down at the right hand of the throne of God."

It is fine to think of future bliss as we endure present trials. C. S. Lewis wrote in *Mere Christianity,* "If you read history you will find that the Christians who did most for the present world were precisely those who thought most of the next. It is since Christians have largely ceased to think of the other world that they have become so ineffective in this."

The Slavery of Indulgence

And take heed to yourselves,
lest at any time your hearts be overcharged with surfeiting,
and drunkenness, and cares of this life,
and so that day come upon you unawares.
— Luke 21:34

READ PROVERBS 23:19-35

For those of us who enjoy eating all too well, here is a story from Belgium. *The Three Edwards,* written by Thomas Costain, tells about a fourteenth-century duke who was greatly overweight. Because of his immense girth, Raynald III was usually called by his Latin nickname *Crassus,* which means "fat."

After a violent quarrel, Raynald's younger brother led a successful revolt against him. Edward captured Raynald, but did not kill him. Instead, he built a room around Raynald in the Nieuwkerk castle and promised him that he could regain his title and property as soon as he was able to leave the room.

This would not have been difficult for most people, since the room had several windows and a door of near-normal size, and none was locked or barred. The problem was Raynald's size. To regain his freedom, he needed to lose weight. But Edward knew his older brother, and each day he sent a variety of delicious foods. Instead of dieting his way out of prison, Raynald grew fatter.

When Duke Edward was accused of cruelty, he had a ready answer: "My brother is not a prisoner. He may leave when he so wills."

For ten years, Raynald remained in the room, unable to squeeze through the doorway. Only after Edward died in battle was the doorway enlarged, enabling him to get out of the room. But by then his health was so ruined that he died within a year.

Raynald came to poverty of health as well as being enslaved to his appetite for excessive food. As our daily reading says, "The drunkard and the glutton shall come to poverty." Our daily reading mentions, too, other types of enslaving appetites. Sexual immorality is one of them. The prostitute and sexually promiscuous woman contributes to the bondage of immoral man, and their sin causes deep problems. As verse 27 says, "A whore is a deep ditch; and a strange woman is a narrow pit."

Consuming alcohol is another enslaving appetite. Although alcohol causes woe, sorrow, contentions, babblings, wounds, red eyes, lack of restraint toward the opposite sex, and uncontrolled speech, yet an alcoholic will "seek it yet again" (v. 35). We first make our habits; then our habits make us.

Temperance at Home

He that is slow to anger is better than the mighty;
and he that ruleth his spirit than he that taketh a city.
— Proverbs 16:32

Read James 1:17-26

A woman cracked an egg into a dish and microwaved it on high for a minute. When the yolk was pierced, the egg blew up, scalding her eyes. Other explosions can occur in a home besides those that do physical harm. Angry outbursts and flaring tempers can build a wall between a husband and wife, wound a child's spirit, give a poor testimony to close neighbors, and spoil your relationship with God.

Don't explode at your spouse. Such situations as a wife who disagrees with her husband about how money should be spent, a husband who sloppily puts newspapers, boots, and pajamas here and there without concern for his wife's attempts to keep the home tidy, a wife who is habitually late, and a husband who selfishly makes decisions can be very provoking and exasperating. But there are better ways than temper outbursts to deal with such problems.

Don't explode at your children. Not only may it crush their spirits; as time goes on, it is also likely to build resentment and bitterness. "Fathers, provoke not your children to wrath" (Ephesians 6:4).

Wrathful jerking of children, shaking, beating, and berating do not belong in a Christian home. How can parents expect their children to develop self-control through discipline when they themselves have lost control of their emotions?

Teenagers should learn to control feelings of anger and frustration. Don't yell, but don't give parents the silent treatment either. Don't slam doors. Take criticism graciously. As the daily reading indicates, each member of the family should be "swift to hear, slow to speak, slow to wrath."

Don't explode at your neighbor. Fences that spoil a view, loud music, farm odors, and a yard that resembles a garbage dump are just a few potential conflicts with neighbors. Outbursts of temper are less likely to improve the situation than courtesy, calm appeals, and reasonable suggestions.

Some people think they have dynamic personalities because they are always exploding. But remember: anger manages everything badly. Therefore, follow Ephesians 4:31 and "let all bitterness, and wrath, and anger, and clamour, and evil speaking, be put away from you, with all malice."

Everyone Needs Temperance

by Katrina Hoover

Every Saturday night Claudia and her family visited Grandpa. Since Grandma died, Grandpa lived by himself. He liked it when they came to see him. Claudia liked to visit him too. She and Grandpa always played a game of chess. Mom would pop popcorn. Dad would read the newspaper. Sometimes he would play chess with Grandpa too.

Tonight Grandpa won the chess game, as usual. Claudia sighed as if she were discouraged, but she really enjoyed playing whether she won or lost.

"You're a good sport," said Grandpa. "When I was your age, I often got angry if I lost. I'm glad you've learned temperance at a young age."

"What's temperance?" Claudia asked.

Grandpa picked up his bowl of popcorn. "Well, let me tell you a story and see if that helps to explain it," said Grandpa. "When I was fourteen—a long time ago!—we used to play softball a lot. We didn't have one of these nice new diamonds with sand and a chain-link backstop. We played on my uncle's big lawn.

"One night it was a really close game. It was getting dark, and we had to finish soon. Our team was at bat, with the bases loaded. I was on third base—maybe that's why I remember it so well. One of my teammates, eighteen-year-old Jim, stood there to coach me.

"Someone said, 'Jim, come to home plate and catch!' (We didn't have quite enough players to cover all the spots, so each team provided its own catcher.)

"Jim said, 'I'm coaching third base. Let someone else catch.'

" 'Just come on, Jim, and catch; it's getting dark!' Jim stomped to home plate, muttering 'Why can't someone else catch?'

"The batter hit, and I ran home as fast as I could. But just before I touched home plate, Jim caught the ball and tagged me. I was out. But then Jim said it was a tie, and since ties go to the runner, I was home safe, and we had won the game.

"But no one agreed with Jim. Everyone else thought I was out, and so did I, so we called it an out. That's when Jim *really* lost his temper.

" 'You want me to play catcher, and then you don't believe me when I say it's safe! Who was the closest to that play? Who knows whether it was safe or not? The first baseman? Are you kidding me?' He threw his glove on the ground as he yelled at us and finally stomped off to his truck and tore out the lane, spinning gravel."

Grandpa paused and chewed a mouthful of popcorn thoughtfully. Claudia stared at him. *"That's* what it means to be temperate?" she asked.

Grandpa chuckled. "Well, I called you temperate with the chess game. So do you think Jim was temperate or not?"

"I would say he was *not,"* said Claudia with a smile. "Did he really act like that when he was eighteen years old?"

"Yes, he really did," answered Grandpa. "We thought he might punch someone. Being upset wasn't the only problem; he also lacked self-control. Temperance means you control yourself and don't do extreme things."

"What do you mean by *extreme?"* Claudia asked next.

"My, my, this girl's full of questions." Grandpa laughed. "It looks like your mom and dad are ready to go home. Tell you what, I'll think of another story for next Saturday night to explain what it means to be temperate and not extreme."

Claudia didn't think of Grandpa's story again until she heard her older brother Scott saying, "Now, that's extreme!"

"What's extreme?" Claudia asked him. "That's the word Grandpa used on Saturday. He didn't tell me what it means yet."

"Fourteen thousand text messages is *extreme,"* Scott said, looking up from the newspaper. "This girl sent her friends fourteen thousand text messages in one month. That's about one every two minutes every day!"

"Ah-h," said Claudia. "So that's what extreme means! She must have a lot of friends!"

"I wouldn't call someone a friend who sent me that many messages," Scott said.

That night for supper, Claudia's mom cooked hot dogs. Scott ate four hot dogs with bread. Then he ate three hot dogs by themselves, just dipping them in ketchup and mustard.

"Seven hot dogs!" Claudia said. "That's extreme!"

"Really?" said Scott, as he reached for another hot dog. He ate that one too. "If you had worked as hard as I did today, you'd eat eight hot dogs too."

"You're not being temperate," said Claudia.

Scott rolled his eyes at her and kept munching.

The next day at school, Claudia's classmate Dylan explained to the teacher how much he had studied for the science test. "I studied for five hours straight," said Dylan. "I didn't go to bed until after midnight. When I did try to go to sleep, I kept seeing the different kinds of clouds we've been studying."

Claudia raised her hand. "Studying that hard is extreme," she said.

"What do you mean?" asked the teacher, a bit surprised.

"Well, my Grandpa told me what temperate means. He told me that people who are not temperate are extreme. They take things too far."

"I see," said the teacher. "Maybe you have a point. I like for my students to study hard. But not getting your sleep doesn't help on a test. We all need to keep our lives in balance."

Dylan turned his head the other way and did not look at Claudia again for a long time.

Saturday, on the way to Grandpa's, Claudia thought about temperance again and wondered what story Grandpa would tell her today. At least she tried to think about that, but her older sister Julia kept talking about clothes and distracting her.

"Mom, what if I don't find a nice coat before I go skating with my friends?" Julia said. "How can I go skating without a coat?"

"You could always wear your old one," Mom said.

"Oh, Mom, I'd be so embarrassed!" said Julia. "I'd rather stay home than wear that old thing. Plus, I want a matching scarf with my new coat."

"Julia, you're so extreme about clothes," Claudia said. "You always have to have everything match. You'd better listen to Grandpa's story about temperance tonight."

"Claudia, stop being such a bossy sister," Julia said.

"Girls, girls," said Mom.

That night, Claudia and Grandpa filled their bowls with popcorn and played their normal game of chess. Claudia lost the game even more quickly than normal, because she was wondering what story Grandpa would have for her tonight. As soon as they finished, Claudia scooped up the chessmen and dumped them into their cardboard box.

"Okay, I'm ready for the story now," she said.

"Story?" said Grandpa.

"Yes," said Claudia. "You told me you were going to tell me another story about temperance." She hoped Grandpa had not forgotten. Then she saw his eyes twinkle, and she knew he had been teasing.

"Well," said Grandpa, "last week I gave you a story from someone else's life. This week I decided to tell you a story about a time when I wasn't temperate. It's always best to look at your own mistakes, you know.

"This story starts the same summer as that softball game," Grandpa said. "I really wanted to make some money, so I decided to raise chickens and sell their eggs. We lived beside a big clinic where a lot of doctors and nurses worked, and they paid a lot of money for farm-fresh brown eggs.

"So my dad helped me buy fifty chicks. When I made money on the eggs, I would pay him back. I took such good care of those chicks! The first few days, I hardly left their box. They were so cute when they were small. The bigger they got, the more room I needed to make for them. I had to build a wire fence so they could go out of the barn for fresh air. I spent a lot of time on that fence, and on the watering pail, and on the feeding troughs. I gave them a special type of feed to keep their eggs from cracking. When they began to lay eggs, I took really good care of those eggs. I collected them twice a day so that none would break. I kept them cooled in the basement and cleaned every one of those eggs by hand and packaged them in used egg cartons.

"Then one day Dad wanted me to help him chop wood for our furnace. I told him I couldn't because I had to clean more eggs to take to market. I complained and begged and argued. Finally Dad told me that if raising chickens was going to take over my whole life, I would have to stop raising them.

"I felt angry at him for a while, but it made me stop and think. And guess what happened? That winter, one cold night, we had a newborn calf in the barn. We put a heat lamp over the calf to keep him warm. Toward morning, a piece of hay caught fire, and by the time we went out to do our chores, smoke was pouring out of the barn, high into the sky."

"Oh, no!" said Claudia. "Did it burn up your chickens?"

"Well, no," Grandpa said. "Actually, the fire wasn't very bad. It was the firefighters who killed my chickens. They sprayed gallons and gallons of water into the barn. The water soaked the chickens, and they froze. At least half of them died."

"Oh, no!" Claudia said again.

"I really struggled to not be angry," Grandpa admitted. "But I think I learned a good lesson. There's nothing in life that we can be sure of keeping just by taking good care of it. Things (and even people) can be destroyed at any time. So it's not worth being extreme or intemperate about anything, except serving the Lord and doing what God wants you to do. You can be extreme about that, and God will bless you."

"Did you lose all your money?" Claudia asked.

"No. I had made a lot of money on the eggs, so I didn't lose money even though the chickens died. But I didn't really make any money after that. But I learned a lesson: don't put all your eggs in one basket!" Grandpa chuckled at his own little joke.

"Do you have any more stories about temperance?" Claudia asked.

"Not this time," Grandpa said. "Maybe next Saturday. I know what: maybe you can tell me a story about temperance now that you know what it means."

"Oh, I already know some people who aren't temperate," said Claudia. "Scott ate eight hot dogs. And Dylan studied his science until midnight. And Julia is always talking about clothes. Those things are extreme, right?"

"I guess they could be," said Grandpa. "They illustrate one meaning of temperance. It's necessary to eat, but we shouldn't overeat. We should study, but we should keep it in balance with other important things. We should pay attention to our clothes, but not be overly concerned about them."

"I think I'm understanding what temperance means," said Claudia thoughtfully.

"Actually, temperance means some other things too. It means to be self-controlled—not like Jim in the softball game. Self-control helps us keep things in balance and not go to an extreme."

Claudia pursed her lips. "So temperance can mean not going to an extreme in things that are okay, like eating and studying and raising hens, and also having self-control with our temper and stuff like that so we don't do wrong things?"

"You've got the picture," said Grandpa. "I heard a preacher say temperance is doing legitimate things in moderation and abstaining from anything that is wrong. By *legitimate* he meant things that are good and necessary. Also, years ago, we used to have temperance lessons in Sunday school—one each quarter. Temperance in those lessons meant not drinking alcohol."

"Well, that's not a problem for me," said Claudia. "In fact, I don't think I have a problem with doing any of the meanings of temperance."

"Well," said Grandpa slowly, "you think about it this week. I think I might be able to think of an area where you are not very temperate."

"Really?" said Claudia, surprised. How could Grandpa think she was extreme! "Aren't you going to tell me what it is now?"

"Oh, no," said Grandpa. "You think about it, and maybe I'll tell you next week, if you haven't figured it out."

Claudia did think about it. She tried to think of a time when she was not temperate. *I don't eat eight hot dogs like Scott,* she thought. *I don't always think about my clothes like Julia. I don't study five hours straight like Dylan.*

Claudia could not think of one thing that she did that was extreme. But she did notice other people being intemperate. Her little brother Carson was not temperate in his fussing. He got extremely fussy when he was tired. She noticed that even her teacher was not always temperate. She got extremely impatient on Monday when a bunch of people raised their hands at the same time. She noticed that her friend Emily talked and talked and talked, and sometimes no one else had a chance to say anything.

But whenever Claudia told someone what she had noticed, the person usually did not want to listen to her. Claudia didn't know why they wouldn't take good advice.

One evening Dad was working at the computer. Julia asked Dad if she could check her e-mail.

"Just wait. I'll be done in fifteen minutes," Dad said.

Julia sat down and worked on her homework for a bit. "Dad, are you finished yet?" she asked. "I think it's been fifteen minutes."

"It's only been ten minutes, Julia," said Dad. "Please have patience. Didn't you already check your e-mail this afternoon?"

"Well, yes," Julia admitted, "but Carmen was going to e-mail me about ice skating, and I didn't get it yet."

Claudia had been listening from the couch. "Julia, now you're being extreme about checking your e-mail," she said. "I think you need a lesson on temperance."

Julia dropped her textbook on the kitchen table. It made a loud thump. "Claudia, when I need a lesson from you, I'll ask," she said shortly.

"Girls!" Dad said. "Julia, you need a lesson on responding politely. Claudia, I think you need a lesson on not being so bossy. Now, I don't want either of you to say another word until I'm finished with the computer. Then you may only talk if you can speak peacefully to each other."

The room was quiet except for Dad's keyboard. Julia kept doing her homework. Claudia was thinking.

Dad said I'm bossy! she thought in dismay. *Maybe that's what Grandpa meant! I'm not temperate because I always look for wrong things in everyone else. It might be okay to correct people sometimes, but I think maybe I've been doing it all the time.*

Claudia felt terrible. She went to bed early. Before she got into bed, she prayed that God would help her not be so bossy anymore.

On Saturday Claudia slowly got her coat and boots to go to Grandpa's. She was afraid of what Grandpa would say. He might scold her for being so bossy.

Claudia paid even less attention to the chess game this week, and Grandpa beat her by even more points than before. Plus, at the end of the game, there was still popcorn left in her bowl. Claudia almost always finished her popcorn before the game was done.

"So, Claudia," Grandpa said, "do you have a story for me this week?"

Claudia sighed. "Yes. I think I figured out what's wrong with me. I'm too bossy. I always tell other people what they do wrong."

Grandpa looked surprised. "Well, Claudia, good for you! I didn't know if you would figure it out. But I don't think that means there's anything *wrong* with you. It just means you need to work on it. Everyone has something they need to try to have more temperance in."

"Really?" Claudia looked surprised.

"Oh, yes," said Grandpa.

"So how should I be less bossy?"

"Well, you know now that it's intemperate and impolite to always tell people what they're doing wrong. Why don't you try something new this week? Think of all the people you called intemperate. Now this week say something nice to each one of them. That's a good way to stop being intemperate in saying mean things."

"Okay," Claudia said. It sounded kind of hard, and maybe not even very much fun. But she didn't want to keep feeling bad about being bossy. She would try it.

That week, Claudia watched carefully for a chance to say something nice to each of the people she had bossed.

She had a great chance on Sunday morning: her brother Scott made scrambled eggs for breakfast.

"These eggs are delicious, Scott," she said. "I like how you put cheese on top."

Scott grinned at her and took another bite.

"Julia, I really like your new dress," Claudia said when Julia came downstairs all ready for church.

Julia looked surprised. "Thank you," she said.

At school, Dylan got another 100 percent. Claudia raised her hand. "Is it just me, or does Dylan get a lot of hundreds?" she asked. "He must really study a lot."

Dylan looked surprised and pleased.

It was funny; once Claudia started trying to notice good things about people, it seemed as if they started doing more good things. That made her think of a new question to ask Grandpa on Saturday night.

When the Saturday night popcorn was popped, Grandpa began setting up the chess pieces for their game. "I'm eager to hear about your week," he said. "Do you want to talk about that first?"

"Oh, no," said Claudia. "I do want to talk about it, but that would be kind of extreme; we always play chess first." Claudia gave Grandpa a wide smile so he would know she was teasing.

"Okay, Miss Claudia," he said. "I guess I'll just have to beat you quickly."

Of course he did. But tonight, even though it was a short game, Claudia finished her whole bowl of popcorn.

"Now," said Grandpa, "how did it go? Did you manage to be less bossy?"

"Yes, I think so," Claudia said. She told Grandpa how she had said nice things to Scott, Julia, and Dylan. She told him that the more good things she said, the more good things seemed to happen.

"I said nice things to people all week! So I have a new question. What if I'm too extremely nice to people? Can you be intemperate in good things?"

Grandpa laughed a long, long laugh. It sounded like a really happy laugh.

"Didn't I tell you that's the nice thing about serving the Lord, Claudia? You can serve the Lord just as hard as you want, and you won't be intemperate. Jesus even died for us—but that doesn't mean He was intemperate. Does that make sense?"

Claudia nodded.

"Now," said Grandpa, "do you think it would be intemperate for us to each have another bowl of popcorn?"

Claudia laughed. "I don't think so," she said. She picked up their empty bowls and hurried to the kitchen.

Questions for Review

1. How did Jim show a lack of temperance during the softball game?
2. In what area was Claudia temperate as she spent time with Grandpa?
3. How was Scott extreme?
4. How was Julia extreme?
5. What nice things could you say about your family members?

Questions for Discussion

1. How did Grandpa show a lack of temperance in his youth?
2. How did Claudia display intemperance?
3. How did Claudia overcome her extreme habit of bossiness and faultfinding?
4. What are some examples of people saying nice things to each other in your family in the last day or two?
5. In what areas could you become more temperate and balanced and less extreme?

GARDENING LESSONS

GARDENING: PAST AND PRESENT

For the LORD shall comfort Zion: he will comfort all her waste places;
and he will make her wilderness like Eden,
and her desert like the garden of the LORD;
joy and gladness shall be found therein,
thanksgiving, and the voice of melody.
— Isaiah 51:3

READ GENESIS 2:1-9

I am interested in horticulture: cultivation of fruits, vegetables, and flowers. I like being in a garden. I think it's a good place to work, to walk, to worship. God placed the first people in a garden where they did the same things. Genesis 3:8 implies that our first parents walked and fellowshipped with the Creator regularly. But they disobeyed, lost their close communion with Him, and were faced with gardening problems—thorns and thistles, sweat and sorrow.

The first Adam was expelled from the Garden because of yielding to Satan and sin. But the second Adam won the victory over Satan and sin in a garden called Gethsemane. In addition, this second Adam won the victory over death in a garden. John 19:41 says, "Now in the place where he was crucified there was a garden; and in the garden a new sepulchre, wherein was never man yet laid."

To work in a garden can do more for a person than provide things for his stomach. According to the Canadian Horticultural Therapy Association, gardening can also alleviate depression, improve your motor skills, boost your self-esteem, and, of course, provide healthy exercise. So, dig in!

However, gardening without God ultimately brings emptiness. Solomon reported, "I made me gardens and orchards, and I planted trees in them of all kind of fruits" (Ecclesiastes 2:5). Yet because his heart was not in tune with his Creator, "All was vanity and vexation of spirit" (Ecclesiastes 2:11).

Jesus must have been familiar with horticulture. He talked of seeds, weeds, vines, pruning, brush for burning, fruit, sowing, and harvest.

Jesus is interested in gardening today. He wants to plant the seeds of truth in our hearts, cultivate them by His grace and Spirit, and have us bear the fruit of the Spirit.

LESSONS FROM GARDENING

And they went forth,
and preached every where,
the Lord working with them.
— Mark 16:20

READ 1 SAMUEL 14:1, 6-13, 23, 45

As I watch things grow in my garden, I often think about God and me working together, and it brings me joy. He provides the soil, the rain, the life in the seeds, and the sun. On my part, I cultivate the soil, plant the seeds, weed, prune, and harvest. I like the way 2 Corinthians 6:1 puts it: "We then, as workers together with him." Spiritually, we can plant and water the truth, but the growth is of God. As 1 Corinthians 3:6, 7 says, "I have planted, Apollos watered; but God gave the increase. So then neither is he that planteth any thing, neither he that watereth; but God that giveth the increase."

In salvation, there is God's part and man's part. God has provided the Word, the Saviour, and regeneration by the Spirit. Our part is to respond with faith in Christ, to yield to the Spirit, and to repent from our sinful ways. After we are saved, we serve as "labourers together with God" (1 Corinthians 3:9). So it was with Jonathan in the daily reading. Thus, the first gardening lesson is cooperation—the importance of being in harmony with God.

The second gardening lesson is patience. As James 5:7, 8 says, "Be patient therefore, brethren, unto the coming of the Lord. Behold, the husbandman waiteth for the precious fruit of the earth, and hath long patience for it, until he receive the early and latter rain. Be ye also patient; stablish your hearts: for the coming of the Lord draweth nigh."

A third lesson is the expectation of growth. A gardener is disappointed if there is no fruit (or little or poor fruit) on the raspberries, the corn, or the apple tree. Second Peter 3:18 says, "Grow in grace, and in the knowledge of our Lord and Saviour Jesus Christ. To him be glory both now and for ever."

The conversion of a soul is a miracle of a moment; the growth of a saint is the work of a lifetime.

If God can make an ugly seed,
With a bit of earth and air
And dew and rain, sunshine and shade,
A flower so wondrous and fair,
What can He make of a soul like you,
With the Bible and faith and prayer,
And the Holy Spirit, if you do His will
And trust in His love and care.

— Author Unknown

What to Plant

Sow to yourselves in righteousness, reap in mercy;
break up your fallow ground:
for it is time to seek the LORD,
till he come and rain righteousness upon you.
— *Hosea 10:12*

Read Ecclesiastes 12:1-6

I encourage everyone to be involved in gardening. Here's what I suggest you plant if you would like to reap a satisfying, bountiful, and eternal harvest.

First, plant five rows of lettuce: let us love one another, let us come boldly to the throne of grace, let us be ready always to give an answer to every man that asks us a reason of the hope that is in us, let us control our tongues, and let us be faithful.

Next, you should include some squash: squash gossip, squash envy, squash careless living, and squash indifference.

Then you should have at least six rows of peas: politeness, prayerfulness, patience, promptness, purity, and perseverance.

Several kinds of berries should be planted: bury pride, bury an unforgiving spirit, bury a hot temper, bury personal idols, and bury bad habits.

Finally, be sure to plant four rows of turnips: turn up for prayer meeting, turn up with a friendly smile, turn up with a consecrated heart, and turn up with a zeal for God.

Don't forget to water, weed, and wait for the fruit of your labors. Be eager to share your gardening knowledge with those who haven't heard. Happy gardening!

Fruit-Bearing

Even so every good tree bringeth forth good fruit;
but a corrupt tree bringeth forth evil fruit.
— Matthew 7:17

Read John 15:1-11

What is needed for fruit-bearing? As verse four of the daily reading indicates, a believer, like a branch, needs to abide in Christ, the Vine. A branch that is disconnected from the vine will be useless and fruitless.

Lawrence of Arabia invited some friends who were sheiks in Arabia to England. (They had supported Britain in a war.) They had a memorable visit, appearing before Parliament, and even meeting the queen. On the last evening before they returned home, Lawrence wondered if there was anything they wanted to take with them to their desert home.

"Yes," they said, leading him up to a hotel room. They pointed to the faucets in the bathtub and said they wanted to take the faucets with them to provide them with running water in the desert. They failed to realize that the faucets needed to be connected to a water source to be useful.

We must be connected to the source of life, Jesus. He said, "Without me ye can do nothing" (v. 5).

A second necessity is water. Verse 3 mentions the Word, which is sometimes compared to water that cleanses and invigorates. Appropriately, we sing "showers of blessings we need." Ezekiel 34:26, 27 says, "I will make them and the places round about my hill a blessing; and I will cause the shower to come down in his season; there shall be showers of blessing. And the tree of the field shall yield her fruit, and the earth shall yield her increase."

A beautiful picture of watering is given by Isaiah 55:10, 11, "For as the rain cometh down, and the snow from heaven, and returneth not thither, but watereth the earth, and maketh it bring forth and bud, that it may give seed to the sower, and bread to the eater: so shall my word be that goeth forth out of my mouth: it shall not return unto me void, but it shall accomplish that which I please."

A third essential is pruning. The husbandman purges the branch as verse two indicates. God, the Husbandman, knows what to prune and how to prune to maximize fruit. God sends trials not to impair us but to improve us. It is better to be pruned to grow than to be cut to burn. Remember that all sunshine and no rain make a desert.

PARABLE OF THE LABORERS

And the grace of our Lord was exceeding abundant
with faith and love which is in Christ Jesus.
— 1 Timothy 1:14

READ MATTHEW 20:1-16

Ever hear complaints in the workplace? I have heard some in the staff room, on the farm, in the shop, even in the kitchen. Things haven't changed much since Jesus told the story in the daily reading. About the only thing people in every walk of life will agree about is that they are underpaid and overcharged. This brings me to the first lesson from the parable.

1. It is easy to grumble. Note, too, that the master wasn't pleased (vv. 13-15). A missionary, Benjamin Weir, was held hostage in Lebanon. He was imprisoned for sixteen months under deplorable conditions. After his release, reporters interviewing him asked, "How did you spend your time?"
   "Counting my blessings," he answered.
   "Blessings?" they reported incredulously.

"Yes. Some days I got to take a shower. Sometimes there were vegetables in my food." He went on, "I could always be thankful for the love of my family."

2. The first shall be last and the last first (v. 16). Things from an eternal perspective may be reversed from what we expect.
3. Motive is important. Did Peter have an inferior motive for service? He had just asked, "What shall we have?" in return for all the disciples had given up to follow Jesus. Jesus warns those who are first in their own eyes.
4. A person can receive the gift of eternal life at any point in life. We can begin our fellowship with and labor for the Master anytime He calls us.
5. It pays to serve Jesus. All were paid (v. 10).
6. We should avoid an evil eye (v. 15). Don't let an envious, critical spirit develop. You don't have time to criticize when you sympathize, harmonize, and evangelize.
7. God is gracious and generous (v. 15). Matthew Henry wrote, "The giving of a whole day's wages to those that had not done the tenth part of a day's work, is designed to show that God distributes His rewards by grace . . . and not of debt. Because we are under grace, and not under the law, even such defective services, done in sincerity, shall not only be accepted, but by free grace richly rewarded."

It is better to trust God's love and liberality than to have a contract. God always gives His best to those who leave the choice with Him.

Parable of Two Sons

And now, Israel, what doth the LORD thy God require of thee, but to fear the LORD thy God, to walk in all his ways, and to love him, and to serve the LORD thy God with all thy heart and with all thy soul.
— Deuteronomy 10:12

READ MATTHEW 21:28-32

The two sons in this parable both had the same father and both had the same command. But their responses were very different. The first son was rude and rebellious, but he repented. The second son knew the right words, but the work never got done. Possibly he had good intentions, but more likely he was a hypocrite who never intended to carry out his father's command to work in the vineyard.

Observe three lessons. First, repentance is necessary. We have all sinned—we all need to repent. John preached repentance (Matthew 3:2). Jesus commanded repentance (Matthew 4:17). Peter urged repentance (Acts 3:19). Paul taught repentance (Acts 17:30).

One day a stern-faced, plainly dressed man stood on a street corner in the busy Chicago downtown. As pedestrians approached, he would solemnly raise his right hand and point to the person nearest him, then intone loudly, "Guilty." He would then pause for a few moments, resuming his rigid stance, before repeating his gesture and indictment.

The effect on people was eerie. They would stare at him, hesitate, edge away, and then hurriedly move on. They no doubt thought he was crazy, but he was right in his evaluation. "There is none righteous, no, not one" (Romans 3:10).

Second, there is hope for the rebellious. The first son represents the obvious sinners—the immoral and the dishonest. If they reverse their direction in life, they enter the kingdom of God.

Third, it is hard to penetrate religious pretense with the message of a hypocrite's need and God's mercy. The chief priests and elders to whom Jesus told the story were self-righteous and thought they needed no Saviour. A Jew would move out of the way of a prostitute or tax collector so that they would avoid touching even their shadows.

In a forest, some huge trees tower above other trees and appear to be the very picture of strength and maturity. However, loggers will sometimes not even bother to cut down these huge trees. You may ask, "Why leave them? A tree that big must contain twice the amount of lumber as a smaller tree."

However, huge trees are frequently rotten on the inside. They are often blown over in a strong windstorm because, while they appear to be the picture of strength, in fact, their hollowness makes them weak. Hypocrites are the same—they appear strong on the outside but are hollow and rotten on the inside.

PARABLE OF THE WICKED FARM MANAGER

He came unto his own,
and his own received him not.
—John 1:11

READ MATTHEW 21:33-46

Police in California tried hard to find a stolen vehicle so they could talk to the thief. They searched and placed announcements on the radio trying to contact the thief for his own safety.

You see, the owner of the car had put a box of crackers laced with poison on the front seat. The car owner had intended to use the crackers as rat bait. Greater than the desire to reclaim the Volkswagen was the wish to potentially save the thief's life.

The parable in the daily reading contains the concept of Jesus being sent into the world to save those who were doing wrong. Luke 19:10 says, "The Son of man is come to seek and to save that which was lost."

Another lesson to be learned is that by nature people reject God's messengers, His Son, and their accountability to Him. Though God sent His only Son, the Jews resisted and rejected Him instead of reverencing Him. As in the story, so was reality a few days later when the Jews said, "Come, let us kill him."

A third lesson has to do with judgment. Condemnation awaits those who crucify the Son (v. 41). Hebrews 6:4-6 gives this solemn warning: "It is impossible for those who were once enlightened, and have tasted of the heavenly gift, and were made partakers of the Holy Ghost, and have tasted the good word of God, and the powers of the world to come, if they shall fall away, to renew them again unto repentance; seeing they crucify to themselves the Son of God afresh, and put him to an open shame."

Finally, let us permit Jesus to make us broken, rather than having the rock crush us in judgment. The scribes and Pharisees sensed that Jesus spoke about them, and "they sought to lay hands on him," thereby proving the main part of the parable.

May *we* reverence the divine householder's Son.

The Miracle Garden

by Katrina Hoover

Nicholas and Julia have a great plan. They are going to each plant a garden and sell the vegetables to make money. What are they going to do with the money at the end of the summer? They don't know yet, but they'll have lots of time to think about it while they take care of the garden.

Nicholas is twelve years old; Julia is ten. They have two little brothers who are too small to plant their own gardens. They can help Mom with her garden, though, so Nicholas and Julia won't have to help as much. Plus, Dad likes to help too, when he gets home from work and on the weekends. Dad is a veterinary surgeon; he goes to farms and helps sick animals get well. Sometimes he is home for a few hours and then gets called out to a farm to treat a sick cow.

Nicholas and Julia are homeschooled. Mom and Dad told them they can count their gardens as part of their science class if they work hard and write a report at the end of the summer.

A few weeks before the end of school, Dad borrowed a tractor from a neighbor and worked the garden soil to make it ready to plant. He added an extra plot to the end of Mom's garden so there would be room for Nicholas and Julia's gardens.

Dad drove the tractor up to the side of the shed and climbed off. "Well, what do you think?" he asked Nicholas and Julia. "Do you think you'll be able to fill that space with plants?"

"Of course, Dad!" said Nicholas.

"I think the space looks too small," said Julia.

"Oh, just wait until you're out there weeding," said Dad. "You'll probably think the garden is way too big then."

Dad helped the children divide the extra garden into two pieces, one for Nicholas and one for Julia. "I think the ground is ready to plant," he told them. "Do you have all the seeds you need?"

"Go get the jug, Nicholas," said Julia. "This is going to be so much fun!"

Nicholas and Julia had gone to a garden center with Mom to pick out their seeds. Julia had picked out bean seeds, pea seeds, onion sets, and seed potatoes. Nicholas was more adventurous: he bought watermelon and pumpkin seeds, as well as tomatoes and broccoli. But mostly the two children bought corn seeds; Dad had told them that they could probably make the most money with sweet corn.

The seed packets were stored in a plastic jug with a wide mouth. Nicholas turned the jug upside down and shook the packets out onto the new green grass. Julia picked out her packets, and Nicholas picked out his.

Julia shivered a little in the cool evening air. "Dad, what if we plant the seeds and then it gets too cold and they freeze?"

"It will be fine," said Dad. "We can always cover them."

The dry dirt felt wonderful after all the mud and slop of spring. Dad showed them how to use a string so they could hoe straight rows in the freshly tilled garden. He showed them how to drop the seeds into the rows and cover them with the hoe. But he did not help them much; the children wanted to do this project by themselves.

By the time the sun set, the garden was all planted. The seeds hid under a flat cover of dry soil. Small wooden posts marked the ends of each row so the children would not accidentally walk over their seeds.

"Dad, what if they don't come up?" Julia asked.

"Julia, why are you so worried about everything?" Nicholas asked. "First you're worried that the plants will come up and freeze. Now you're worried that they won't come up at all. Haven't you ever planted a garden before?"

"No, I haven't, and neither have you," said Julia.

"Well, I've helped with Mom's," said Nicholas, "and the plants always come up."

"Well, well," said Dad. "You two are going to be working together a lot this summer. You may as well start by speaking kindly to each other. Anyway, Julia's right; it is a miracle that those hard, dry seeds turn into green plants."

"How can it be a miracle?" asked Nicholas. "We learn how it works in school. I thought miracles were only when you couldn't figure it out."

"You can learn in school what happens," said Dad. "But no one can tell you why it happens. Only God knows the mystery of life."

The next morning, Julia dashed out to the garden. She knew the plants would not be up yet, but she just wanted to look at the garden again. She tiptoed between the rows of buried seeds. She tried to imagine rows of plants. How could those dry old seeds turn into beautiful green plants? Dad was right; it was a mystery.

For the first few days, Nicholas and Julia watched the garden closely. They couldn't wait to see the plants come out of the ground.

On Saturday Dad did not have to go to work. When Nicholas woke up, he looked out the window and saw Dad walking in the garden. He saw Dad stop and look closely at the ground. Dad walked a few more steps and bent down again, lightly brushing dirt aside.

"Julia!" Nicholas yelled, pulling on his clothes. "I think some of our plants came up! Dad's out in the garden and he keeps looking at something."

Sure enough, the corn rows were dotted with small yellow-green tips of leaf blades. Here was a plant, there was a plant, here were three plants. Julia and Nicholas danced beside the rows with delight.

"Hey, I think more of Julia's are up than mine," Nicholas said.

"Who's worrying now?" asked Julia with a laugh.

Nicholas ignored her.

"You might have planted yours a bit deeper," said Dad. "I'm sure yours will come up too."

Dad moved on and checked the plants in Mom's garden.

"I have an idea!" said Nicholas. "You know how Mom said we need to write a report at the end of the summer? Let's ask her if we can take pictures to go with it!"

"Oh, yes!" said Julia. For once, the two agreed completely. They dashed across the lawn to the house.

"Well . . ." Mom said at first.

"Please, Mom!" said Nicholas. "We'll take good care of the camera. We'll only use it every now and then, when there's something new."

"Okay," said Mom, "but you need my permission every time you use it. A camera is not a toy."

They didn't have much to take a picture of yet, but Nicholas and Julia took thirty-five pictures of their garden that morning.

By Monday morning, there was even more to catch on camera. The children could see the rows now, marked with spotty lines of light-green plants. There were even a few weeds, which the children quickly picked out.

"I'm so glad we're doing gardens," said Julia as she and Nicholas reviewed their pictures, deleting the ones they didn't want.

"I know," said Nicholas. "It's fun and easy."

Nicholas moved their pictures to Dad's computer. Dad showed them how to start a picture file named "Gardens." In that file, they started two files: "Nicholas's garden" and "Julia's garden." Every time they took pictures of their gardens, the pictures went onto the computer in those files.

On sunny days, the children loved to be out in their gardens, pulling every little weed they could find. They could not believe how much the plants were growing.

Then it rained for two days. Julia went out to the garden once between showers. When she tried to step into the garden, her foot sank into the ground. Worse yet, she saw a whole forest of tiny weeds that she did not remember seeing before.

"Mom," Julia said, "my garden is getting terribly weedy!"

"That's what the rain does," said Mom. "The rain will help your plants grow, but it will also help the weeds grow. And when the sun comes out nice and warm, the weeds will really grow. Weeds are just like Satan; they always want to spoil everything good. If you want your garden to be nice, you'll have to fight those weeds, just like we need to fight Satan when he tempts us to do wrong."

The next day the sun shone and dried out the ground, but the children still sank into the garden when they tried to walk in it. The plants were growing very fast, but the weeds seemed to be growing even faster. They could almost see the weeds pushing their heads higher and higher into the air.

As soon as the ground had dried enough, Dad tilled between the rows of all three gardens.

"It looks better already!" said Nicholas. "But there are still lots of weeds."

"You have to be persistent with weeds," said Dad. "Get them out by the roots, or they'll keep coming back again and again. Weeds are just like sins in our lives—if we let even a little bit of them go, they'll keep coming back."

"You sound like Mom," said Julia. "She said the weeds are like Satan."

Dad laughed. "Gardens are a lot like life," he said. "That's why Mom and I both thought of the same thing."

It took the children almost all day to weed the garden. By the end of the day, their hands were stained brown and green from the dirt and weeds. Their knees were dirty from kneeling beside the rows, and the backs of their necks were burnt from the sun. But the gardens looked beautiful!

"It's such a good feeling to kill all the weeds," said Nicholas at supper. "But that was a lot of work."

"You should have put sunscreen on your neck, Julia," Mom said. She could see that Julia was in pain. "Don't forget it tomorrow."

The next weekend the whole family went camping with their cousins and had a great time. Nicholas and Julia told their cousins about their gardens, but then they forgot about them in the fun of boating, hiking, and playing games.

They could not believe what they saw when they came back home. Julia was spreading a sleeping bag out on the lawn to air when she looked up at the garden.

"Look at our gardens!" she called to Nicholas, who was cleaning campfire tools.

"I know; I saw them," said Nicholas.

The vegetable plants had grown to twice their size. The sturdy corn plants stood nearly a foot tall. But the weeds! A new crop of weeds had sprung up. The children would have to weed the garden all over again.

"You can weed this afternoon after we have all the camping things put away," said Mom.

The afternoon was steamy hot. Julia could feel the sun beating down on her skull through her hair. Nicholas said he was getting a sunburn through his shirt. Just like Dad had said, the garden looked huge.

"I have an idea," said Nicholas, looking down his three long rows of corn. "I'm going to hoe dirt over these weeds. That way, I'll be hilling the corn and killing the weeds at the same time."

"Won't the weeds grow through the dirt?" Julia asked.

"Not if I put enough on!"

Julia watched Nicholas for a few minutes as he heaped dirt at the base of the cornstalks. His row did look nice when it was done, but wouldn't the weeds grow through? She turned back to her own corn rows and kept pulling the weeds. It took a long time, but she remembered what Dad had said about pulling the weeds out by the roots.

Nicholas finished all three of his rows in the time it took Julia to do one row. "I'm going to do my whole garden like this," he said, heading for his tomatoes. "This is fantastic!"

Julia kept hoeing, even after Nicholas had finished his whole garden. She barely finished before suppertime. And her garden didn't look one bit nicer than Nicholas's garden!

"Hmmm," Dad said when Julia explained how Nicholas had finished so quickly. "Remember how I said to pull the weeds by the roots, because weeds are just like sin? You did the right thing. Covering them up looks good for a while, but just wait . . ."

A week later, the gardens had sprouted weeds again. But the weeds growing in Julia's garden were small, new weeds. Nicholas's garden also had little weeds, but it also had tall, strong weeds that poked their heads through the dirt.

Nicholas hoed away in sullen silence. He knew it was his fault that the weeds had not died. Had he ruined his garden? The large weeds had large roots that left gaping holes behind. Some of the weeds had grown so big that when Nicholas pulled them out, he pulled a vegetable plant out too. When he finished his first corn row, he looked back at the large weeds lying wilted on the ground. They made his whole garden look ugly. Drops of sweat slid down Nicholas's face, and he turned unhappily to the next row.

This time, Julia finished first. She went along her rows, gathering the biggest weeds into a bushel basket. She dumped the weeds into the ditch. Her garden looked wonderful.

"Shall I pick up your big weeds too?" Julia asked.

"You may if you want to," Nicholas said. He did not want to ask his sister for help, but he knew it would look a lot nicer with the big weeds taken away.

Nicholas kept working. Pulling the weeds and hilling the plants kept him so busy that he stopped thinking about being miserable. Instead, he tried to make the rows look as nice as possible. By the time he finished, Julia had picked up all the weeds and both gardens looked very nice. Nicholas felt so much better that he even managed to thank his sister.

Sweat soaked Nicholas's shirt and Julia's dress. They saw huge, billowing clouds. The sky had turned a strange shade of gray. A restless wind tossed the tree branches.

"I think it's going to storm," said Nicholas. "I'm glad we're done." He took a last look at the perfect gardens, and they went inside.

The storm hit right before supper. Mom had just set a pot of soup on the table when rain began to pour. It got dark outside, even though the sun would not set for hours. The wind fired the rain against the windows, making it sound like hail.

CRASH! Thunder boomed, rattling the old house. Lightning flashed, and flashed, and flashed again, like a giant light bulb flickering on and off. The little boys looked scared. Julia and Nicholas watched quietly out the window.

Dad listened to the weather forecast; there was a severe storm warning.

"Let's eat supper in the basement," said Dad. "Just in case."

It was kind of fun to have a picnic in the basement. The crashes of thunder sounded farther away, and the wind didn't seem as scary since they were safe underground. Then the sound of rain hitting the basement window changed to a pinging noise.

"It's hailing," said Dad. "I hope the gardens will be okay."

Nicholas and Julia looked at each other in alarm. They hadn't thought of the gardens getting damaged. But as the hailstones began to pile up outside the basement window, Nicholas felt sick. Some of those hailstones were really big! Surely they would not damage the gardens that looked so nice!

As soon as the storm died, the entire family rushed outside. Normally, Nicholas would have collected handfuls of the hailstones and tried to pick out the layers of ice. This time, however, he went straight to the garden.

"Oh, no!" said Mom, as they got close enough to see the destruction. The bean leaves and watermelon leaves were torn and broken. Several tomato stalks had snapped. But nothing looked as horrible as the corn.

The hail had torn the leaves from the corn plants. Except for a few straggly leaves, only sad and hopeless stalks remained. Both Nicholas and Julia wanted to cry. Even Mom and Dad looked a little sad.

"We'll just have to wait and see what happens," said Dad. "Maybe they will grow new leaves."

"Why did this have to happen?" Nicholas asked. "We just hoed the garden! If I had known this was going to happen, I wouldn't have gone to all that work!"

"Remember how we said that a garden is a lot like life?" Dad asked. "Bad things happen all the time, and we don't know why. But we need to believe that God can make it turn out for our good."

When Julia went to bed that night, the crippled stalks of corn popped into her mind every time she closed her eyes. If only she could push a button and make the garden look as it had a few hours before! All their hard work, gone in a five-minute hailstorm!

A few weeks later, Nicholas and Julia weeded their gardens again. Both gardens looked much better. The bean plants had new leaves; the watermelon plants shot out long green runners. Even the cornstalks had grown new leaves. Dad said the gardens would eventually catch up. But would the corn be ready in time, before the cold weather came? Or would the frost kill it?

Long before Nicholas and Julia's corn ripened, other gardeners put out signs by the road saying SWEET CORN FOR SALE.

"Dad," said Julia, "even if our corn does get ready, everyone will be tired of sweet corn. No one will want to buy our corn."

"Well," said Dad, "there's nothing to do but wait and see. Do you see the tassels growing on the corn?" Dad pointed to the furry white shoots at the top of each stalk. "That means you'll have corn soon."

The ears of corn started out so small. Nicholas and Julia checked them every day. The ears got fatter and fatter, and the silk at the ends of each ear began to turn brown.

"Well, I think you might be able to start selling corn tomorrow," said Dad one night. "Why don't we try a few ears for supper tonight just to test them?"

The ears looked a little young yet, but Mom dropped them into a pot of boiling water. When they were done, the children buttered and salted them.

"Let's both take a bite at the same time," said Nicholas. "One, two, three, bite!"

Nicholas and Julia chewed for a few seconds.

"Mm-m-m-m!" said Julia.

"Delicious!" said Nicholas.

Even Mom and Dad agreed that the corn was very sweet and tasty.

"You know," said Dad, "I haven't seen so many corn stands lately. I think most people's patches are finished. You might be the only ones who still have sweet corn to sell."

Nicholas and Julia set up their stand with great care. They borrowed two card tables from Mom and put them beside the road. Nicholas piled tomatoes in a box. Julia made bunches of onions. Beneath the table, Nicholas placed several watermelons and Julia put a basket of her potatoes. Mom helped them decide what prices to put on the signs.

Devon, a neighbor, stopped at the stand a few hours after they had finished setting it up.

"Mm-m-m-m, sweet corn again!" he said. "Our garden's been out of corn for a few weeks already. How do you manage to have corn so late in the season?" Devon bought two dozen ears for a family gathering.

As soon as he left, Nicholas did a cartwheel.

"Our first sale!" Julia shouted, running to the house to tell Mom.

Every day the children sold corn. Often people said how glad they were to see that someone still had corn.

At the end of the summer, Dad helped the children pack up their stand.

"You know what title I'm going to use for my garden report?" Julia said. "I'm going to call it 'The Miracle Garden.' Not just because the seeds growing is a miracle, but because it's a miracle that our corn made it through the hailstorm. And it's a miracle that we could still sell our corn even though it was so late."

"It's amazing what God can do with something that looks like it's ruined," said Dad. "I'm eager to read your report."

Questions for Review

1. What were some crops Nicholas and Julia planted in their gardens?
2. What lesson did Nicholas learn about weeds?
3. How are weeds like sin?
4. What kind thing did Julia do for Nicholas?
5. In what way was it good that the hail damaged the corn and kept them from having early corn?

Questions for Discussion

1. What principles for living are illustrated in growing a garden?
2. In what ways was the garden of Julia and Nicholas a miracle garden?

3. What Bible verse does this story remind you of?
4. Has your family ever had a big disappointment that turned out to be a blessing after all?
5. What lessons has your family learned from planting things?

WONDERS OF PLANTS

The Biggest Trees

When thou shalt besiege a city a long time,
in making war against it to take it,
thou shalt not destroy the trees thereof by forcing an ax against them:
for thou mayest eat of them,
and thou shalt not cut them down
(for the tree of the field is man's life) to employ them in the siege.
— Deuteronomy 20:19

READ GENESIS 1:9-17

When God created plants as told in the daily reading, His creativity was incredible. Scientists think there are over 350,000 species of plants. Some are microscopic; others are immense. I am fascinated by the tallest plants—trees.

I would like to see a giant sequoia in California—the largest of all living things. If transplanted to a city street, the trunk would block the street from curb to curb. If you were to climb the tree, you would typically need to climb 120 feet to reach the first bough. If you cut off the first bough and placed it upright in the ground, it would be seventy feet high and have a circumference of twenty-two feet. A relative of the sequoia, the California redwood, is taller—360 feet. Sequoias are not quite as tall but are bigger in diameter.

One tree, called General Sherman, is 272 feet high, has a circumference at its base of 102 feet, and its branches begin at 130 feet.

The greatness of these trees points to their Creator. Ezekiel 17:24 says, "All the trees of the field shall know that I the LORD have brought down the high tree."

Another amazing thing about the sequoia is its tremendous age. Some of them sprouted more than three thousand years ago—before King David ruled Israel.

Unfortunately, many of these great trees have been cut down by loggers or by people who wanted the adventure and challenge of cutting one down. The few sequoias that remain are located in one place—the western slopes of the Sierra Nevadas in California. God warned Israel against indiscriminately cutting and wasting trees, as indicated in the theme verse. God gave the Israelites rules because trees are so valuable.

Trees give praise to their Creator. As Psalm 96:12, 13 says, "Let the field be joyful, and all that is therein: then shall all the trees of the wood rejoice before the LORD: for he cometh, for he cometh to judge the earth: he shall judge the world with righteousness, and the people with his truth."

As you look up high at the sequoia, keep on looking higher to the high and lofty One who inhabits eternity.

The Fiercest Plants

Lest Satan should get an advantage of us:
for we are not ignorant of his devices.
— 2 Corinthians 2:11

READ 2 CORINTHIANS 11:1-15

For many years, I was unaware that some plants eat animals. Having grown up on a farm, I knew, of course, that animals eat plants: cows like alfalfa, pigs eat corn, horses chew timothy grass. But God has designed some plants to eat small forms of animal life. Consider a few of the five hundred varieties that are carnivorous.

Sundews have leaves covered with red or orange hairs, each tipped with a shiny drop that looks deceptively like honey. But when a fly, ant, or other insect touches the droplet, it discovers that the fluid is powerful glue. As the insect struggles to get free, it makes the surrounding hairs bend over, and it soon becomes coated with gluey goo. The little creature suffocates. The sundew then secretes an enzyme that digests the catch.

Butterworts catch insects in a sticky secretion on the long, tapered leaves arranged in a rosette at the base of the plant. The leaves often curl over the trapped prey. Then the plant secretes digestive enzymes. When the "meal" has been digested, the leaf unrolls and is ready to act again.

The pitcher plant has bright colors that are attractive to insects. It also has an aroma coming from its nectar. In addition, its leaves are very slippery. When an insect lands on the leaf, it can't keep itself from sliding down past many little hairs. These hairs are one-directional, allowing the little creatures to get into the center of the flower, but not out again. The insect then is digested in a liquid at the bottom of the pitcher.

Satan would love to deceive you (1 Peter 5:8). As the theme verse says, we are not unaware of his tactics. Our daily reading indicates his deception. He doesn't use glue, bright colors, or attractive aromas, but he does use sinful companions, a carnal nature, and short-term pleasures. There is no escape by ourselves—we need a Saviour to rescue and liberate us. "If the Son therefore shall make you free, ye shall be free indeed" (John 8:36). To have control over temptation, we must allow Christ to control us.

THE MOST USEFUL PLANT

On the next day much people that were come to the feast,
when they heard that Jesus was coming to Jerusalem,
took branches of palm trees, and went forth to meet him, and cried,
Hosanna: Blessed is the King of Israel that cometh in the name of the Lord.
—John 12:12, 13

READ PSALM 92

One man who had spent his life caring for a grove of palms said, "If you can count all the stars that you can see in the sky, then you can count all the ways that coconuts serve us." He was correct, for a coconut palm has over one thousand uses.

Palms provide food. The date palm of Bible lands provides a sweet fruit with many uses. The coconut palm, which is more common, is used for protein—a single nut has as much protein as a four-ounce steak. The liquid makes a good drink—about two glasses full, which contain about two tablespoons of sugar, plus minerals and vitamins, pure and sterile. (In fact, during World War II, military doctors found that they could drip the coconut water, instead of a sterile glucose solution, directly into a patient's veins.) The nut meat tastes good and is used widely in baked goods. When the nut meat is squeezed, it provides coconut milk, which is widely used in Asian and Indian cooking. The biggest use, however, is coconut oil for cooking.

Palms provide the raw materials for many manufactured goods—fibers to make ropes and upholstery, fronds to be woven into furnishings and clothing, trunks to provide building materials, and roots to be used for dye.

Palms provide oil for dozens of industrial uses—shampoos, soaps, toothpaste, shaving cream, paints, synthetic rubber, plastics, and margarine, to name a few.

Coconut shells can be turned into cups, jugs, spoons, toys, lampshades, or teapots.

As our daily reading says, believers should flourish like a palm. We should live upright lives that serve God and people. Therefore, care for the sick, comfort the elderly, feed hungry children, clothe the destitute, share the Gospel, love the brotherhood, do good unto all men, serve God acceptably with reverence and godly fear.

Evidently palm tree branches—a symbol of peace, beauty, and honor—will be in Heaven, for Revelation 7:9 says, "After this I beheld, and, lo, a great multitude, which no man could number, of all nations, and kindreds, and people, and tongues, stood before the throne, and before the Lamb, clothed with white robes, and palms in their hands."

The Largest Seed

And God said, Let the earth bring forth grass,
the herb yielding seed, and the fruit tree yielding fruit after his kind,
whose seed is in itself, upon the earth: and it was so.
— Genesis 1:11

Read Luke 8:9-15

The biggest seed of all is the *coco-de-mer* that grows on a palm on the Seychelles Islands in the Pacific. It can be eighteen inches long and eight inches thick, weighing up to fifty pounds.

This does not mean the nuts grow into the biggest trees. There is little correlation between the size of the seed and the size of the plant. The world's tallest tree, the redwood, grows from a seed that is only one-sixteenth of an inch long. Orchid seeds are so tiny that it takes thirty million of them to make an ounce. These seeds travel as dust in the air.

Some seeds need to be planted. Ecclesiastes 11:6 says, "In the morning sow thy seed, and in the evening withhold not thine hand: for thou knowest not whether shall prosper, either this or that, or whether they both shall be alike good." But the biggest seed doesn't need anyone to plant it. It floats from its island location to another island where it may sprout and take root.

The Seychelles nut palm is interesting in more than the size of its seed. Its straight, tough trunk reaches up to ninety feet in height. At the top are giant, fan-shaped leaves which often measure twenty-five feet in length.

For centuries the source of the coco-de-mer (coconut of the sea) was a mystery to the people of India and other coastal people along the Indian Ocean. The trees simply appeared along the shore.

A palm doesn't produce its first fruit until it reaches thirty years of age. The nut may take two years to mature. It is like the ordinary coconut except that it is bigger and is bi-lobed. At first it is edible as a green coconut, but eventually the interior "meat" becomes as hard as ivory.

Coco-de-mer may be the biggest seed, but the most important "seed" is that referred to in the daily reading—the Word of God. As it is received, nurtured, and obeyed, it brings forth fruit abundantly and eternally. Thank God we can be "born again, not of corruptible seed, but of incorruptible, by the word of God, which liveth and abideth for ever" (1 Peter 1:23). Other books were given for our information—the Bible was given for our transformation.

A Very Fragrant Plant

Yea, the fir trees rejoice at thee,
and the cedars of Lebanon.
— Isaiah 14:8

Read 1 Kings 6:9-18

Another tree that the righteous are like is the cedar. "The righteous . . . shall grow like a cedar in Lebanon" (Psalm 92:12). How are Christians like a cedar?

Like a cedar, we should be upright. The magnificent cedar of Lebanon is often 120 feet in height. The western red cedar of the American Northwest may reach over 200 feet in height. Amos 2:9 says, "Yet destroyed I the Amorite before them, whose height was like the height of the cedars." The Christian should live an upright, godly life pointing to God. Psalm 37:37 says, "Mark the perfect man, and behold the upright: for the end of that man is peace."

The cedar tree is strong. Some are forty feet in circumference. Believers are to be "strong in the Lord, and in the power of his might" (Ephesians 6:10).

The cedar tree is useful. While living, it gives shade and looks beautiful. When cut down, it provides durable wood that resists rotting. It is relatively soft and easily sawn, planed, and molded. Solomon's temple was made from cedar. He used cedar pillars, as well as cedar boards for ceiling, walls, and floor. Christians make up the temple of God today. We should be steadfast and spiritually durable; we should resist the rot of sin; we should be easy to work with.

Cedar wood has a unique beauty. It has a warm red tone, solid and quite free from knots. Solomon's temple was intended to be beautiful, so cedar was a fitting wood to use. The Christian should display a unique beauty—the beauty of holiness. Psalm 96:9 says, "O worship the LORD in the beauty of holiness."

Cedar is especially known for its attractive aroma. While growing, it exudes a fragrant gum or balsam. I love the smell of cedar chests. The Christian should have the fragrance of Christ's character permeating his life as he follows Christ. As Ephesians 5:2 says, "Walk in love, as Christ also hath loved us, and hath given himself for us an offering and a sacrifice to God for a sweetsmelling savour."

The cedar praises God and so should we. Psalm 148:9, 12, 13 says "Fruitful trees, and all cedars: . . . both young men, and maidens; old men, and children: Let them praise the name of the LORD."

Praise God for the beautiful, fragrant, useful cedar.

The Tallest Grass

He causeth the grass to grow for the cattle,
and herb for the service of man:
that he may bring forth food out of the earth.
— Psalm 104:14

READ DEUTERONOMY 11:13-21

Grass is a blessing from God, as shown by the daily reading. In the beginning, "God said, Let the earth bring forth grass" (Genesis 1:11). Grass grows in nearly all environments: in deserts and swamps, in tropical regions and in the subarctic areas, on big mountains and amidst small rocks. Psalm 147:8 says God "maketh grass to grow upon the mountains."

There are six main types of grasses. First, there is the kind I mow with a lawn mower. Second, there are grasses used for hay and grazing. Third, ornamental grasses grow tall and beautiful in parks and flower gardens. Fourth, sugarcane grows seven to fifteen feet high. Fifth, there are cereal grasses such as wheat, rice, and corn. 1 Corinthians 15:37 makes reference to growing wheat or some other grain. A sixth kind is woody grasses such as bamboo.

Bamboo is the tallest grass. It is much taller than the prairie grasses that grow taller than a horse. It is taller than corn in Mexico that grows to a height of twenty feet. A stalk of bamboo may reach a height of 120 feet and be thirteen inches thick at the bottom.

Bamboo is surprisingly strong. Scientists have compared the strength of laminated bamboo and found that its breaking point is about equal to steel. It makes a very suitable reinforcement for concrete work.

Bamboo has a tremendous variety of uses, especially in Asia. People may live in bamboo houses, sit on bamboo chairs, and prepare food in bamboo containers. Their sandals may be made of bamboo strips and their covers at night may be bamboo mats. They may eat young bamboo shoots as vegetables. They may keep animals in bamboo cages or use bamboo as a fence.

Bamboo is a gift from God that benefits millions and millions of people. James 1:17 says, "Every good gift and every perfect gift is from above, and cometh down from the Father of lights, with whom is no variableness, neither shadow of turning."

THE THICKEST PLANT

The fruit of the righteous is a tree of life;
and he that winneth souls is wise.
— Proverbs 11:30

READ GENESIS 2:15-24

Trees are mentioned in the Bible from Genesis to Revelation. The daily reading mentions the tree of life and the tree of knowledge of good and evil. In the last chapter of the Bible, verse 14 says, "Blessed are they that do his commandments, that they may have right to the tree of life, and may enter in through the gates into the city."

The Bible mentions many kinds of trees still present on the earth—sycamore, fig, chestnut, cypress, fir, mulberry, olive, pine, pomegranate, cassia, almond, green bay tree, box tree, myrtle, teal, oak, and willow.

The earth's thickest tree is not mentioned in the Bible—the baobab. I am fascinated by this tree. One in Tanzania has a circumference of over 130 feet. They typically grow to be about sixty feet tall. Some of these trees are two thousand years old. The trunk makes the African think of the wrinkled skin of an elephant, pinkish-gray or a copper color. It produces a fruit called monkey bread—a gourd-like shape that dangles from the tree like a lantern on a long ropy stem.

Much of the tree can be eaten. The pulp of the fruit can be eaten raw or boiled. Its black seeds are fairly appetizing and when ground can be used as a substitute for coffee. The leaves, which resemble spinach, are rich in vitamins, and the tender young shoots are similar to asparagus. The roots, bark, and leaves are used as medicines. The trees are often hollow. This attracts bees, so natives suspend beehives in them.

Other uses include red dye from the roots, fuel from the seeds, cups from the fruit's hard shell, and waterproof hats from the bark.

Some African tribes believe that the rain god, Rasa, lives in a heavenly baobab tree. I believe that God made the baobab and other trees that we might thank and worship the Creator.

© iStockphoto.com/Prill Mediendesign & Fotografie

The Greatest Plants

by Howard Bean

"Look at the size of that tree straight ahead!" exclaimed Luke as the Walters family came around a sharp bend on the Bruce Trail. "That's awesome!"

"How tall do you think that tree is, Dad?" asked Melissa.

"That is a tall tree for here in southern Ontario," said their father. He pursed his lips and scratched the back of his head thoughtfully. "It's got to be over one hundred feet tall."

"How tall is that in meters, Dad? I'm trying to learn both types of measurements in school, but I get confused."

"Oh, it's about thirty-five meters."

"That makes it taller than Tom Applebaum's silo. It's thirty meters high," said Luke.

"Miss Weber at school told us the biggest trees in Canada grow in British Columbia, along the coast where they get lots of rain. I think she said they get to be ninety meters high. That's almost three times taller than that tree," said Melissa.

"Mother, do you remember how small we felt looking at the redwoods in California on our wedding trip?" asked Dad.

"I sure do. They were immense. They made me think of the Creator as I looked up and up. They are truly awesome—you know, they filled me with awe."

"Are those the biggest trees in the world?" asked Luke.

"Yes, they are," answered Mother. "Well, actually, it depends on what you mean by biggest. Redwoods are the tallest living trees in the world, but some other California trees are actually larger in total size—the giant sequoia.

"The what?" asked Luke. "Socoola?"

"Not quite. Sequoia—that's S-E-Q-U-O-I-A."

"Sequoia," repeated Luke. "What are they like?"

"Well, the giant sequoia is quite tall too," said Dad, "but not as tall as a redwood. I also recall that their first branches are way up in the air. You'd have a hard time climbing up one, Luke. They are also very big around. We actually drove our car right through the middle of one."

"I'd like to do that sometime," said Luke.

"I was really fascinated by a fallen sequoia we saw. I remember that a horse and rider could travel through the hollow trunk without the rider having to duck his head."

"I can't imagine a tree that big," said Melissa.

Dad went on. "I remember that they estimated the height of that tree based on the circumference—you know, the distance around—and they figured it stood over four hundred feet tall."

© Miguel V.

"How does that compare with the height of a redwood?" asked Melissa.

"I don't recall for sure," said Dad. "Do you know, Mother?"

"Actually, I do," said Mother. "I was looking over the scrapbook we made of our wedding trip just last Wednesday. I had taken it along when I stayed with Grandma. I can't remember everything I wrote, but I remember the tallest living tree then standing was 367 feet high."

Dad interrupted her. "I just now remember a newspaper article saying that they just found one at 379 feet."

Luke whistled. "That's way over three times taller than that tree ahead of us."

Mother went on, "The biggest sequoia, General Sherman, is over 270 feet high and is 36 feet across at its base. It contains over 50,000 cubic feet of wood, weighing about 1,000 tons. I also remember it's about 3,600 years old, which means it was alive long before the Apostle Paul or Daniel or Jonah or Elijah."

"How can they live so long?" asked Melissa. "Wouldn't forest fires and disease kill them?"

Dad answered, "As I recall, there are two reasons they live so long. For one thing, the bark on those big fellows is about a foot thick. Also, I think there's something about the sap that makes it hard to catch fire. A lightning bolt is about the only thing that will kill it. Now I think we've rested long enough. Let's get going. According to my map we will be getting into a swampy area pretty soon."

"I think there is a pond near the trail up here. Maybe we can find a plant that eats animals."

"Pardon me," said Melissa, "did you say a plant that eats animals? Don't you mean an animal that eats plants?"

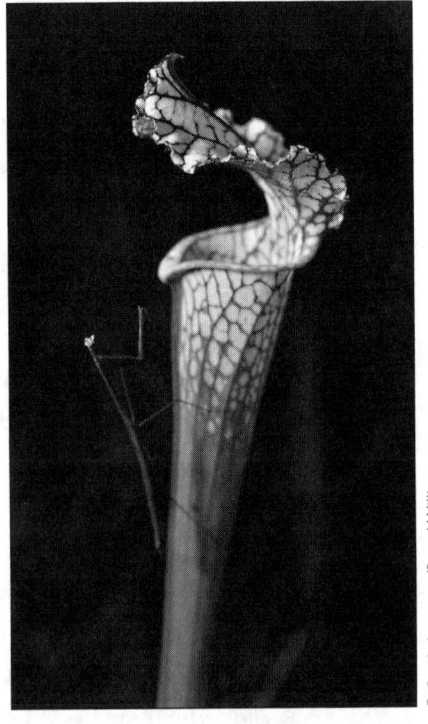

© iStockphoto.com/Russel Williams

"We might see an animal that eats plants too, but I meant a plant that eats tiny animals," said Dad.

"What kind of plant is that?" asked Luke.

"Well, there are several carnivorous—or animal-eating—plants. I read an article recently about them. The bladderwort family of plants is the most common kind. They're small, usually yellow plants that grow in the water. Where the leaves join the stems is a tiny air-filled pouch. The pouch has a single opening surrounded by bristles. If an insect pushes against the little bristles, that pouch pops open. Water rushes into the pouch and sucks in the insect along with it. The 'door' can't be opened from the inside, so the insect is caught and the plant has a meal."

"That would be a terrible feeling, to be caught with no way of escape," said Melissa. "I hate being in closed-in places."

"Isn't one of them called a pitcher plant?" asked Mother. "I think it has leaves that remind a person of a pitcher."

"That's right," said Dad. "The sides of the pitcher are waxy. An insect landing on it slides right down into the water at the bottom of the pitcher. Stiff hairs pointing downward keep the insects from climbing out.

"Those pitcher plants are sometimes called hunters' cups, because the fluid in them is drinkable. They hold at least a swallow or two of water."

"Ugh," said Melissa. "What if there are dead insects in the water?"

"You just have to be careful, I guess," said Dad. "My favorite animal-eating plant is the Venus flytrap. It has two parts, something like an open clamshell, lined by hairs that act as triggers. If an insect touches a couple of hairs, *snap,* it's caught. The leaf stays shut until the plant digests the insect. If it misses, the leaf opens again in thirty minutes or so."

"Let's talk about something else," said Melissa. "This kind of talk is going to spoil my appetite for lunch."

"What kind of tree is that on the left?" asked Melissa.

"C'mon, Melissa, you should know that," said Luke. "That's a beech. Isn't it, Dad?" he added.

"Yes."

"Isn't that the kind you carved your initials in the bark of when you were a boy?"

"Yeah, I'm ashamed to say I did. Not a good thing. It harms the tree and allows bugs to get into the trunk, I've heard."

"That's a pine tree. I know that one at least," Melissa said. "I think it's such a nice-looking tree. But not as nice as a palm. I just love looking at pictures of palm trees along a sandy beach."

"What's so wonderful about a palm tree?" asked Luke.

"Well, for one thing," said Melissa, "its life cycle is sort of human. It doesn't bear fruit till it is about thirteen years old, the age when a child becomes a man or woman. It bears fruit till about sixty and dies at about eighty.

"For another thing," she went on, "it's different from apple trees and most trees that bear fruit once a year. The coconut palm has twelve different crops growing on it at any given time. It produces about one hundred nuts per year."

"How do you know so much about the coconut palm?" asked Dad. "Pretty impressive."

"I did a project earlier this year at school. Want to know some more stuff?"

"Sure," said Dad as they walked side by side on the trail.

"Well, I don't remember everything, but I can tell about some of the ways people use it. The shell can be made into cups, or if you carve a handle, it becomes a jug. It can be made into a spoon, a knife handle, a toy, or a lampshade. It makes good charcoal. The hairs of the husk can be woven into a rope or broom. Strips of leaves can be made into hats, mats, or baskets. What else? Oh, yes, the coconut oil is even used to make ice cream."

"I don't think of a coconut palm as being very important to me," said Mother. "But it must really be important in tropical areas."

"What kind of nuts are these?" asked Luke as his family gathered around to examine the handful he had picked up.

"I'm not sure." Dad looked around at the nearby trees. "It might be some kind of a butternut."

"I like the feel of them," said Luke, "but they're not nearly as big as a kind of nut our teacher was telling us about in science class the other day. She said the biggest nut is like two coconuts fastened together. It's huge—about the weight of four gallons of milk. She filled four gallon jugs and let us try to lift all four of them at once to get the idea of how heavy one nut can be.

"She said for years and years people couldn't figure out where the big things came from, floating in from the ocean. There were some pretty wild tales. Some sailors claimed there were underwater trees where the nuts grew."

© Karelj

"What are the nuts called?" asked Mother.

"I'm not sure. Coco-something or other," said Luke.

"Have you heard of them, Dad?" asked Mother.

"No, not that I remember," replied Dad.

Luke went on. "Another wild tale was about a big

bird—a vulture or something—that lived in the trees where these great nuts grew just above the ocean. This bird supposedly fed on tigers and elephants and stuff. Ships that got too close to the trees got tipped over by giant waves around the great trees."

"I don't believe any of that," said Melissa as they started walking again.

"I don't either," said Luke. "But kings thought the huge seeds were really special. They said only rulers could have the big nuts. They thought that water stored in the partly hollowed-out shells could keep poison from killing them."

"I don't believe that either," said Melissa, "but it would be fun to see one sometime."

"Well, at this point," said Dad, "I think we'll have to be satisfied with seeing ordinary nuts and seeds."

"Look at the grove of cedar trees." Mother pointed. "Aren't they lovely?"

"Yes, I like their shape," said Dad, "but I also like to use cedar wood. That's what I made our deck out of. You helped me, Luke. Remember how nice the cedar smelled?"

"Yeah, that was fun."

Mother asked, "Did you know cedar was important in Bible times?"

"Is that what Jesus' cross was made of?" asked Luke.

"Well, I doubt it. We don't really know. We do know Solomon used it."

"Ah, that was for the temple, wasn't it?" said Melissa.

"Yes, and I think David's palace had a lot of cedar too," said Mother.

"I really like the smell of my cedar chest," said Melissa, "and I hope the cedar liner keeps the moths and stuff from spoiling the things in it."

"Look at that tall grass!" exclaimed Luke. "That grass is taller than I am. Maybe even taller than you, Dad."

"It is really tall," agreed Dad. "But God made some grass grow ten times taller than that grass."

"Huh?" said Luke. "You must mean back in the days before Noah's Flood. Our Sunday school teacher told us she thinks there were giants living then. Maybe the grass was gigantic then too."

© GaylaLin

"Well, I don't know about that," said Dad. "But I'm referring to grass that grows over one hundred feet tall."

"That sounds crazy, Dad. Just think what it would be like to take a lawn mower to that! That's taller than the barns and silos and trees around here. Are you kidding, Dad?"

"I think he is probably thinking of a plant that scientists call a grass, but you wouldn't think it looks like grass at all," said Mom. Then she asked Dad, "Are you referring to that missionary letter we got from the Hubers in the Philippines last week?"

"Yes," Dad chuckled. "It's called bamboo. Scientists call it a grass, but it's pretty tough stuff. In Asia they use it for building houses, even bridges."

"Don't pandas eat bamboo shoots?" asked Melissa.

"That's right. So do gorillas. And some people like the tender shoots too."

"What I find really fascinating," said Mother, "is how fast they grow—something like three feet in a day."

"No wonder they get so tall!" said Melissa.

"Your dad wasn't joking when he said bamboo is ten times taller than that grass over there," said Mother. "One kind grows up to 120 feet."

"I'd really like to see bamboo plants sometime," said Luke, "but I'm glad to stick with slower growing grasses for our lawn. It grows plenty fast to suit me. Mowing the lawn always makes me hungry. And speaking of food, when are we going to eat our lunch?"

"It is past twelve," said Mother. "Let's look for a nice spot to stop and eat."

After a while they climbed to a rock section where some larger rocks made inviting places to sit and eat their sandwiches and chips. The trees weren't as tall here, and a few were quite misshapen.

"You know what I think is the weirdest looking tree I've ever seen?" asked Luke. "It's that one in Africa that looks like it's growing upside down, like its roots are up in the air."

"What tree is that?" asked Mother.

"I forgot what it's called. Remember at school, Melissa, when a missionary from Nigeria showed us pictures of it. You know—it's really fat and there are not many leaves on it and it looks like it's having a bad-hair day all the time."

"Oh, yeah, I know now which tree you mean. It's a . . . uh . . . it starts with *b*, I think."

"Is it baobab?" asked Father. "When I was a boy I read stories about the Jungle Doctor. He talked about baobab trees."

"That's the one," said Melissa. "Yeah, it's really thick. Enormous. The missionary said that in one town there is a bus stop in a hollow baobab. Thirty people can easily wait in it for the bus."

"Well, I don't think any bus is going to pick us up along this trail," said Dad, "so I think we'd better get hiking again."

Questions for Review

1. What are the names of several of the plants the Walters family talked about?
2. What is the name of the biggest living thing in the world?

3. How is the tallest plant different from the largest plant?
4. What is an example of a plant that eats animals?
5. What is the world's tallest grass called?

Questions for Discussion

1. Of all the plants the Walters family mentioned, which is the most amazing to you?
2. To what two trees does the Bible compare the righteous?
3. How is a godly person like a palm tree (or a cedar tree)?
4. What is your favorite plant?
5. Would you like to have a contest between two groups in your family in which each side tries to name the most kinds of plants? (Parents and children, or boys versus girls, for example.)

WEEDS

Weeding Your Garden

For all have sinned,
and come short of the glory of God.
— Romans 3:23

Read Genesis 3:8-19

From the time I was ten years of age to the time I turned twenty, my attitudes changed toward a number of things: my enjoyment of climbing trees, my attitude toward girls, and my appreciation for gardening. But one thing remained the same—my dislike for weeds.

A weed is a plant that is troublesome and unwanted where it is growing. It grows to the injury of the desired crop. Think of weeds in your experience as undesirable things and sins in your life.

Weeds, like sin, go back to the fall of man. Spiritually, weeds started in the Garden of Eden as our first parents disobeyed God's explicit command not to eat the fruit of the tree of the knowledge of good and evil. Physically, Adam and Eve's sin brought a curse to the ground. "Thorns also and thistles shall it bring forth to thee" (Genesis 3:18).

In nature, weeds are classified in two groups. Common weeds generally grow from seeds and are fairly easy to kill—for example, pigweed. Noxious weeds are harder to eliminate. They are often perennial and are spread by underground stems. Twitch, or quack grass, is one example.

Some temptations to sin may be more difficult for you to deal with than others. You may not be tempted with profanity, drunkenness, or slothfulness, but struggle with bitterness, gossip, sexual lust, anger, or prayerlessness. But all sins are noxious to the human race and have brought no end of trouble over the centuries.

Weeds, like sin, appear without effort. No farmer or gardener deliberately plants weeds. Some weed seeds come from within the soil of the garden. Likewise, much sin arises from within a person's heart. Ephesians 2:3 says, "We all had our conversation in times past in the lusts of our flesh, fulfilling the desires of the flesh and of the mind; and were by nature the children of wrath, even as others."

Some weed seeds come from the surrounding fields and environment. Dandelions and thistles are carried through the air. Likewise, some temptations come from our environment through speech, peer pressure, and bad examples. 1 Corinthians 15:33 says, "Be not deceived: evil communications corrupt good manners."

No matter where temptations come from, the pleasures of sin are for a season, but its wages are for eternity.

Weeds Grow Fast

Then when lust hath conceived,
it bringeth forth sin:
and sin, when it is finished,
bringeth forth death.
—James 1:15

READ GENESIS 4:1-16

Before I left home for a two-week vacation, I had the garden free of weeds. When I came back, I noticed many little weeds growing and the little ones I had missed had grown amazingly big. I soon got my hoe, hands, and rototiller busy.

Spiritually, if I don't cultivate my relationship with God, sins will appear. I need to cultivate the soil of my heart with prayer, Bible reading, meditation, fellowship, and spiritual exercise.

In the garden of Cain's heart, some weeds began to grow—the weeds of disobedience to God, envy, and anger. He refused correction from God; then he murdered his brother and tried to evade personal responsibility. What a harvest he reaped: a curse, alienation, fear, and loneliness. Sin would have few takers if its results occurred immediately.

Eve was full of hope and optimism about this first child. (See verse 1 of today's reading.) Many Christian parents today feel the same. A tiny baby joins the home and brings joy. Before long, however, the parents notice little weeds beginning to show themselves. Among the pretty flowers of rosy cheeks, cute dimples, pleasant coos, and heart-warming smiles, the parents observe the weeds sprouting from a sinful nature.

Discipline and correction are not only for little hearts; they are also needed in the hearts of adults. Take David, for example, a man after God's own heart. Instead of cultivating the soil of his heart during idle time, he allowed the seed of lust to sprout into the ugly weed of adultery. More weeds sprouted and grew fast—deception, evil scheming, murder, and lying.

When a Christian falls, there will usually be little indiscretions first. Therefore, it is imperative to deal with the "little" sins. Weeding is hard work, but not weeding is ultimately much harder than weeding. Sin is not hurtful because it is forbidden—it is forbidden because it is hurtful.

A note for parents and caregivers of little children: Waiting to weed until the plants are a little bigger will allow the weeds to grow too. It is so much easier to weed the garden when the weeds are still small. Little weeds in little hearts are also much easier to remove than bigger weeds. Do not procrastinate; do it now while the child is young.

Weeds Choke

And some fell among thorns;
and the thorns sprang up with it,
and choked it.
— Luke 8:7

Read Matthew 13:1-9, 22

When I was a boy, my father sent me to weed a small cornfield of about one acre. We had been very busy getting the hay crop into the barn, so this field had been neglected. I don't remember if my dad thought the field was too small to spray with herbicides or if it had been forgotten.

The corn was not growing well; the weeds were. They looked like they had been on steroids. They were tough, tall, and had roots like eagles' claws. I don't think I'm exaggerating to say there were tens of thousands of weeds standing higher than the three-foot-high spindly cornstalks.

I began to pull them, but after a while my dad told me to stop. The corn looked weak and the worth of the anticipated crop would not be equal to the labor. The weeds had choked the good seed.

"Wherefore lay apart all filthiness and superfluity of naughtiness, and receive with meekness the engrafted word, which is able to save your souls" (James 1:21). The phrase *superfluity of naughtiness* gives the idea of weeds crowding out garden plants by rampant growth. Get rid of the choking weeds with meekness so that the implanted Word can flourish.

Deal with the thorns mentioned in our Scripture reading. Don't let cares choke. This means worries, anxieties, the *what if*s that run counter to trust. Our work is to cast care: God's work is to take care. What God promises, God will provide. As someone said, "If God sees the sparrow fall, paints the lily straight and tall, gives the sky its azure hue, certainly He cares for you."

Don't let riches choke. The love of money is a root (1 Timothy 6:10). It sends up weed sprouts from its underground stem of sin. Here's the sprout of materialism. There's the thistle of coveting. Over there are the thorns of shoplifting, cheating on income tax, and taking extended coffee breaks on the company's time.

Don't let pleasures choke. Avoid sinful pleasures. They are sure to kill your crop of holiness. Avoid legitimate pleasures if they interfere with personal devotions, church attendance, and Christian service.

Weeds in the United States do billions of dollars of damage each year. Sins do much more harm, keeping souls from joy, peace, and Heaven.

IDENTIFYING WEEDS

Is not thy wickedness great?
and thine iniquities infinite?
—Job 22:5

READ 2 TIMOTHY 3:1-13

What weeds grow in your area? I've had the dubious pleasure of getting acquainted with quite a variety of weeds: burdock, ragweed, dandelion, thistles, pigweed, lamb's-quarter, creeping Charlie, wild carrot, plantain, and poison ivy, to name a few.

Sins have a lot of variety. Galatians 5:19-21 places them in contrast to the fruit of the Holy Spirit. "Now the works of the flesh are manifest, which are these; Adultery, fornication, uncleanness, lasciviousness, idolatry, witchcraft, hatred, variance, emulations, wrath, strife, seditions, heresies, envyings, murders, drunkenness, revellings, and such like: of the which I tell you before, as I have also told you in time past, that they which do such things shall not inherit the kingdom of God."

Count the number of sins mentioned in the daily reading in verses 2-4. As time goes on, things don't get any better, according to verse 13. One may go wrong in many directions but right in only one.

Thank God, these variations of sin can all be forsaken and forgiven. That's the way it was with the Corinthian Christians. Paul wrote to them, "Be not deceived: neither fornicators, nor idolaters, nor adulterers, nor effeminate, nor abusers of themselves with mankind, nor thieves, nor covetous, nor drunkards, nor revilers, nor extortioners, shall inherit the kingdom of God. And such were some of you: but ye are washed, but ye are sanctified, but ye are justified in the name of the Lord Jesus, and by the Spirit of our God" (1 Corinthians 6:9-11).

When we meet Christ at the *cross* of Calvary, He *crosses* out our sins. Christ's cleansing power can remove the most stubborn weeds of sin—drunkenness, covetousness, an immoral lifestyle, and self-righteousness.

Not only is there a variety of sin, there is also a variety of opinion about what constitutes sin. Consider, for instance, how people, even professing Christians, think about gambling, divorce and remarriage, swearing of oaths, lawsuits, and gay "marriages."

But God's Word declares a clear line between what is right and wrong. We need not be confused. "Sin is the transgression of the law" (1 John 3:4). "All unrighteousness is sin" (1 John 5:17).

Making sin legal does not make it harmless. Sin is not judged by the way we see it but by the way God sees it.

Keep Weeding

Knowing this, that our old man is crucified with him,
that the body of sin might be destroyed,
that henceforth we should not serve sin.
— Romans 6:6

Read Colossians 3:1-10

Do you know of any garden that has never had a weed? I know of no person who has never had or doesn't have any weeds of sin. "There is none righteous, no, not one" (Romans 3:10).

At conversion, as you receive Christ, your sins are all gone. The garden of your soul is weed-free. Jesus' blood makes the garden clean "from all unrighteousness" (1 John 1:9).

However, in our humanity we sometimes yield to temptation and sin, although we do not make a practice of sinning. The garden of our heart is not overrun with weeds, but some sprout and grow and need to be killed. Our daily reading tells us to mortify, that is, put to death the sins that tend to sprout.

On the farm where I grew up we had a lot of trouble with twitch grass in our garden, which spread vigorously underground. I hacked off with my hoe what I could see, but that only temporarily solved the problem. Only by digging up the roots and exposing them to the sun could the problem be eliminated. Likewise, we need to expose sin by confession. The confession first and always is to God. David said, "I will confess my transgressions unto the LORD; and thou forgavest the iniquity of my sin" (Psalm 32:5). Often we need to confess, also, to other people. "Confess your faults one to another, and pray one for another, that ye may be healed" (James 5:16).

Sometimes I pull at a weed and it breaks off, leaving the root firmly in the ground. That's not a solution to the weed problem. We need to deal with the root. As John the Baptist said, "Now also the axe is laid unto the root of the trees" (Matthew 3:10).

We need to keep weeding in our lives. Even though we are up-to-date spiritually with all our sins under the blood, we need to give continuing attention to the garden of our souls. In my youth, my pastor explained to me that sanctification is both instantaneous and progressive. Although all sin is forgiven (instantaneous), yet we also need to grow in holiness (progressive). As 2 Corinthians 7:1 says, "Having therefore these promises, dearly beloved, let us cleanse ourselves from all filthiness of the flesh and spirit, perfecting holiness in the fear of God."

Weeding Is Work

Let all bitterness, and wrath, and anger,
and clamour, and evil speaking,
be put away from you, with all malice.
— Ephesians 4:31

Read Acts 5:1-11

Does weeding get done by wishful thinking? by good intentions? by procrastinating? The best time to do weeding is between yesterday and tomorrow. Procrastination is the fertilizer that makes difficulties grow.

Check the garden of your heart often. "Examine yourselves, whether ye be in the faith; prove your own selves" (2 Corinthians 13:5). Ask for the help of the heavenly Gardener. "Search me, O God, and know my heart: try me, and know my thoughts: and see if there be any wicked way in me, and lead me in the way everlasting" (Psalm 139:23, 24).

I can work up quite a sweat weeding the garden. Reaching down repeatedly and pulling up vigorously takes some effort if you go as fast as possible. So does energetic hoeing. The Hebrew writer says, "Lift up the hands which hang down, and the feeble knees; . . . Looking diligently lest any man fail of the grace of God; lest any root of bitterness springing up trouble you, and thereby many be defiled" (Hebrews

12:12, 15). The weed called bitterness has an especially tough root that makes it difficult to remove. It takes the spade of God's grace and an earnest desire to be done with it.

Not only in our personal lives but also in the large garden of the church is weeding necessary. As shown in today's reading, the apostolic church had some work to do in removing the hypocrisy of Ananias and Sapphira.

The church at Pergamos should have done some weeding. Jesus told them, "I have a few things against thee, because thou hast there them that hold the doctrine of Balaam, who taught Balac to cast a stumblingblock before the children of Israel, to eat things sacrificed unto idols, and to commit fornication" (Revelation 2:14).

So should have the church at Thyatira. "I have a few things against thee, because thou sufferest that woman Jezebel, which calleth herself a prophetess, to teach and to seduce my servants to commit fornication, and to eat things sacrificed unto idols" (Revelation 2:20).

It is easier just to let the desired plants and weeds grow together. But this does not produce a beautiful and bountiful garden.

Weeding Is Worth It

But he that received seed into the good ground
is he that heareth the word, and understandeth it;
which also beareth fruit, and bringeth forth,
some an hundredfold, some sixty, some thirty.
— Matthew 13:23

Read 1 Thessalonians 4:9-18

The Museum of Science and Industry in Chicago had a fascinating display. It showed a checkerboard with one grain of wheat on the first square, two on the second, four on the third, then eight, sixteen, thirty-two, sixty-four, and so on until they could no longer fit the seeds on the square. Then it asked the question, "At this rate of doubling each successive square, how much would you have on the sixty-fourth square?"

You could punch a button at the bottom of the display to find out. The answer? Nine sextillion—enough grain to cover the entire subcontinent of India fifty feet deep. Incredible!

A field or garden with good soil and weed control can produce a bountiful harvest. So can a soul that is weeded. Galatians 6:9 says, "And let us not be weary in well doing: for in due season we shall reap, if we faint not."

Not only can a garden be bountiful, but also beautiful. A holy life is a lovely life. Psalm 96:9 speaks of the "beauty of holiness." Today's reading tells of beautiful things in the garden of one's soul—virtues such as love, honesty, industriousness, generosity, and comfort.

A well-weeded life is also an orderly life. I dislike a garden that is a mass of weeds in which you can hardly even tell if there are rows of flowers and fruit.

Furthermore, a well-weeded life brings glory to the heavenly Gardener. Jesus said, "Herein is my Father glorified, that ye bear much fruit; so shall ye be my disciples" (John 15:8).

What is the garden of your life like? Are there little weeds that need attention? big thistles that may cause some pain to remove? unsightly grasses that are smothering the fruit of the Spirit?

Cooperate with the Holy Spirit to remove those weeds. Then the beautiful fruit of the Spirit will bless you and others, and God will be pleased. Separate yourself from fellowship with the world, or the world will separate you from fellowship with God.

The Ugly Weed

by Janelle (Erb) Kuepfer

Violet gazed dreamily up at the clouds. She lay on her back in the middle of the buckwheat field, eyeing the big cloud above her—the cloud that looked just like a lollipop. She licked her lips as she watched the wind whip another layer onto her lollipop. Violet loved spending her spare moments lying in the back field, watching the clouds and dreaming.

Another cloud, shaped like a stagecoach, rolled in beside the lollipop. Violet sat up with a start. How could she have forgotten? Today was Monday, and that meant a stagecoach would arrive. One of these Mondays, her cousin Molly was coming to town with her parents by stagecoach for a visit. Maybe they would arrive today!

Violet ran out of the wheat field toward the store that sat in front of it. Out of breath, she arrived at the store and looked around inside. There was only one customer in the store, discussing a bolt of fabric with Ma. Stepping behind the counter, Violet gazed hungrily at the barrels of candy in the glass showcase. *What does it matter if I just take one?* Dipping her hand into the peppermint barrel, she pulled out a smooth round peppermint, popped it into her mouth, and tucked it into her cheek.

Peering through the glass she had polished that morning, she checked to see if Ma was watching. To her dismay, she met Ma's disapproving eyes. *Ma must have seen me take the peppermint! Oh, no! Should I put it back?* She dismissed the ridiculous thought the moment it came. Ma and Pa forbade her to take anything from the store without asking, including candy. But today really was a special day, wasn't it? Her cousin Molly might be coming, after all! She sucked hard on the peppermint, willing it to dissolve.

But her cheek still bulged with the peppermint when Ma and the customer came to the counter to settle their goods. Ma brushed by her without saying anything, but her eyes told Violet she had seen everything. Violet carefully wrapped the material in the brown paper bag while the customer settled her account with Ma.

As soon as she left and the store was empty, Ma turned to Violet. "Violet, did I just see you take a peppermint?"

"Yes, Ma," Violet's soft voice trembled as the last of the peppermint dissolved and slipped down her throat. "I'm sorry. I shouldn't have taken it."

"Being sorry is not enough." Ma's lips were thin, her voice firm. "You have directly disobeyed us. Did you already forget what Pa said would happen if you disobeyed?" Her next words were drowned out by a clatter of horses' hooves on the street, followed by several shouts. Ma and Violet looked out the doorway just in time to see the stagecoach rattle past the store.

"The stagecoach!" Ma exclaimed. "Ted and Rose! And Molly! They could be along! Oh, I do hope so!" Together they rushed from the store just in time to see Uncle Ted, dusty but smiling, emerging from the coach.

Ma gripped Violet's shoulder and said quickly, "I will talk to Pa tonight and tell him what you have done," before she ran to meet her sister.

"Let's play doll, Molly. I have an extra doll you may play with," Violet suggested the next day.

"I brought my own doll along," Molly replied. "Ma packed it into her trunk. I'll go and ask her for it." She ran off to find her Ma.

Violet picked up Patty, a cornhusk doll Pa had made for her birthday last year. She poked one of Patty's eyes lightly. The brown button was growing loose. *I hope Ma will teach me how to sew it back on Patty's face,* Violet thought. "Then you'd feel better, wouldn't you, Patty!" She kissed the scratchy face. Reaching under her bed, she brought out Patty's burlap blanket.

Violet looked up from her doll when Molly skipped into her bedroom. "This is Lucy," Molly offered, holding out her own cornhusk doll for Violet to see. Violet hardly noticed the doll. She stared in wonder at Lucy's blanket. Gently she fingered the soft fabric. "A real cloth blanket!" she breathed.

"Ma made it for me for Christmas," Molly happily explained. "She had some leftover scraps of fabric, so she made a blanket for Lucy."

"Oh. I like it." Violet remembered her manners. But deep inside, Patty's burlap blanket embarrassed her. *All I have is a scratchy blanket for a scratchy doll!* she thought bitterly. *If only I could have a blanket made out of fabric. If Ma ever has scraps of fabric left over, I'll ask her to make me a blanket!* she thought. *Oh, well, I love Patty even though I don't like her blanket. Molly can have her silly blanket.*

The two girls spent most of the afternoon playing with their dolls. Not another word was spoken about Lucy's blanket. But as the day wore on, Violet wished more and more for a blanket just like Lucy's.

When Ma called them for supper, the girls put away their dolls. Violet laid her sleeping Patty on the bed. She watched Molly wrap Lucy in her blanket and place her gently on the floor in the corner of the bedroom.

As the two girls went to bed that night, Molly stated, "I'm so thirsty. I need a drink. And I forgot to kiss Ma and Pa goodnight." She hurried to the kitchen where the adults were quietly chatting.

"Okay," Violet replied as she climbed under the old quilt. Then she paused. An idea popped into her head. She knew it was a very bad idea, and she shook her head to get rid of it. But instead of going away, it continued to grow.

Here's your perfect chance, a little voice deep inside her head told her. *Take Molly's doll blanket and hide it. When they return home, you can bring it out and say Molly left it here. Nothing can be done about it then.*

No! another voice whispered. *Ma and Pa said taking things that aren't yours is stealing. Don't take the blanket! Remember how it hurt last night when Pa punished you for taking the peppermint?*

Molly won't really know you took it, the first voice whispered. *Maybe she'll think she mislaid it. Quickly take it before she comes back!*

Violet jumped out of bed. Before she could stop herself, she swept the coveted blanket off Lucy. Arranging Lucy just how she had found her, she tucked the blanket under her mattress as far as she could reach.

Violet had just settled under the covers when Molly pattered into the room. She climbed into bed, whispered a goodnight to Violet, and fell asleep shortly.

Going to sleep for Violet, however, was not so easy. It seemed every time she closed her eyes, she could see the blanket dancing in front of her, mocking her. She almost got up and returned Lucy's blanket, but she was afraid Molly would awaken and wonder what she was doing. At last she fell into a fitful sleep.

The two families had planned a picnic in the woods for the next day. Violet's usual morning duties in the store, dusting and sweeping, kept her and Molly busy most of the morning.

She avoided Molly as much as she could, but it was almost impossible, as they worked together. Several times she almost told Molly what she had done, but her mouth went dry and her tongue wouldn't form the words. Feeling miserable and guilty, she finally decided that at her first chance, she would return the blanket before anyone noticed it was missing. But she had no chance. When they finished with the morning jobs, Ma asked the girls to help her and Aunt Rose prepare their picnic lunch.

"Hey, Violet!" Molly exclaimed as they took turns fishing pickles from a jar. "Let's take our dolls with us on the picnic!" She looked over at Aunt Rose for approval.

Aunt Rose smiled and said, "You may take them along if you promise to take good care of them." Ma nodded in agreement.

"We will, won't we, Violet?" Molly smiled at Violet.

"Of course," Violet agreed. She tried to smile back. *I need to get Lucy's blanket back before Molly discovers it's missing!* Her heart pounded. *Why, oh, why did I do such a foolish thing?* A sweat broke out on her forehead and her hands felt clammy. Setting her fork down, she picked up the empty pickle jar to carry it to the counter. Without warning, her clammy hands lost their grip on the jar, and it fell to the floor with a loud crash, shattering. Sticky pickle juice splashed everywhere.

The women jumped and Molly shrieked. Her skirt was covered with pickle juice. Shards of glass lay around Violet's feet.

"Are you all right, Violet?" Ma asked, stepping over the mess to check out her daughter. "Did you get cut?"

"I-I don't think so," Violet stammered, not moving.

Just then the kitchen door opened and the men stepped in. "Whoa! What's going on?" Pa looked around at the mess. "Is everyone okay?"

"You can't go on the picnic looking and smelling like this!" Aunt Rose teased Molly. She whisked her off to Violet's bedroom to change into another dress while Ma explained what had happened.

Violet's heart sank. *I hope Molly doesn't notice the missing blanket. Oh, if only I could have put it back before Molly went in there!*

But it appeared to be too late. She heard excited voices in the bedroom. Then Molly peered into the kitchen. "We can't find Lucy's blanket. I can't remember where I left it last, but I'm sure I wrapped it around Lucy last night. Violet, do you remember?"

Violet's face turned red. She hurried into the bedroom, hoping the others wouldn't follow. But Ma's footsteps were close behind. Her tone was stern as she asked, "Violet, do you know where the blanket is?"

Violet hesitated. Should she tell them why she had taken it, or should she pretend she had just hidden it as a joke? One glance at Ma, and her decision was made. Ma looked like she already knew what Violet had done.

"I took it," Violet confessed softly.

Ma nodded her head sternly. "Where is it?" she asked.

Violet walked to her bed and lifted a corner of the mattress. The beautiful blanket lay there, and Molly rushed over and grabbed it. She held the blanket tightly and stood beside Aunt Rose.

Violet stared at the floor, dreading what was to come. She sensed Ma asking Aunt Rose and Molly to leave. Silence reigned until Pa entered the bedroom. He sighed; then he knelt in front of Violet.

"Why did you do it, Violet? Stealing is wrong. God told us in one of the Ten Commandments, 'Thou shalt not steal.' Have you already forgotten the lesson you learned last night?"

Violet hung her head, ashamed.

"A bad habit, or a sin like stealing, is like a weed, Violet. If you do not stop it while it is small, it will only grow bigger and bigger. Weeds that aren't pulled when they are small will grow and grow. Their roots become tough and strong and resist being pulled from the ground."

"I'm sorry, Pa. I never want to steal again," Violet said with tears in her eyes after Pa had punished her.

"If you are tempted to steal again, remember the weeds, and don't let them grow," Pa instructed. "And ask God to help you choose right. Now, is there someone else you should ask for forgiveness?"

Together they went in search of Molly.

"Ma, may I please have that doll?" Violet begged several weeks later. "One of those real dolls in the store. Please, Ma?"

"There's nothing wrong with the doll you have, Violet. And besides, we don't have any spare money to buy a real doll," Ma said firmly. Then she added, "Before you play with it or call it your own, it must be paid for."

"Of course, Ma. I won't steal that doll. I'm trying to pull that weed, just like Pa explained. I've been saving my money. When I have enough, I'm going to buy the doll," she decided.

But two days later on Sunday morning, the nagging weed began to sprout again. At church, the minister announced the offering. He said it would be given to the poor families in town, those who didn't have enough money to buy things they needed.

Violet's ears perked up. Like popcorn, little ideas began to pop into her mind. *My family deserves some money. Didn't Ma say we have no spare money? I'm sure if Pastor Parker knew that, he would give us some of the offering.*

Violet smiled to herself. She tried to convince herself that her parents would be grateful. To ask the pastor for money would be too bold, she decided. *I know,* she thought, *I'll do it when the offering basket comes around. I'll put in my nickel like usual. But this time, I'll also take out some money. Hopefully no one will see me. But I'm not stealing,* she tried to console herself. *We deserve the money.*

Violet was surprised how easy it was to exchange her nickel for a dollar bill. The folded bill fit perfectly into the palm of her hand. And nobody seemed to notice her fumbling.

Now she had to decide where to put the dollar bill when she got home. She thought of putting it on the kitchen table, as if it had come from nowhere. But Pa and Ma would probably ask if she knew where it came from. *I'll hide it in my room for now until I think of a good place to put it.*

But Violet didn't need to wait. She heard Ma and Pa discussing something on the way home from church. They both had stern looks on their faces, and it didn't take long to find out why. Arriving home, Ma and Pa made her sit down at the kitchen table. Pa stood in front of her and asked, "Violet, did you take something today at church that wasn't yours?"

Violet was quite sure Pa knew she had taken the money. She confessed to him what she had done. With a sinking heart, she realized the weed had grown big and tall.

After listening to her confession and punishing her once more, Pa looked over at Ma. He was quiet for a moment; then he turned to Violet. "Now, Violet, tomorrow there's something else that needs to be done to make this right. You'll need to tell Pastor Parker what you've done and tell him you're sorry. That will help you remember never to steal again, even when you're tempted."

Morning came just after Violet had fallen asleep, or so it seemed. She waited to get out of bed until she heard Ma setting the table for breakfast.

Breakfast was eaten in silence. Violet only picked at her food. At last Pa laid down his fork, cleared his throat, and said, "Violet, right after you wash the breakfast dishes, we are going to visit Pastor Parker. Why don't you start thinking about what you are going to tell him."

Tears swam in Violet's eyes, but she nodded. She couldn't wait to have this day behind her. She knew Pa would make her return the money she had stolen.

Pa continued, "When we come home, I have something else for you to do. This is part of your punishment and will help serve as a reminder of the lesson we're trying to teach you."

Violet nodded, but didn't say anything. Silently, she washed the dishes. When she had finished, she found Pa in the barn and told him she was ready to go. She reached into her pocket to be sure the dollar bill was still there. It gave her a sharp paper cut.

All too soon they arrived at Pastor Parker's house. He met them at the door with a welcoming smile, one that Violet couldn't return.

"Violet has something to tell you, Pastor," Pa said, prompting Violet to speak.

The pastor looked at Violet and smiled encouragingly.

Her tears were dropping fast as the words rushed out of her mouth. "I'm sorry, Pastor Parker. Yesterday, after I put my nickel in the offering basket, I stole a dollar bill out of the basket. I wanted Ma to buy me a doll, but she said we didn't have enough money. When you said the offering was for poor families, I thought Ma and Pa could use some money. I knew it was wrong to take the money, but I did it anyway. I wanted the doll so badly." She pulled the dollar bill out of her pocket and handed it to the pastor. "This is yours, Pastor, and I am very sorry."

The minister took it and looked gravely at her. Then he knelt in front of Violet and said, "This isn't my money either, Violet. When we place money in the offering basket, we are giving it to God. He has only chosen me to give it to those who need it. I forgive you, Violet, and I know that if you ask God to forgive you, He will. When He saw you steal the money, I'm sure it made Him sad. But now you made Him happy by returning the money and confessing your sin. If you ask Him to, He will help you remember that stealing is wrong. Shall we ask Him right now?"

Violet nodded. The three joined hands on the front porch as Pastor Parker prayed.

Violet felt a little relieved on the way back home. But she wondered what else Pa had for her punishment.

She didn't have long to wait. When they got home, Pa led her to the garden. "Ma and I have decided that you will weed these three rows of vegetables." He pointed to two rows of carrots and a row of corn. "As you weed, I want you to think about the ugly weed in your life. When you are finished weeding, come up to the house, and we will meet you in there." With that, he turned and headed for the store.

Bending over, Violet tackled the weeds from the first row. Ma had told her how important it was to pull the root in order to get rid of the weed, so she made sure it came along with the plant. *This is easy enough,* she thought as she pulled the weeds, one after the other. Her pail was almost full when she reached the end of the first row of carrots. Pausing for a moment, she glanced at the next row. It had more weeds—taller weeds.

She dumped her pail full of weeds on a pile in the field and walked to the second row. Pulling at the weed, she grunted a little until the stalk snapped off at the roots. The roots remained in the ground, leaving Violet holding the stalk and leaves. She dug into the ground around the root, trying to free it from the soil packed around it. The root resisted stubbornly, but at last it came out, at least most of it. Violet could see some of the roots were missing. She went on to the next one and the same thing happened.

Gazing down the row, Violet sighed. This row was going to be a lot more work than the last one. The weeds stubbornly clung to the ground. *Pa said I'm supposed to think about the weed in my life. He must mean my stealing. I wonder what that has to do with the weeds in the garden? Some of these weeds are big and others are small. The big ones sure are hard to pull.*

The light suddenly dawned. *It's what he told me the other day. The bigger a sin gets, the harder it is to get rid of it.* She yanked at another stubborn weed. A blister had formed on her finger and thumb, and it hurt each time a weed scraped against it.

Finally she reached the end of the carrot row. As she dumped her pail of weeds, she looked back at the row she had just weeded. The carrots were definitely smaller than the plants in the row beside them and they did not look nearly as healthy. Here and there she had accidentally pulled the carrot tops with the weeds.

Walking up to the corn row, she could see weeds that she and Ma had missed earlier that spring. The tough, prickly stalks had grown almost as tall as the corn. Bravely, she braced her feet and gripped the first weed. She pulled, but nothing happened. She pulled again. This time her hands slipped and she ripped off a few leaves.

Planting her feet more firmly, she glared at the weed and pulled with all her might. She heard a snap, and before she knew it, she was on the ground with only the top of the weed gripped in her hands.

Tears stung her eyes as she pulled again at the weed. A few more pieces broke off, but Violet could not pull the root from the soil. Its roots had grown too strong. She broke it off near the ground and moved on to the next weed. There the same thing happened. As she went from one weed to the next, Pa's words from a few weeks before, rang in her mind. "If you do not stop a bad habit while it is small, it will only grow bigger and bigger. Weeds that aren't pulled when they are small will grow and grow. Their roots become tough and strong and resist being pulled from the ground."

Violet was ashamed. *I am just like this tough old weed. I've never really "pulled" my weed of stealing. Each time I do it, my root gets stronger and stronger. Ma and I didn't notice these weeds when they were tiny, and so they grew and grew, just like my stealing. Well, I'm going to pull my "weed." I don't want to be like a tough, old, stubborn weed.* She snapped off the last weed, emptied her pail, and hurried into the house. She couldn't wait to tell Ma and Pa what she had discovered.

Questions for Review

1. What was the weed Violet had growing in her life?
2. What were three things she stole?
3. How did Ma try to help her deal with the weed?
4. Why did Violet need to visit the preacher?
5. When is the best time to deal with weeds?

Questions for Discussion

1. What were the results of Violet stealing the doll blanket?
2. Do you think Violet will steal any more?
3. What are some examples (other than stealing) of weeds that might grow in a child's life?
4. Has a weed been dealt with in your family?
5. Is there a weed you or your family should be working to remove?

SOWING AND REAPING

The Results of Sowing

Be not deceived; God is not mocked:
for whatsoever a man soweth,
that shall he also reap.
— Galatians 6:7

READ JUDGES 16:15-30

You would, no doubt, seriously question my mental abilities if I told you the following:

- If I plant corn, I expect turnips to grow from the corn seed.
- If I plant carrots, I look for pea plants to push through the ground from the seeds.
- If I plant an apple seed, I anticipate that a walnut tree will grow from the seed.

How is it then that many people act as though they can sow habits of sin and expect to have a life filled with happiness and harmony? No wonder our verse says, "Be not deceived." The deception is widespread that ingesting the poison of sin will have no adverse consequences and that taking the fire of immorality into one's bosom will not lead to burns and death. Such thoughts are as delusional as thinking that jumping from an airplane at three thousand feet without a parachute will result in a safe, enjoyable landing.

As our daily reading shows, sowing sin leads to a harvest of spiritual blindness and bondage. The same principle holds true in the lives of them who have never been God's people, as illustrated by the fate of the Philistines.

I have been told by those who work closely with delinquent teens that there is a disconnect in the minds of such youth between their choices and the consequences. They typically fail to see that their state of bondage, grief, unemployment, loneliness, and problems with the law is a result of their choices of bad associates, rejection of authority, and the pursuit of ungodly pleasures. They feel they didn't get the breaks, were treated unfairly, and weren't lucky.

Lord Byron, a skilled English poet who spent his life in pursuit of pleasure, wrote despairingly near the end of his short life,

> "The thorns I have reaped are of the tree I planted.
> They have torn me and I bleed.
> I should have known what fruit would spring
> from such a tree."

There is a happy side to the law of sowing and reaping. Although it is true that if we sow "to the flesh," we reap trouble, disappointment, and death, it is equally true that if we sow "to the Spirit," we shall reap a blessed and beautiful harvest of desirable results. If I plant sweet corn seed, I reap a wonderful harvest of delicious corn. The next six devotionals will show both the positive and negative consequences of sowing and reaping.

GETTING WHAT YOU DON'T WANT

Even as I have seen, they that plow iniquity,
and sow wickedness, reap the same.
—Job 4:8

READ 3 JOHN

Ungodly people do things to get what they want and end up getting what they don't want.

For example, a thirty-two-year-old man in Oklahoma decided to pursue fun and fame by painting graffiti on a sixty-four-foot water tower. He lost his balance and fell to his death. He got what he wasn't trying to get. Proverbs 11:27 says, "He that seeketh mischief, it shall come unto him." This is in contrast to the godly person. "He that diligently seeketh good procureth favour."

Several hundred generations ago, my ancestors were trying to get satisfaction, pleasure, and wisdom as they reached out and took forbidden fruit in a beautiful park. What they got was pain and punishment, guilt and grief, danger and death.

Another of my distant relatives, a man called Diotrephes, wanted to get something: preeminence—presumably things such as power, fame, influence, honor, and reputation. In his attempt to get these things, he got rebuke, dishonor, and abasement. How would you like the words in our daily reading to be written about you by the Apostle of Love (vv. 9-10)?

A man who lived years ago near the Dead Sea wanted to own lots. In fact, Lot was his name. He thought he could gain lots by getting the best land—the grazing ground near the well-watered plain of Jordan near Sodom, a city known for its wickedness and sin. By taking the best land away from Uncle Abram, he got what he wanted. But he also got what he didn't want—destruction of his possessions, a pillar of salt for a wife, and the wicked conniving of his two daughters.

The prodigal son desired freedom mingled with pleasure. To that end, he "gathered all together, and took his journey into a far country, and there wasted his substance with riotous living" (Luke 15:13). But before long he got what he hadn't sought—poverty, pigs' feed, and loneliness.

Sin may temporarily bring you the things you want. But ultimately it will also bring you the things you absolutely don't want. The pleasures of sin are "for a season," but the wages are for eternity. A person always pays for sin with the coin of sorrow. Sin must be dealt with in one of two ways: punishment or pardon. Therefore, seek pardon available only through Jesus Christ.

The Weight of the Crop

For I acknowledge my transgressions:
and my sin is ever before me.
— Psalm 51:3

Read Psalm 51:7-17

In a town in Ontario, a transport truck was parked in the yard of a trucking company, loaded with three large coils of steel. Two men drove their fairly new F-150 pickup close to the truck, intending to steal one of the coils. The price of metal was very high in 2008, and they knew they could get a lot of money for the steel.

They were able to roll it off the transport onto the bed of their pickup. Unfortunately for them, they had no idea how heavy one coil is. They stared in disbelief as the steel flattened the pickup.

The owner of the transport emerged from the office where he had been watching the procedure. He said, "You've got two choices. We can call the police, or you can get a crane to put the steel back on the transport."

King David also thought he had an attractive, feasible plan. Commit adultery with Bathsheba, arrange the death of her husband, and life would continue smoothly. But as our daily reading shows, he soon experienced the crushing weight of guilt. Adultery is a guilt-edged invitation to tragedy. He put it this way in Psalm 38:4-6: "Mine iniquities are gone over mine head: as an heavy burden they are too heavy for me. My wounds stink and are corrupt because of my foolishness. I am troubled; I am bowed down greatly."

The Lord was merciful to David as he confessed and repented of his sin. Christians today testify of the relief and joy of being delivered from the soul-crushing weight of guilt.

The law of sowing and reaping still stands. It is a spiritual (and mathematical) law: Sin will add to your troubles, subtract from your energy, multiply your difficulties, and divide you from God's help. The wages of sin never are reduced.

If I repent of a life of sin, although I cannot entirely erase the consequences of my past sins, I can begin to sow to the Spirit. If a piece of material in an upholstery shop is cut too short, you cannot stretch it to fit the part that it was planned for. However, although it cannot be used where originally intended, it can be useful elsewhere or on another piece of furniture. Christ can still use and bless us no matter what the sins of the past.

The wages of sin is death. Quit before payday.

Helping Yourself by Helping Others

As we have therefore opportunity,
let us do good unto all men,
especially unto them who are of the household of faith.
— *Galatians 6:10*

Read John 4:31-38

Not only does sowing of wrong lead to undesirable reaping, but the sowing of unselfishness brings good reaping.

Consider the observations of an Austrian physician, Viktor Frankl, who was put into one of Hitler's prisons. He along with other Jews faced cruel atrocities. Their living conditions were abysmal. Their working conditions were depressing. Their medical care was virtually nonexistent.

Dr. Frankl gave what little medical help he could to the diseased and dying. Over time, he made some very perceptive observations, which he recorded in his book *Man's Search for Meaning*.

He discovered that the people who kept their strength and sanity the longest were the ones who tried to help other prisoners and who shared what little they had. In other words, their physical and mental health seemed strengthened by their compassion, service to others, and focus on something other than themselves.

Dr. Frankl concluded that if a person faces life's challenges by trying to make life better for others, the effort strengthens that person's psychological and physical stamina. Serving others stimulates one's energy rather than depleting it. Serving others enhances one's well-being.

This illustrates and corresponds to the teaching of Scripture. Jesus said, "It is more blessed to give than to receive" (Acts 20:35).

Christ, while doing spiritual service in Samaria, stated to His disciples who had urged Him to eat, "I have meat to eat that ye know not of" (v. 32 of our daily reading). He pointed out the connection between serving others and receiving personal benefit in verse 36.

In the object lesson given by Jesus of humble service in the feetwashing ordinance, Jesus concluded His lesson by pointing out a benefit of obediently serving others. "If ye know these things, happy are ye if ye do them" (John 13:17).

Now let's make application to service in church offices in the brotherhood. If you want to be happy, serve the church and the Lord. Unselfish service to others will prove to be the best medicine for your own ills.

Grim Education

Whoso curseth his father or his mother,
his lamp shall be put out in obscure darkness.
— Proverbs 20:20

Read Genesis 47:5-12

Once there was an old man who lived with his adult married son. His eyes were dim and his hands trembled. When he sat at the kitchen table, his spoon sometimes missed his mouth, or the broth dribbled out of his mouth onto the tablecloth.

This sight did not enhance the appetites of his son or his daughter-in-law. After a while, the woman decided she had had enough. The old man's sloppiness was interfering with her happiness and peace of mind. So she and her husband gently but firmly took the old man by the arm and guided him to the corner of the kitchen. There they gave him a stool to sit on and an earthenware bowl to eat from. From then on he always ate in the corner, looking with moist, longing eyes at the table.

One day his trembling hands could not hold the bowl and it fell to the floor and broke.

"If you are a pig," said the daughter-in-law, "you must eat out of a trough." So they made him a little wooden trough and gave him his meals in that.

The couple had a four-year-old son whom they doted over. One evening they noticed the boy playing rather intently with some pieces of wood.

"What are you doing?" asked his father.

"I'm making a trough," he told them, smiling up at them for their approval. "It's to feed you and Mommy out of when I am big."

The man and wife looked at each other across the table in silence. Then tears came to their eyes. They went to the corner and took the old man by the arm and led him to the table. They set him on a comfortable chair and gave him his food on a plate. This story by Grimm concludes with the old man always eating at the table thereafter, with no complaint if he spilled some food.

Proverbs 23:22 says, "Despise not thy mother when she is old." This would make a good motto at the entrance of our old folks' homes.

Parents wonder why the streams are bitter when they themselves have poisoned the fountain. It's hard to train a child in a way the parents don't go themselves.

The Bible says, "Honour thy father and thy mother," and there is no expiration date on the command.

Not a Defective Detective

For God shall bring every work into judgment, with every secret thing, whether it be good, or whether it be evil.
— Ecclesiastes 12:14

READ JOHN 8:1-12

Ralph York, 23, had a brief and botched flirt with crime. He stole a mountain bike in broad daylight from a garage in Port Dalhousie, Ontario. He then fled and hid behind a building—not realizing it was the Port Dalhousie community police office—when a Niagara police officer happened to pull in. York thought he was surrounded and dove into a nearby pond, swimming frantically to get away. As York neared the other shore, he saw another police car and assumed that police officer was also on his trail. In fact, that police car was only pulling into a gasoline station. So York swam back, emerged from the water, and walked down the street dripping wet—right toward another police car on routine patrol. Mr. York felt so flustered and guilty that he blurted out a full confession to the surprised officers.

The Bible says, "Be sure your sin will find you out" (Numbers 32:23). Sometimes, as in the case of Mr. York, one's conscience and consciousness of guilt brings about sin's exposure. It was conscience that caused the accusers in our daily reading to leave behind them an implication of wrongdoing. Christ said, "He that is without sin among you, let him first cast a stone at her. . . . And they which heard it, being convicted by their own conscience, went out one by one" (vv. 7, 9).

In addition to sin being found out by conscience, sin can also be exposed by circumstances. For example, in Hamilton, Ontario, a Christmas shopping spree with a stolen credit card came to an abrupt end when the thief came face to face with the card's owner—a cashier. The thief had shopped at ten stores, buying over six hundred dollars' worth of merchandise, before heading to one more store. But the cashier recognized her own name on the Visa card—a card that Visa had sent but which had never arrived. She recognized the customer as a woman from her apartment building.

Sin is the greatest detective. Be *sure* your sin will find you out. Whether by conscience or circumstances, sin has a way of exposing the sinner. Often sin becomes known in this life. If covered up here and not taken away by the blood of Jesus, it will humiliate and damn us in the existence to come. Sin is an effective detective; don't let it get on your trail.

Reaping a Good Crop

And let us not be weary in well doing:
for in due season we shall reap, if we faint not.
— Galatians 6:9

Read Ruth 2:1-16

A shepherd had a problem with his neighbors' dogs killing his sheep. He thought of the usual possibilities to try to deal with the problem—fences, shotguns, lawsuits. But he decided on a better idea. To every neighbor's child he gave a lamb or two as a pet. After some time, as his neighbors had their own small flocks, they began to tie up their dogs.

Good sowing may result in a problem being solved. Or it may result in a wonderful reputation. For example, David Livingstone used his doctor skills to help the people in the wilds of Africa; he worked to end slave trade; he shared the Good News of Jesus. Long after he had died on his knees in Africa, he was referred to by the native people as "the kind doctor."

Another benefit of sowing seeds of kindness is illustrated by a taxi driver who was unusually friendly and cheerful. Asked why, he said, "It all started when I heard about a taxi driver who was so kind to a passenger that the man remembered him in his will with a bequest of

$65,000. So I thought I would try it. Maybe if I was polite and helpful, somebody might leave me something. But after I tried it, I decided that I would do it just for the fun of it."

Seeds of thoughtfulness can even improve the abilities of others. At least, according to some results presented in 1995 at the American Association for the Advancement of Science, kindness helps doctors to diagnose an illness. In an experiment, researchers gave fifty percent of forty-four doctors a bag of candy as a token of appreciation for their help in the study. The other twenty-two received nothing. As the physicians studied the symptoms of a hypothetical patient, those who had received a gift were far more likely to make a correct diagnosis. The research concluded that pleasant-feeling states contribute to helpfulness. The songwriter had it right in the words, "Little deeds of kindness, little words of love, make our earth an Eden like the heaven above."

As shown in the daily reading, Ruth, who was kind to her mother-in-law, reaped a crop of kindness from her future husband. If you would be arrested for being kind, would enough evidence be found to convict you?

Sowing and Reaping—You Get What You Plant

by Katrina Hoover

Nicholas watched with interest as Dad sewed the cow's stomach shut. Nicholas loved going on vet calls with Dad. Any farm visit was interesting, but he especially liked watching surgeries.

"How did you learn to sew those stitches so fast?" Nicholas asked in awe as Dad's needle moved in and around the thread, or suture, as Dad called it.

Dad laughed. "You start slowly and carefully," he said. "If you learn to do it right the first time, it's not hard later. But people who are sloppy when they first learn are often sloppy later." Dad quit talking and tied a knot in the suture.

On the way home, Dad asked, "Are you and Julia planning to plant gardens again this summer?"

"Oh, of course," said Nicholas. "But this year we're just thinking of doing one big garden and sharing the money we make."

"That will work if you share the work equally," Dad said. "You know, the ground is dry enough, I think you could plant some early crops tonight, like peas and potatoes."

"Really?" said Nicholas. "I thought we'd have to wait a long time yet."

When they got home, Nicholas found Julia and the two sketched their garden plans on a piece of scrap paper. They included a large plot for corn and smaller sections for tomatoes, beans, and peas. They decided they would try growing some pumpkins as well.

"Dad said we can plant peas and potatoes tonight," Nicholas said.

"Yes, Mom said they like cool weather. Do you think we can go to the garden center and buy seed potatoes and peas?"

With permission from Mom, the two set off on their bikes. They lived in the country, but a man who lived just down the road had built a garden center where he sold seeds and gardening supplies.

The neighbor's fifteen-year-old son, Peter, helped them pick out their seeds. He told them which potatoes were early and which were good for baking. He showed them the Howden pumpkin seeds that would make large, deep-orange pumpkins and the seeds that would yield good pie pumpkins.

"I have an idea, Julia," Nicholas said. "We still have those pumpkin seeds in the basement that we took out of a pumpkin we bought last year. Let's just plant those."

"Sure," said Julia. "We won't have to spend extra on seeds."

"Well," said Peter, "that might not work. Often pumpkins are hybrids, which means their seeds might not grow into pumpkins like themselves."

"Oh, I think ours will work," said Nicholas. "Peter, what do you do all day between customers?"

"Video games," Peter said. "I just set a new record this morning." Peter invited Nicholas and Julia to take a look.

"You get points for doing stuff. Like if I run this guy over and kill him, I get big points. If the guy just gets injured, I don't get quite as many points. It's really fun, and it's challenging too."

Nicholas and Julia paid for their purchases and biked home. They spread their seeds on the porch and began to cut the seed potatoes into smaller pieces. Mom helped because she wanted to plant potatoes too.

"Mom, why do we have to cut these potatoes up?" Julia asked. "Why not just plant the whole potato?"

"Wouldn't you rather have three plants from each potato than just one? Plus, you get nicer potatoes if not so many are trying to grow side by side." Mom kept right on dividing potatoes as she talked. "Okay, as soon as we finish here, we'll plant the potatoes, and then you two can plant your peas."

After they finished planting potatoes, Nicholas took a hoe and began making a row for the peas.

"Shouldn't we use the string like we did before?" Julia asked.

"Oh, don't worry," said Nicholas, "I can make a straight line without a string. We're just doing two rows today. We'll use the string when we do the main garden."

Nicholas and Julia dropped the pea seeds into the furrow and covered them with dirt. It was so exciting to be planting again.

In a week, the little plants pushed up their heads and began to shake off the dirt. "Your plants look very nice," said Dad. "But these pea rows are really crooked. What happened to your string?"

Nicholas laughed uneasily. "Well, I didn't figure we'd need the string for just a couple of rows."

"Ah, you didn't use the string," Dad said. "The other day you asked me how I learned to make such nice stitches in a surgery. Remember what I told you about being sloppy when you first do something?"

Nicholas nodded.

"Now your garden will be crooked for the rest of the summer, and there's nothing to do about it. We might even end up tilling some of those peas where the two rows are too close together."

Nicholas sighed. "I didn't think about that," he said.

"Well, it won't wreck the garden," Dad said. "It will just be a good reminder. Things will always grow like you plant them, whether it's peas and potatoes or stitching in a surgery."

Julia forgot about Dad's words as she set the table for supper that night.

"Julia," said Mom, "remember how I told you to put the silverware around the plate? This doesn't look nice, with the knife and fork and spoon just piled any which way. If you learn to do it that way, you'll be sloppy for the rest of your life."

Nicholas grinned at Julia. "At least I'm not the only one who gets talked to for being sloppy," Nicholas said.

"Well, at least I can still change mine," said Julia as she rearranged the silverware.

"You won't be able to if you make it a bad habit," said Mom. "It's hard work to learn to do something right the first time, but once you learn it, it's easy."

The next day, Nicholas and Julia hilled potatoes. They piled dirt around each potato plant and pulled all the small weeds. The extra dirt would help the plants make more new potatoes.

"You'll need to hill them several times," said Dad. "It's a lot of work, but it's worth it."

"Everything Dad and Mom talks about is work," said Julia. "I guess they really think we need to learn this lesson about doing things right the first time."

Nicholas and Julia planted the rest of the garden with pumpkins, tomatoes, and green beans. They used the pumpkin seeds from the basement.

"These look like perfectly good seeds," said Julia. "I can't believe they wouldn't work. Peter probably just wanted us to buy more."

The pumpkin seeds sprouted and made beautiful plants with broad green leaves. As the plants grew bigger, they sent out long runners and soon produced huge yellow flowers that kept the bees buzzing with delight.

The children were hilling the potatoes for the last time when Peter rode in the lane on his scooter. "Nicholas! You've got to come see my new weight set!" he shouted over to the garden.

"Sure thing!" Nicholas called. "Do you mind if I run over for a few minutes?" Nicholas asked Julia. "You can stop hilling until I come back."

Julia agreed and flopped under a shade tree nearby.

A few minutes later, Mom came by and asked for Nicholas.

"He went to see Peter's weight set," Julia said. "Didn't he ask you?"

"No," said Mom.

"Mom, why are the tomatoes on this side of the garden smaller than the ones in the middle?" Julia asked.

Mom looked at the tomatoes. "Um-m-m . . . I'm not sure," she said. "Oh, look at the shade! See how the shade tree blocks the sun? That's probably why those are smaller."

That night at the supper table, Dad and Mom talked to Nicholas about his visit to Peter. "You need to get permission before you leave," Dad said. "Plus, Peter is not the kind of boy I want you hanging out with all the time."

"But I was just looking at his weight set!" Nicholas protested.

"I know," said Dad. "But the words he says and the games he plays will still stick in your mind even if you are only with him for a few minutes. It's very important to choose good friends."

"It's like the tomatoes at the end of your garden," said Mom. "The tree shades them just a few hours each day, but did you see how much smaller they are than the others that are always in the sun? If you spend time with shady friends, your character won't grow."

"We're talking about planting *again?"* said Julia.

"Gardens are just like life," said Mom. "Julia, pass the potatoes again. These are some of your hard-earned red potatoes. Aren't they delicious?"

Nicholas and Julia always did the supper dishes. Tonight Nicholas didn't say much as he brought the plates to Julia. Julia could tell he was still thinking about Peter.

"Let's go look at the garden a little," said Julia. "I don't feel like doing the dishes right now."

The two went out and walked up and down the rows of plants. They had managed to keep ahead of the weeds; the garden looked beautiful. The pumpkin plants were the nicest looking of all. The hollow green runners grew so long that they grew into the bean row and got all tangled up with the bean plants.

"Wait, what's this?" Nicholas asked as he studied the pumpkin row. "Is this a weed?"

"It looks like a tomato plant," said Julia.

Mom was working in her garden and came over. "Are you done with the dishes already?" she asked.

"No," said Julia. "We just came out to look at the garden. What's this plant in our pumpkin row? It looks like a tomato plant."

"It is a tomato plant, if I see right," said Mom. "I guess a tomato seed got mixed up with your pumpkin seeds."

"It's in the way!" said Nicholas. "It's taking up the space that our pumpkins need." He reached down and pulled it out with one twist.

"Hm-m-m," said Mom, "that reminds me of two children who made a visit to look at their garden when they were supposed to be washing dishes."

"Mom!" said Nicholas and Julia together. "Not another lesson from the garden!"

"Gardens are a lot like life," said Mom with a smile. The children could tell that Mom was having fun, seeing how many lessons she could find from the garden.

"Remember when we talked about using every part of the potato?" Mom said with another smile. "Dad and I want to use every possible lesson we can from this garden."

Nicholas and Julia couldn't help laughing. Mom had just thought of a gardening lesson about gardening lessons. They hurried back to the house to do the dishes.

Every now and then Peter invited Nicholas to his house. Dad and Mom sometimes said he could go if he didn't stay long.

"Hey, Nic," Peter said one day, "how about coming for my birthday party? A couple of friends and I are going out for pizza and hanging around town for a while. Then we're coming back to my house for the night. Don't know if we'll sleep much, but we'll have fun!"

"I'll need to ask my parents," said Nicholas.

"Your parents are really picky," said Peter. "My dad doesn't care what I do."

"Yeah, I guess they are," said Nicholas.

He was not surprised when Mom said no. Actually, Nicholas didn't mind, because he didn't know Peter's friends. Still, as he and Julia worked in the garden that night, he thought about how much fun it would have been to go out for pizza.

"Nicholas!" Julia called. She was bent over the pumpkin row, almost covered by the large leaves that were beginning to take over the garden. "Come look at this weird pumpkin!"

Nicholas dashed across the garden. *Now* what? He found an open patch of dirt beside Julia and peered into the leaves. The prickly runners and stems scratched his skin as he parted them.

Lying against the warm dirt was the strangest looking "pumpkin" they had ever seen. It had a long, slender neck and a wide, fat bottom and green and orange stripes that jogged and jagged around the "pumpkin" like a maze.

"That doesn't look anything like the pumpkins from last year," said Nicholas.

"I'm not even sure if it *is* a pumpkin," said Julia.

Nicholas called Dad over to see the strange fruit. Soon the whole family was standing and staring. Julia took a picture of it.

"Well, maybe it's just a sick one," said Dad. "But I'm guessing they'll all look like that."

"Will we be able to eat them?" Nicholas asked.

"Or sell them?" Julia asked.

"I don't think I would either eat one or buy one," said Mom.

"Hey!" Nicholas said to Julia. "Mom didn't think of a lesson to teach us. That's amazing!"

"Actually, I have one for you," said Dad. "It's a lesson about following advice. Didn't you say that Peter told you this might happen?"

"But Dad, you always tell me not to listen to Peter!" said Nicholas.

"Now, Nicholas," said Dad, "you know more about proper behavior than Peter does, so you should not follow his behavior. But

Peter knows more about gardens than you do. If someone knows better than you, you should follow his advice. Sometimes by the time you realize it was good advice it's too late to change. You could plant new pumpkins now, but they would never be ready before the frost."

Several days after the birthday party, Dad called Nicholas over to his recliner. "Take a look at this newspaper notice," Dad said. "A group of boys was forced by police to leave McDonald's because of disorderly conduct. See the list of names?" Peter's name was on the list; the date was the night of the birthday party.

"What does disorderly conduct mean?" Nicholas asked.

"Bad behavior," Dad said. "It must have been pretty violent if the McDonald's workers called the police. I'm glad you weren't at that party, Nicholas."

Nicholas didn't say anything, but he was glad too.

Nicholas and Julia kept watching the pumpkin plants, hoping to find something normal. They could not. Every fruit that developed on the showy plants was misshapen and strange. The pumpkin crop was a complete failure.

"Well, some people might buy them for fall decorations," said Nicholas. "But I don't think we should tell people they're for eating."

"You're right," said Julia. "What if they're poisonous?"

They both laughed.

"Well, we've had enough garden adventures for one summer," said Nicholas. "Hopefully nothing else bad happens."

"If anything does happen, I'm sure Mom or Dad will have a lesson for us," laughed Julia.

"Have you looked at the Indian corn lately?" Nicholas asked. "At least we'll have that to sell in the fall."

"If it's ready; didn't Dad say it would take a long time?"

Julia and Nicholas walked over to the Indian corn row. The stalks towered over the regular corn. They were a deep red, almost purplish color.

"Dad was right; the ears are still really small," Nicholas said. "Hopefully, they'll be ready."

For several weeks, everything went well. The summer crops flourished; the fall crops were on schedule. Even the strange pumpkins grew rapidly.

One night Nicholas and Julia picked their first batch of sweet corn to taste before beginning to sell. They carried their basket to the side of their garden to take off the husks.

"This is really weird," said Nicholas. "Look at this kernel!"

Nicholas had the husk half off. He brushed away the silk. Julia leaned over to have a look.

"It's blue!"

"Yeah. Or kind of a gray color." Nicholas stripped the rest of the husk and found several more strange-colored kernels.

Julia's first ear was completely yellow. She picked up a second ear and tore back the husk. This ear, too, had blue kernels.

"There's Dad coming home," Julia said. "Let's show him."

They raced across the lawn with the ears of corn.

Dad stepped out of his vet truck, smelling like barns as usual, his overalls smeared with dirt. "Something serious must be happening for me to get this much attention," he said with a smile.

Julia and Nicholas held out their discolored ears. "Why are they blue, Dad?" Nicholas asked.

Dad looked at the corn and frowned. "I don't know. Did you buy the seed from the garden center?"

They nodded.

"Jump in my truck, if you can stand the smell," Dad said. "I'll run you down to show it to Peter or his dad."

Even though the truck usually smelled bad, Nicholas and Julia liked riding in it. In fact, they didn't really think the smell was bad; it was just the vet truck smell.

They arrived at the garden shop just before Peter flipped the "closed" sign over.

His dad took a look at the corn. "It looks like it cross-pollinated with Indian corn," he said. "Did you plant Indian corn anywhere near the sweet corn?"

Julia and Nicholas stared at him and then at each other.

"Yes," said Nicholas. "Our Indian corn row is right beside the other corn."

"Ah, yes, that explains it."

"How does that happen?" Dad asked.

"Cross-pollination ruins only the seeds of a plant. It doesn't matter for most vegetables," Peter's dad said, "because we usually don't eat the seeds. If two squash plants cross-pollinate, you'll never know the difference unless you try to plant the seeds. But we eat the seeds of a corn plant, so we notice it right away."

Nicholas got up the courage to ask the dreadful question. "Is the corn ruined?"

Peter's dad frowned. "Well, I guess you can cook it and see," he said. "But I'm afraid it might not be very sweet. Even if just a few kernels are dark, the flavor of the ear may be ruined."

"How far away from the Indian corn does the sweet corn need to be?" Dad asked.

"At least one hundred feet," Peter's dad said.

Nicholas's heart sank. "Our garden isn't even one hundred feet long!" he exclaimed.

"I'm sorry," said Peter's dad. "We should have remembered to warn you about the Indian corn when you bought it. We have extra corn this year; you may have some of ours if you pick it yourself."

"Really?" Nicholas asked.

"Sure. Peter, go show Nicholas and Julia that extra corner of the patch."

Peter led the way down a field lane to a huge patch of corn. Peter snaked his way into the patch and gathered an armload of corn for Nicholas and Julia.

"Here's some for your supper," said Peter. "You can even sell some if you pick it in the next few days. All our corn goes to market, so you won't be taking our customers."

"Thanks a lot!" said Nicholas.

Dad, Nicholas, and Julia piled back into the vet truck.

"You know what?" Dad said as they drove the short stretch of road home. "Peter's dad told me he wishes Peter would be more like you, Nicholas. He says he thinks it's really neat that you work hard and don't play violent games or cause trouble in town."

"Really?" said Nicholas, surprised. He figured Peter and his dad would make fun of him and his family.

"Well, it's just like you've learned this summer," Dad said. "Are you ready for a lesson review? You get whatever you plant. If Peter's dad gives Peter violent games, he can expect him to get into trouble with the police. If you plant Indian corn beside sweet corn, you can expect trouble."

"Or if you plant seeds from a hybrid pumpkin," Nicholas said with a disgusted grin.

"Or if you plant tomatoes in the shade," Julia added.

"Or if you don't use a string to plant your peas," Nicholas said.

"What a lot of stupid things we've done this summer!" Julia said.

They were all laughing as they climbed from the truck.

Questions for Review

1. What were some crops that the children planted?
2. Why didn't Nicholas's dad and mom want him to spend a lot of time with Peter?
3. Why did the children use the pumpkin seeds from the basement?
4. What lesson did Nicholas learn from not using a string to make a straight line?
5. What problem did Julia have when she set the table?

Questions for Discussion

1. Why were the pumpkins the children grew so weird?
2. Why was the sweet corn not usable?
3. Has your family made any mistakes when gardening?
4. Why should children follow the instructions of parents about spending time with neighbor children?
5. How is gardening a lot like life?

Themes, Titles, Verses, and Readings

Love

The Importance of Love	Ephesians 5:2	John 15:12-17
Love God	Psalm 18:1	Matthew 22:34-40
Love Your Neighbor	1 John 4:20	Luke 10:25-37
Love Your Enemies	Romans 12:20	Matthew 5:38-48
Love the Stranger	Matthew 25:35	Exodus 22:21-27
Love Your Spouse	Titus 2:4	Ephesians 5:25-33
Love Your Children	Matthew 3:17	Titus 2:1-8

Joy

Jesus and Great Joy	Hebrews 12:2	Luke 15:3-10
Attempts to Find Joy	Jeremiah 2:13	Luke 15:11-20
Steps to Salvation's Joy	2 Peter 3:9	Luke 15:21-32
The Joy of the Prodigal's Return	Luke 15:10	Acts 16:26-34
Be of Good Cheer	Matthew 14:27	Matthew 9:1-8
Joy Amidst Trials	James 1:2	Acts 16:19-25
The Joy of the Lord Is Your Strength	Nehemiah 8:10	Philippians 4:4-13

Peace

Jesus: Prince of Peace	Ephesians 2:13, 14	Isaiah 9:1-7
Peace From the Prince of Peace	Romans 8:6	John 14:23-29
Peace in Spite of Grief	Psalm 29:11	Psalm 119:161-176
Peace at Home	Psalm 34:14	Colossians 3:12-21
Restoring Peace	James 5:16	Genesis 33:1-11
Making Peace, Not Pieces	Matthew 5:9	Joshua 22:10-34
Though Trials Should Come	2 Kings 4:26	Psalm 46

Longsuffering

I Want It Now	James 1:4	Romans 15:1-7
Patience of God	Romans 15:5	Psalm 86
Learn Patience from James and Job	James 5:11	James 5:1-11
Causes of Impatience	Hebrews 10:36	Acts 27:1-25
Developing Patience	Romans 12:12	Romans 5:1-8
Sweet Fruit of Patience	Ecclesiastes 7:8	Psalm 37:1-11
Patience in Daily Life	1 Thessalonians 5:14	Genesis 40:1-15, 20-23; 41:1

Gentleness

God's Kindness	Psalm 69:16	Isaiah 63:7-16
Kindness of Christ	Hebrews 5:2	Matthew 20:29-34
Kindness at Home	Ephesians 4:32	Matthew 1:18-25
Kindness to Siblings	Colossians 3:12	Genesis 50:15-21
Kindness to the Handicapped	1 Thessalonians 5:14	2 Samuel 9:1-13
Kindness in the Community	1 John 3:17	Acts 28:1-10
Kindness at Church	2 Peter 1:5-7	Jeremiah 38:6-13

Goodness

Barnabas: A Good Man	1 Thessalonians 1:3	Acts 11:22-30
Brave Esther	Joshua 1:9	Esther 4:5-16
Helpful Aaron	Exodus 4:14	Exodus 4:27-30; 17:9-13
Lydia: A Good Businesswoman	Philippians 1:6	Acts 16:9-16
Jethro: A Wise Adviser	Proverbs 12:15	Exodus 18:7-26
President of the Dorcas Society	James 1:27	Acts 9:36-43
Jonathan: A True Friend	Proverbs 17:17	1 Samuel 18:1-4; 23:14-18

Faith

Jesus Is Faithful	Hebrews 3:1, 2	Hebrews 10:12-23
Faith in Abraham's Shield	Hebrews 11:11	Genesis 15:1-7
Holy and Wholly Committed	Deuteronomy 1:36	Numbers 13:26-33; 14:1-9
A Dying Leader's Challenge: Be Faithful	Joshua 24:31	Joshua 24:1, 11-27
Diligent Deborah	Judges 5:1, 2	Judges 4:1-16
Let Your Heart Be Steadfast	Matthew 10:28	Psalm 115:1-13
Faithful Unto Death	Revelation 2:10	Acts 7:54-60

Meekness

Meekness of Jesus	Matthew 20:28	Philippians 2:1-8
The Need for Meekness	Zephaniah 2:3	John 13:1-17
Meekness in Relation to God	Psalm 22:26	Isaiah 6:1-8
The Value of Meekness	1 Peter 3:9	Luke 9:51-56
Meekness Demonstrated	Matthew 5:5	Ephesians 4:1-13

Meekness in Action	Romans 12:18	Titus 3:1-8
Meekness in Building Relationships	Psalm 37:11	Philemon 1-21

Temperance

Be Temperate	2 Timothy 2:3	1 Corinthians 9:24-27
Developing Self-Control	Daniel 1:8	2 Timothy 1:1-10
How to Grow the Fruit of Temperance	Galatians 5:25	Ephesians 5:8-20
What Esau Saw	Hebrews 12:16, 17	Genesis 25:27-34
Importance of Self-Control	1 Corinthians 9:25	Hebrews 11:23-28
The Slavery of Indulgence	Luke 21:34	Proverbs 23:19-35
Temperance at Home	Proverbs 16:32	James 1:17-26

Gardening Lessons

Gardening: Past and Present	Isaiah 51:3	Genesis 2:1-9
Lessons From Gardening	Mark 16:20	1 Samuel 14:1, 6-13, 23, 45
What to Plant	Hosea 10:12	Ecclesiastes 12:1-6
Fruit-Bearing	Matthew 7:17	John 15:1-11
Parable of the Laborers	1 Timothy 1:14	Matthew 20:1-16
Parable of Two Sons	Deuteronomy 10:12	Matthew 21:28-32
Parable of the Wicked Farm Manager	John 1:11	Matthew 21:33-46

Wonders of Plants

The Biggest Trees	Deuteronomy 20:19	Genesis 1:9-17
The Fiercest Plants	2 Corinthians 2:11	2 Corinthians 11:1-15
The Most Useful Plants	John 12:12, 13	Psalm 92
The Largest Seed	Genesis 1:11	Luke 8:9-15

A Very Fragrant Plant	Isaiah 14:8	1 Kings 6:9-18
The Tallest Grass	Psalm 104:14	Deuteronomy 11:13-21
The Thickest Plant	Proverbs 11:30	Genesis 2:15-24

Weeds

Weeding Your Garden	Romans 3:23	Genesis 3:8-19
Weeds Grow Fast	James 1:15	Genesis 4:1-16
Weeds Choke	Luke 8:7	Matthew 13:1-9, 22
Identifying Weeds	Job 22:5	2 Timothy 3:1-13
Keep Weeding	Romans 6:6	Colossians 3:1-10
Weeding Is Work	Ephesians 4:31	Acts 5:1-11
Weeding Is Worth It	Matthew 13:23	1 Thessalonians 4:9-18

Sowing and Reaping

The Results of Sowing	Galatians 6:7	Judges 16:15-30
Getting What You Don't Want	Job 4:8	3 John
The Weight of the Crop	Psalm 51:3	Psalm 51:7-17
Helping Yourself by Helping Others	Galatians 6:10	John 4:31-38
Grim Education	Proverbs 20:20	Genesis 47:5-12
Not a Defective Detective	Ecclesiastes 12:14	John 8:1-12
Reaping a Good Crop	Galatians 6:9	Ruth 2:1-16

Christian Light Publications, Inc., is a nonprofit, conservative Mennonite publishing company providing Christ-centered, Biblical literature including books, Gospel tracts, Sunday school materials, summer Bible school materials, and a full curriculum for Christian day schools and homeschools. Though produced primarily in English, some books, tracts, and school materials are also available in Spanish.

For more information about the ministry of CLP or its publications, or for spiritual help, please contact us at:

Christian Light Publications, Inc.
P. O. Box 1212
Harrisonburg, VA 22803-1212

Telephone—540-434-0768
Fax—540-433-8896
E-mail—info@clp.org
www.clp.org